Conducting Research in Educational Contexts

Also available from Continuum

Developing a Questionnaire 2nd edition, Bill Gillham

Educational Research, Jerry Wellington

Educational Research and Inquiry, Dimitra Hartas

Ethics in Research, Ian Gregory

Observation Techniques, Bill Gillham

Philosophy of Educational Research, Richard Pring

Research Questions, Richard Andrews

Researching Education 2nd edition, David Scott and Robin Usher

Small-Scale Social Survey Methods, Bill Gillham

Conducting Research in Educational Contexts

Tehmina N. Basit

continuum

Continuum International Publishing Group

The Tower Building
11 York Road
London SE1 7NX

80 Maiden Lane
Suite 704, New York
NY 10038

www.continuumbooks.com

British Library Cataloguing-in-Publication Data
A catalogue record for this book is available from the British Library.

ISBN: 978-0-8264-8688-2 (hardcover)
       978-0-8264-8689-9 (paperback)

Library of Congress Cataloging-in-Publication Data
Basit, Tehmina N.
Conducting research in educational contexts / Tehmina N. Basit.
    p. cm.
ISBN 978-0-8264-8688-2 (hardback)
ISBN 978-0-8264-8689-9 (pbk.)
Education–Research–Methodology. I. Title.
LB1028.B358 2010
370.7'2–dc22
2009030007

Typeset by Newgen Imaging Systems Pvt Ltd, Chennai, India
Printed and bound in Great Britain by CPI Antony Rowe Ltd,
Chippenham, Wiltshire

For Abdul Basit

Contents

Part 1 Getting Started

Part 2 Gathering Data

Part 3 Making Sense of Data

Acknowledgements

I am indebted to a number of people and organizations for helping me in writing this book:

The master's and doctoral students whom I have taught over the years and whose questions and comments have informed my thinking and writing.

The University of Wolverhampton School of Education for support; and the Library staff, Joan Blackhurst and her team, for their help.

Chris Comber, Miriam David, Olwen McNamara, Mike Rickhuss, Ian Stronach and Sally Tomlinson for their insightful comments on various chapters.

Alison Clark, Christina Garbutt and Ania Leslie-Wujastyk at Continuum; Alexandra Webster, formerly from Continuum; and Pattabiraman Muralidharan from Newgen Imaging Systems, for their support at various stages of development of the book.

My husband, Abdul Basit, for criticism, comments, discussions, proofreading, and sorting out computer problems. I dedicate this book to him.

* * *

I gratefully acknowledge the permission granted by the following publishers and authors to include materials in the book:

- Taylor and Francis and the journal, *Educational Research*, Vol. 45, for reproducing two figures from my paper, Manual or Electronic: the Role of Coding in Qualitative Data Analysis.
- RoutledgeFalmer for material from Wragg, E. C. (1999) *An Introduction to Classroom Observation* (second edition).
- Sage Publications for material from Mason, J. (2002) *Qualitative Researching* (second edition); and from Alaszewski, A. (2006) *Using Diaries for Social Research*.
- Continuum Publishing for material from Gorard, S. (2003) *Quantitative Methods in Social Sciences*.
- Open University Press for material from Hopkins, D. (2008) *A Teacher's Guide to Classroom Research* (fourth edition).

List of Tables and Figures

Tables

Figures

Introduction: passionate enquiries

This book has been written as a result of a number of years of teaching educational research methods to diverse groups of students embarking on research in educational contexts. These range from postgraduates conducting a research project for an MA or MSc to those undertaking a PhD, or EdD – the practitioner doctorate in education offered at many British universities. Essentially, the book is aimed at novice researchers who are carrying out research for the first time. They include those who have years of experience as educational practitioners, but never had the time or the opportunity to get involved in research.

The purpose of research is to develop knowledge for, in, and of, society (Pring, 2004). Educational research endeavours to examine educational phenomena to learn from them and to improve existing knowledge, policy and practice. Research in education draws on a number of disciplines including anthropology, history, philosophy, politics, psychology and sociology. It is concerned with issues to do with teaching and learning across the educational spectrum, ranging from early years to primary and secondary schooling, further and higher education, and lifelong learning. Government policy, curriculum, pedagogy, school effectiveness and improvement, student attainment, students' and parents' viewpoints and experiences, training and professional development of teachers, social inclusion, social justice, gender, leadership and management are just some of the areas that lend themselves to educational inquiry. In short, educational research deals with a wide range of issues to do with education and how it is perceived, experienced, evaluated and improved, and how we learn from studying various phenomena and generate new knowledge.

Giddens (1979) points to the 'double hermeneutic' that researchers have to live with, that is, they interpret a world that is already interpreted by the research participants. The researchers seek the true meaning in the interpretations of the participants and elucidate them further to reveal the truth. Pring (2004) argues that:

> The overriding principle which informs research would seem to be that of finding the truth. This is much more than telling the truth, although it does of course include that. The purpose of undertaking research is the production of new knowledge. The reasons for seeking new knowledge are several: the improvement of practice, a knowledge-base for developing policy, increased accountability, solving problems which the researchers find interesting. The reasons, however, are not the most important point for the moment. The characterisation of research as the production of new knowledge is. (p. 146)

Education and educational research are closely linked to politics and decision-making. Educational research follows the tradition of social science research and draws on the same paradigms, employing similar methodologies and using the same methods as other social sciences. Research in education is scientific research as, in common with other sciences, its purpose is the search for truth and is carried out in a logical and methodical manner. Howard and Sharpe (1983) observe that:

> Most people associate the word 'research' with activities which are substantially removed from day-to-day life, and which are pursued by outstandingly gifted persons with an unusual level of commitment . . . We would argue that the pursuit is not restricted to this type of person, and indeed can prove to be a stimulating and satisfying experience for many people . . . with a trained and enquiring mind. (p. 6)

Nevertheless, it is crucial to have knowledge of research methods to conduct research. Stake (1995: 15) argues that 'the design of all research requires conceptual organisation, ideas to express needed understanding, conceptual bridges from what is already known, cognitive structures to guide data gathering, and outlines for presenting interpretations to others.' While some of us are better researchers to begin with than the rest of us, merely because we have innate skills that enable us to carry out research in a much better way, there is no reason why the rest of us cannot hone our research skills with experience. However, it is important to reflect on our research practice as we go along and learn from our mistakes, so that we do not repeat the same mistakes in subsequent research projects.

Beginner researchers usually find the mechanics of research intimidating. This step-by-step book instructing them how to start a research project, and then guiding them through the various phases to the end result in an uncomplicated manner, aims to motivate novice researchers to embark on the exhilarating experience of educational research. The book is intended as a confidence-booster and an inspiration for students carrying out educational investigations for the first time. It will give them an insight into the thinking and planning that constitute a research project, taking them through the process to the end product. It will be invaluable for postgraduates undertaking masters and doctoral studies. Furthermore, teachers and lecturers preoccupied with more teaching and less research will find reading about research in simple terms reassuring and will see it as something that can be accomplished. The book is written in simple English in a reader-friendly way to make it accessible to novice researchers. The chapters do not assume a great deal of prior knowledge of the readers. Yet, this book will take the readers further from their current level and enhance their understanding of research by illuminating and demystifying the various research processes.

Educational research is a process carried out in educational contexts to further our understanding of educational phenomena, to illuminate and elucidate events, to learn from effective practice, and to seek to improve practice that is unhelpful. This kind of research is helpful for practising teachers as well as those researchers who are studying for higher degrees, whether they are teachers or full-time researchers. McNamara (2002: 15) observes that 'recently, there has been a sea change in the opportunities available for teachers to engage both in *doing* teacher research projects and in *using* existing findings from the wider research and evidence base.' She however notes the marked absence of research-informed culture in schools despite such initiatives.

Research is a systematic enquiry made public (Stenhouse, 1975). It is 'a systematic, critical and self-critical enquiry, which aims to contribute to the advancement of knowledge and wisdom' (Bassey, 1999: 38). It is the process of arriving at dependable solutions to problems through the planned and systematic collection, analysis and interpretation of data (Mouly, 1978). It involves seeking through methodical processes to add to one's own body of knowledge, and to that of others, by the discovery of nontrivial facts and insights (Howard and Sharpe, 1983). It should be systematic, credible, verifiable, justifiable, useful, valuable and trustworthy (Lincoln and Guba, 1985). The relevant policy arenas should find usefulness and meaning in the study; and the study should be useful for practitioners (Marshall and Rossman, 2006). As can be seen, the focus in the definitions above is on the process being systematic, advancing knowledge, solving problems and offering solutions.

Pring (2004) argues that research can only be educational if it relates to educational practice. He draws a distinction between:

> Research which is firmly embedded within the social sciences and which may well be relevant to education; and research which arises from distinctively educational concerns and which draws upon, but is not to be reduced to, the knowledge which has accumulated within those sciences. The distinction may sometimes be blurred and it may be that educationally relevant research may often be properly placed in the disciplines of psychology, sociology or philosophy. But it can only be relevant if it relates to the 'practice of education' – to the activities, engaged in on the whole by teachers, which have those characteristics which pick them out as educational. (p. 9)

Contemplating research

Once we have decided to embark on a research project, we have to consider several questions. Taking inspiration from Kipling's (1974) concepts in 'I Keep Six Honest Serving Men' from 'The Elephant's Child', these questions will be as follows:

1. *What* are we going to investigate?
What is the research construct that we aim to examine? Do we want to look at, for example, aspirations, attainment, behaviour, leadership, perceptions, social justice, or teaching and learning? Or do we want to explore more than one construct?

2. *Why* are we choosing this issue?
What is the rationale for deciding to investigate this particular topic and why is it significant? Why is it important to examine this issue at this particular time?

3. *When* do we want to undertake the research?
When do we wish to do our fieldwork, in case of empirical research; and library research, in case of a theoretical study? When do we want to commence and complete the various phases in our study?

4. *How* are we going to conduct the research?
What paradigm, methodology, approach and methods do we intend to work with to gather our data and analyse them and what is the justification for using them? Do they fit the purpose of our research? Do we want to work with more than one of them? How will we deal with issues of validity, reliability and ethics?

5. *Where* are we carrying out our research?
What is the setting of our study? Is it one or more educational establishments – a school, an FE College, a University? Or are we choosing participants linked to education, but seeing them away from the educational institution, such as the parents of students?

6. *Who* are we intending to focus on?
Do we wish to target school pupils, parents, teachers, headteachers, governors, support staff, lecturers, or university students, or more than one group?

We conduct research because we feel passionate about an area of inquiry; an idea that had been germinating in our minds, perhaps for years, before we decided to do something about it. A research project carried out for a master's or doctoral degree is one of the ways in which such an idea can be brought to fruition. Quality research is about the search for truth, the commitment to carry it out in an ethical manner, the ability to generate reliable and valid data, and to present the findings in a way that practitioners, policy makers and other researchers – present and future – can benefit from them. Meaningful research is also about generating new theories, whether in the form of grounded theory, or by refuting or developing existing theories. Further, research is futile if it does not generate sufficient knowledge to enable us to make recommendations for improving the status quo, and striving for social justice, to make the world a better place for us and for our future generations.

Activity

The reality of research
What images, words and phrases come to your mind when you think of 'research'?

What are the different educational contexts in which you can conduct research?

What kinds of issues can you examine in educational research?

Stance of the researcher

Educational research is a form of social science research and, like other social sciences, seeks to discover, explain and interpret social reality mainly in two different ways by working within the positivist or the interpretivist paradigms. These two modes of looking at the social world are underpinned by ontological and epistemological notions.

Ontological assumptions are concerned with the grounds of knowledge, the belief in what exists, what is real; the very nature of being and the essence of the social phenomenon being examined. It has to do with the researcher's view of what constitutes social reality. The researcher decides whether social reality is external to individuals, is imposed on them from the outside world, and is hard and objective; or if reality is the product of the subjects' own perception and cognition.

Epistemological assumptions are concerned with methods; the very basis and nature of knowledge; the proof that can be accepted of valid knowledge and how it is attained and conveyed to others. It has to do with the researcher's view of how knowledge is acquired and how it is communicated to the reader. If knowledge is viewed as objective and tangible, then the researcher needs to be in the role of the observer and follow the methods favoured by the natural sciences, such as experiments. However, if knowledge is regarded as personal and subjective, then the researcher seeks more interaction with the subjects through interviews to explain the social phenomena as the research participants perceive it.

Thus, ontology is about 'Being' and epistemology is about 'Knowing'. Ontology and epistemology lead to methodological considerations. Methodology is the theory of research methods and involves the creation of reliable and valid knowledge. According to Kaplan (1973) methodology describes and analyses the methods used; reveals their limitations and resources; clarifies their presuppositions and consequences, and relates their potentialities to the frontiers of knowledge. In short, methodology encompasses the whole process of educational research.

The choice of appropriate research methods is extremely important for an apposite methodology. Methods denote the range of techniques that are available to educational researchers to gather data to help them to interpret the social phenomena under scrutiny. These include questionnaires, interviews, observations, and diaries amongst others. The researchers need to ensure that the methods used are right for a specific research project and reliable and valid data can be collected through these methods.

Ontology and epistemology affect the researchers' stance or positionality, which in turn determines the methodology and methods chosen by them to conduct a research project. Axiology, which refers to the nature of values and value judgements, is another important consideration. This represents the researchers' principles and beliefs which lead them to make specific judgements and decisions. Researchers' stance can be influenced by a number of factors which impinge on how they view social reality and the nature of knowledge. These include their age, gender, social class, ethnicity, religion, educational level, place of residence, place of work, occupation, political views and so forth. While this may indicate as if researchers bring bias and baggage to the research, resulting in the collection of skewed data leading to distorted analysis, we have to remember that no research is totally value-free as all research is carried out by humans. Even when sophisticated tools are used to gather and analyse data, it is an individual who interprets the findings of the research and conveys them to an audience. It is therefore important that researchers exercise reflexivity, i.e. critical self-examination. They need to ponder, as they embark on research, where they are coming from; what they want to investigate; when, where, and how they want to examine those phenomena; why this will be the best possible way of carrying out their research; and how they can ensure that their research is carried out in an ethical manner. Hopkins (2008), discussing research in the classroom highlights the ethical responsibility of the researchers towards their own biases:

> Our own background, values and beliefs and cultural understandings inevitably have an impact on our decisions about the research. We construct reality through our own ideas and 'truths' which many, and justifiably, would argue is 'our truth'. However, research needs to be as objective as possible, and as any claim to objectivity or to a 'value free' position is an illusion, personal biases have to be identified throughout the research process and strategies to minimise them have to be employed. (p. 203)

Structure of the book

This book complements other books on research methods. It will act as a definitive resource for new and early career researchers offering what they need to know before embarking on a research project. It will tell them the difference between paradigms, methodologies, approaches and methods – terms which are so often discussed to mean one thing by one author and something else by another. The book will consider a range of methods to choose from, enabling the researchers to select the most appropriate one for their topic and context.

The book is divided into three parts that follow the lifecycle of a research project: Getting Started, Gathering Data and Making Sense of Data. Each part focuses on a particular phase of research and discusses what researchers need to know at that point in their research. Significantly, the book draws attention to the difficulties faced by researchers, thus pointing out that a research project is not a neat and tidy package, but can be messy and frustrating. Yet, it also shows how a complete project can emerge from what appears chaotic at earlier stages. I hope that structuring the book in this way makes it intellectually creative and exciting for the readers, as each phase in the stages of development of a research project leads to the next phase, the outcome of which is not fully anticipated, and culminates with the writing up of the project. This prevents the research journey from becoming mundane and predictable.

The three chapters in Part 1 deal with the initial stages of research. Chapter 1 discusses the two main research paradigms: the positivist and the interpretive, and critical theory. It then introduces the quantitative and qualitative methodologies, and the eclectic methodology. It proceeds to explain the various approaches to research, such as case study, ethnography, action research, survey and experimental design. Chapter 2 contemplates the different steps in project design. It looks at searching and reviewing the literature, the role of theory, choosing the hypotheses or research questions, and selecting the sample. Chapter 3 examines the issues that need to be taken into consideration when designing and conducting research. These include validity and reliability, triangulation, ethics, access, piloting and generalizability.

Part 2 focuses on the collection of data. Chapter 4 discusses in detail the design and use of questionnaires in educational research. It presents examples of various kinds of questions, both closed and open-ended, that can be asked in questionnaires, and discusses the kinds of data that can be generated through the use of this method. Chapter 5 examines the different types of research interviews. These include structured, semi-structured and unstructured interviews, focus groups, telephone and email interviews, life histories and narratives. It also looks at the design and structure of interview schedules. Chapter 6 contemplates the use of observation as a method of gathering data. This includes a discussion of structured and unstructured observation, and participant and nonparticipant observation. It also looks at observation checklists and video recording of observation in educational contexts. Chapter 7 discusses the use of various kinds of documents as methods of data collection in educational research. These include diaries, logs, journals and blogs.

The final part of the book considers the analysis, interpretation and reporting of data. Chapter 8 looks at ways in which quantitative data can be analysed. This includes analysing numerical data by using tables, histograms, bar charts, and spreadsheets. It briefly illustrates how quantitative data can be analysed by using the statistical package SPSS. Chapter 9 deals with the analysis of qualitative data. It discusses the role of coding, and the generation of grounded theory. It then demonstrates how textual data can be coded by using an electronic package such as NUD*IST NVivo. Chapter 10 explains the process of academic writing and ways in which the findings of an educational research project can be written for different kinds of assessment and audience. It discusses how a research report, dissertation, thesis, and journal article can be composed.

Part 1
Getting Started

Research Paradigms and Approaches: choosing models and traditions

1

Chapter Outline

This chapter will discuss the two main research paradigms: the positivist and the interpretive, followed by the third paradigm, critical theory. It will then introduce the quantitative and qualitative methodologies, and then the eclectic methodology. It will proceed to explain the various approaches to research, such as case study, ethnography, action research, survey and the experimental design.

Research paradigms

Educational research presents two contrasting notions of the social sciences. On the one hand is the positivist paradigm which is the more established and conventional view that the social sciences are similar to the natural sciences and can discover and determine human behaviour by observing it first hand; on the other hand is the interpretive paradigm, the view that human behaviour needs to be described and explained by individuals in the way it is perceived by them. Burrell and Morgan (1979) argue that in the former, social reality is objective and external to individuals and imposes itself on their consciousness from without; in the latter, it is the product of individual consciousness and cognition.

Paradigms are models, perspectives or conceptual frameworks that help us to organize our thoughts, beliefs, views and practices into a logical whole and consequently inform our research design. According to Bassey (1999), paradigms are:

> A network of coherent ideas about the nature of the world and the function of researchers which, adhered to by a group of researchers, conditions the patterns of their thinking and underpins their research actions. (p. 42)

The positivist paradigm

Also known as the normative paradigm, this is the traditional view of educational research, very similar to the hard, natural sciences, where truth can only seen to be discovered by observing, experimenting on, or interrogating a large number of subjects, resulting in findings that can be statistically analysed, and are therefore believed to be generalizable. This sees social reality as objective, observable, controllable and measurable, with patterns and causality.

The interpretive paradigm

Also called the naturalistic paradigm, this relates to a nontraditional view of educational research, which is nevertheless as rigorous as research in the natural sciences and that conducted within a positivist paradigm. It focuses on smaller numbers and in-depth analyses of human behaviour and perceptions, acknowledging differences as well as similarities. Researchers working in this paradigm are not interested in generalizing from their findings. This paradigm interprets social reality the way it is viewed by the research participants;

a phenomenon termed by Habermas (1984: 109) as 'double hermeneutic', indicating the interpretation of an already interpreted world.

Critical theory

The positivist and the interpretive paradigms have been criticized for offering partial versions of social phenomena by focusing merely on the technical and hermeneutic aspects of research and failing to address the ideological and political perspectives. Critical theory is meant to prescribe what society should comprise and how individuals should behave. The most common examples of critical theory are Critical Race Theory and Feminist Research. The purpose here is not merely to interpret and report on a social situation, but to change it for the benefit of society. Critical research aims to emancipate and empower the disempowered and those who are facing inequality and discrimination. It seeks to advance freedom and democracy for the betterment of individuals and society. Nevertheless, research conducted within both the positivist and the interpretive paradigms does encompass critical theory. This is evident when research critiques an existent situation and offers recommendations for improvement, social justice, empowerment and emancipation. Thus critical theory is a necessary component of educational research carried out in the positivist and interpretive paradigms.

The positivist and interpretive paradigms subscribe to two specific methodologies: the quantitative methodology and the qualitative methodology respectively.

Research methodologies

Quantitative methodology

This methodology claims researcher objectivity and value freedom. It regards the social world as hard and objective and similar to the natural world. It assumes that clear cause and effect relationships can be established while scrutinizing human behaviour. It also takes the stance that reliable and valid knowledge of the social world is discovered in the same way that natural scientists discover knowledge about the physical world. Knowledge is gained only through our senses, for example, by seeing or hearing; and anything that cannot be sensed directly cannot constitute social reality. Furthermore, facts can be substantiated only if they have been tested scientifically, or recounted by a large number of people.

Quantitative methodology favours the hypothetic-deductive model, based on the premise that valid and reliable knowledge can only be generated by developing and testing hypotheses. It assumes that social phenomena can be split into smaller events in the form of variables, which can be isolated and manipulated. It is concerned with gathering numerical data, thus quantifying and measuring social reality, which can then be analysed statistically. This methodology claims to produce generalizable findings.

Approaches to quantitative methodology include Survey and Experimental Design. Even Case Study and Action Research sometimes employ a quantitative methodology, though in combination with a qualitative methodology (see below).

Qualitative methodology

Qualitative research includes 'any type of research that produces findings not arrived at by means of statistical procedures or other means of quantification' (Strauss and Corbin, 1998: 10–11). This methodology is based on the premise that the social world is very different from the natural world and what we see is not necessarily the truth. Reality is subjective and the social world has no objective existence independent of individuals' views, perceptions and behaviour. Cause and effect statements cannot always be made to explain social events. Social reality is *created* by human experience rather than just being *discovered* by individuals. Qualitative methodology thus subscribes to the alternative notion of the social world focusing on the subjective views of research participants and enabling the researcher to explain social reality as it is perceived and created by the research participants themselves.

Qualitative methodology investigates the quality of relationships, activities, situations or materials, and there is a greater emphasis on holistic description, that is, on describing in detail what happens in a specific situation (Fraenkel and Wallen, 1990). It aims to describe events, perceptions and views scientifically, thus illuminating social phenomena. The purpose of this kind of inquiry is to achieve *depth* rather than *breadth*. This is done by presenting the information textually and without the use of numerical data. The focus is on a detailed exploration of a small number of examples or participants who can elucidate a particular aspect of social reality. The researchers thus endeavour to understand the social world as it is experienced, lived or felt by the research participants. This methodology does not claim to produce findings that are generalizable, though the research can be replicable and transferable to other

similar contexts. Qualitative methodology is more responsive to the participants, but more arduous, stressful and time-consuming for the researchers.

Approaches to qualitative methodology include Case study, Ethnography,
Action research, and Life history or Narrative.

Mixed methods or eclectic methodology

A combination of quantitative and qualitative methodologies is increasingly
being favoured by educational researchers. Though it does not suit every
researcher or research problem, this mixed methods or eclectic methodology
enables us to carry out large-scale surveys or experiments to gather and analyse generalizable data followed by in-depth investigation of a smaller number
of issues with a smaller proportion of participants. For example, hundreds of
subjects can be approached to convey their brief views through a questionnaire or take part in an educational experiment thus generating quantitative
data. This can be complemented by the collection of qualitative data to look at
a fewer instances more closely through semi-structured interviews or unstructured observation. Researchers need to be cognizant of the benefits of using
the eclectic methodology and consider whether this is the best way of addressing their research questions, and if it will result in robust interpretations of the
phenomena under consideration.

Cresswell (2003: 18–20) explicates the three methodologies as follows:

> A *quantitative* methodology is one in which the investigator primarily uses
> postpositivist claims for developing knowledge (i.e. cause and effect thinking,
> reduction to specific variables and hypotheses and questions, use of measurement
> and observation, and the test of theories), employs strategies of inquiry such as
> experiments and surveys and collects data on predetermined instruments that
> yield statistical data.

> Alternatively, a *qualitative* methodology is one in which the inquirer often makes
> knowledge claims based primarily on constructivist perspectives (i.e. the multiple
> meanings of individual experiences, meanings socially and historically constructed,
> with an intent of developing a theory or pattern); or advocacy/participatory per-
> spectives (i.e. political, issue-oriented, collaborative, or change oriented) or both. It
> also uses strategies of inquiry such as narratives, phenomenologies, ethnographies,
> grounded theory studies, or case studies. The researcher collects open-ended,
> emerging data with the primary intent of emerging themes from the data.

> Finally, in *mixed methods*, the researcher tends to base knowledge claims on
> pragmatic grounds (e.g. consequence-oriented, problem-centred and pluralistic).
> It employs strategies of inquiry that involve collecting data either simultaneously

or sequentially to best understand research problems. The data collection also involves gathering both numeric information (e.g. on instruments) as well as text information (e.g. on interviews) so that the final database represents both quantitative and qualitative information.

Research spotlight

Eid (2008) carried out a mixed methods study to examine young Bahraini citizens' civic and political knowledge and understanding. Her conceptual framework comprised three domains: citizenship, community and identity; rights, responsibilities and law; and democracy, political literacy and government. Data were gathered by administering a questionnaire to 460 male and female students, aged 17–18 years, in the final year of secondary school. This was followed by in-depth interviews with a stratified sample of 22 young people. The findings indicated a noticeable understanding of the conceptions of citizenship among young people, sufficient understanding of their rights and responsibilities, some knowledge of democracy, but little understanding of politics and government. While they showed an awareness of issues affecting their community, they were less involved in community associations and activities.

Approaches to research

Educational research, like other social science research, is seen by Kirk and Miller (1986: 60) as a four phase affair:

1. The first stage is of **invention**, in which the researcher formulates a research design and a plan of action. This will also involve the generation of hypotheses or research questions, looking at ethical issues and the ways to ensure the validity and reliability of the research.
2. The second step is of **discovery**, which refers to data collection and uncovering social reality by methods such as experiments, interviews and observation.
3. The third phase is of **interpretation**, which produces an understanding of social phenomena as a result of data analysis.
4. The final phase is of **explanation**, which produces a message that is communicated to an audience in the form of a thesis, report, presentation, paper or book.

However, before a researcher embarks on these four phases of research, the initial phase is of thinking about research, familiarizing ourselves with the context in which we are conducting our investigation by reading about research carried out by other researchers in that field and related fields, and most importantly by reading about the methods that can be employed to conduct our research and choosing those that fit our purpose.

Researchers need to familiarize themselves with the various approaches that lend themselves to educational inquiry. This will enable them to choose the most suitable approach for their study and the most appropriate methods of data collection. Below are the most popular approaches that can be undertaken to conduct research in educational contexts.

Case study

A case study provides a unique portrayal of real people in a real social situation by means of vivid accounts of events, feelings and perceptions. It is the study of an instance in action (Adelman et al., 1980); one instance meant to illuminate other similar cases or phenomena, and intended to demonstrate a more general notion of the social world. This instance can be one pupil, a group of female students, a single sex class, a multiethnic primary school, a geography department in a secondary school, an initial teacher training institution, a group of medical students, a charitable organization and so forth.

It is perfectly legitimate to conduct a case study of a single individual as well as a group of individuals seen as a single case. The researcher seeks greater understanding of the case in order to appreciate its uniqueness and complexity, and its embeddedness and interaction with its contexts (Stake, 1995: 16). The emphasis upon the uniqueness of events or actions, shaped by the meanings of the research participants in the situation, points to the importance of study of the unique case or the instance (Pring, 2004: 40). In a case study, the phenomenon under study is not readily distinguishable from its context (Yin, 1993: 3).

Case studies provide a natural basis for generalization (Adelman et al., 1980). Generalizations can be made about the instance or the group, or from the instance to the group. However, these are not statistical generalizations as case study researchers do not claim to generalize to the whole population, rather, as Stake (1994) notes, this kind of research lends itself to naturalistic generalization. Robson (2002) argues that case studies offer analytical generalizations, which means that they develop theories from one case which can help researchers to understand other similar cases, phenomena and situations. A single instance can tell us about the class of instances that the case relates to. For example, a multicultural inner city primary school can illuminate significant elements of similar inner city multicultural primary schools, including their strengths and weaknesses.

A case study presents a rich description and details of the lived experiences of specific cases or individuals and offers an understanding of how these individuals perceive the various phenomena in the social world and their effect on themselves. This kind of research approach needs to be conducted in an environment where the researcher can access the case to be studied. For example, a study of newly qualified primary teachers will usually be carried out in primary schools, and a study of senior managers in a college of further education will be undertaken at such a college. While traditionally case study was conducted by using observation as the sole method, interviews and documents are becoming increasingly popular, as are multiple methods using all of the above.

Different types of case study have been identified by researchers. However, there is considerable overlap in their views and the different types noted by them are not mutually exclusive, as can be seen below:

1. Exploratory, as a pilot to other studies or research questions
2. Descriptive, providing narrative accounts
3. Explanatory, testing theories
4. Interpretative, developing conceptual categories to examine initial assumptions
5. Evaluative, explaining and judging
6. Intrinsic, understanding the particular case in question
7. Instrumental, examining a particular case to gain insight into an issue or a theory
8. Collective, gaining a fuller picture by means of a group of individual studies
9. Historical case study
10. Psychological case study
11. Sociological case study
12. Ethnographic case study
13. Action research case study
14. Educational case study.

(Source: Merriam, 1988; Stake , 1994; Yin, 2009)

Adelman et al. (1980) argue that case study data are strong in reality because case studies are down-to-earth and attention-holding and are in harmony with the reader's own experience. Paradoxically, case study data are difficult to organize. Case studies recognize the complexity and embeddedness of social truths. By careful examination of social settings, case studies can look at discrepancies between participants' perceptions. They can provide archives of rich descriptive material that can allow subsequent reinterpretations, which may be different from the interpretations of the initial case study. Insights from case studies may be directly interpreted and put into action for improvement of policy and practice. Case studies are accessible as they are reported in a straightforward and less esoteric manner and allow the readers to make their own judgements about the implications of the research.

Case study research is ideally suited for a lone researcher specifically the one enrolled on a master's or doctoral programme. It essentially examines a case in depth. However, it can be conducted using both the qualitative and quantitative methodologies. At one end of the continuum are the data gathered through unstructured observation and unstructured or semi-structured interviews; at the other end are data collected through questionnaires and structured observation. Case study research is very similar to ethnographic research. The fundamental principles and techniques are the same in both these approaches.

Research spotlight

Social Relations in a Secondary School by Hargreaves (1967) is a case study of a secondary modern school which examined the social relations between teachers and pupils, and among pupils. The study used participant observation conducted during two school terms when the researcher was present in school every day. Other methods used for data collection were questionnaires, interviews and informal discussions.

Research spotlight

Beachside Comprehensive by Ball (1981) is a case study of a coeducational comprehensive school. It involved participant observation, interviews with teachers and pupils, and small-scale questionnaire and sociometric studies for data collection.

Ethnography

Ethno-graphy is literally the writing of culture. This is a tradition that educational research has adopted from cultural anthropology. The idea is to create a vivid portrayal of the culture or group being studied. In this research approach, the researcher usually undertakes participant observation of a situation over a long period of time. However, increasingly, interviewing is also being used as a method of data collection in ethnographic research, particularly in ethnographic case studies.

Woods (1986) observes that ethnography is:

> Concerned with what people are, how they behave, how they interact together. It aims to uncover their beliefs, values, perspectives, motivations, and how all these things develop or change over time or from situation to situation . . . It is *their* meanings and interpretations that count. This means learning *their* language and customs with all their nuances . . . [They have] constructed their own highly distinctive cultural realities, and if we are to understand them, we need to penetrate their boundaries. (p. 4)

LeCompte and Preissle (1993: 39–45) argue that ethnographic approaches are concerned more with description, rather than prediction, induction rather than deduction, generation rather than verification of theory, construction rather than enumeration and subjectivities rather than objective knowledge. As regards knowledge, they distinguish between *emic* approaches, as in the term 'phonemic', where the concern is to catch the subjective meanings placed on situations by participants; and *etic* approaches as in the term 'phonetic', where the intention is to identify and understand the objective or researcher's meaning and constructions of a situation.

According to Pring (2004), ethnography:

> Refers to that kind of research which takes seriously the perspectives and the interactions of the members of the social groups being studied. It is based on the premise that social reality cannot be understood except through the rules which structure the relations between members of the group and which make it possible for each to interpret the actions, gestures and words of the others. (p. 106)

Ethnographic research lends itself well to research topics which are not easily quantified (Fraenkel and Wallen, 1990). It can be used in many contexts. Woods (1986: 8–9) maintains that teachers can use the ethnographic approach in evaluating their own teaching, the motivation and learning of their students, and the development of their careers, thus enabling themselves to engage with research and have a direction over it. Cohen et al. (2007) point to critical ethnography, the emerging branch of ethnography that resonates with the critical paradigm. In this, qualitative anthropological research and participant observation is undertaken, with its theoretical basis grounded in critical theory (Carspecken, 1996).

Research spotlight

An example of ethnographic research is *Young, Gifted and Black: Student–Teacher Relations in the Schooling of Black Youth*, which is based on a study conducted by Mac an Ghaill (1988) using participant observation and interviews with students and teachers in which they speak candidly about what they think of each other.

Action research

Action research is a self-critical enquiry which can be effectively used to bring about change on a small scale. As the term indicates, it is research and action together, which is attractive to practitioners as they can understand, inform and reform their practice in this way. This kind of research is conducted by practitioners on their own work to consider its effect on themselves and others whom they work with. It can be carried out, for instance, by one teacher; a group of teachers and senior managers in a school; a group of teachers and outside researchers; or researchers, teachers, Local Authority (LA) personnel, and external sponsors working together as a group.

Elliott (1991) defines action research as:

> The study of a social situation with a view to improving the quality of action within it. It aims to feed practical judgement in concrete situations, and the validity of 'theories' and hypotheses it generates depends not so much on 'scientific' tests of truth as on their usefulness in helping people to act more intelligently and skilfully. In action research 'theories' are not validated independently and then applied to practice. They are validated through practice. (p. 69)

Action research is undertaken *in situ* to improve practice. This can be in teaching and learning, assessment procedures, management and administration, continuing professional development and so on. Kemmis and McTaggart (1988) note that action research involves problem-posing as well as problem-solving. It builds upon educational practitioners' existing skills and experiences as reflective practitioners (Middlewood et al., 1999). While most action research is carried out using the qualitative methodology, quantitative methodology can also be used in action research projects.

For example, a secondary English teacher finds that there is very little involvement of Year 7 boys in classroom interaction, with the result that they are performing poorly in tests. She is not sure whether it is due to her own teaching practice or the boys' apathy. She sets up a small-scale action research project using structured observation and semi-structured interviews with the boys and girls in her class. She finds that due to a combination of some girls' keenness to ask and answer questions, some boys' reluctance to raise their hands to ask or answer a question, the fact that she picked a girl who raised her hand to answer a question rather than putting a boy on the spot, and the pace of teaching were reasons for this gender imbalance. As a result of the research, the teacher adjusts her practice.

Research spotlight

Elliott and Adelman (1976) carried out an action research project from 1973–1975 which was funded by the Ford Foundation. It involved 12 schools and over 40 teachers who conducted action research into the issues of implementing inquiry/discovery methods in their classrooms.

However, the purpose of action research is not merely to improve practice. This research approach can enhance teachers' confidence and feelings of self-esteem, broaden their perspectives and awareness of classroom issues, and lead to change in values, beliefs and attitudes. Carr and Kemmis (1986) view action research as a self-reflective enquiry undertaken by practitioners to improve their practice in order to maximize social justice. Schostak (2002), too, views reflection as a necessary component in action research and sees this research approach as:

> A process of systematic reflection upon circumstances to bring about desired states of affairs. Reflection, whether it is critical of assumptions or simply based upon the acceptance of taken-for-granted presuppositions, aims to produce understandings, explanations, creative insights, syntheses, synergies, useful or delightful patterns as a basis for informing judgements, decision making and action. (p. 192)

Stenhouse (1979) contends that action research should contribute not just to practice, but to a theory of education and teaching so that other teachers can benefit from it. Though action research can successfully be carried out by a lone teacher as researcher, Kemmis and McTaggart (1988) regard action research essentially as a collaborative activity:

> Action research is a form of collective self-reflective enquiry undertaken by participants in social situations in order to improve the rationality and justice of their own social and educational practices, as well as their understanding of these practices and the situations in which these practices are carried out. (p. 5)

Action research is essentially helical whereby practitioner-researchers reflect on their practice, carry out research to inform their understanding of the issues, improve aspects of their practice, reflect on and evaluate the improved practice and consider aspects which still need attention, conduct more research to deal with the areas identified and so on.

Research spotlight

Ebbutt and Elliott (1985) conducted an action research study from 1981–1983 funded by the Schools Council, focusing on the problems of 'teaching for understanding' in the context of the public examination system. The study was carried out in nine schools. The researchers helped teachers to gather and analyse data, but emphasized that the teachers owned the data and were responsible for disseminating the findings.

Survey

Survey is the most widely used method of research in educational contexts and beyond. Surveys are generally concerned with examining large groups and are therefore designed to gather data from large numbers of respondents. They can provide a great deal of information in a relatively short time. Survey findings are claimed to be generalizable, enabling the researcher to make inferences about the wider population with some degree of confidence because of the large numbers investigated. These can be groups of people such as students or teachers, institutions, and even entire countries. This approach is useful for gathering data pertaining to facts, attitudes, behaviour and so on, but these data are largely superficial as surveys are not designed to look at issues in depth. Gorard (2003) notes that:

> The use of a survey is indicated when the data required does not already exist and the research questions are not susceptible to experimental trial for practical reasons such as lack of resources or ethical constraints. (p. 90)

Survey data can be analysed to provide description of, and comparison and contrast between, different groups. For example, a large Europe wide project may investigate widening access to nontraditional students in higher education. For this purpose, a survey can be carried out in a number of higher education institutions of different kinds in various European countries. However, for a student reading for a higher degree, it will be viable to carry out only a small-scale survey confined to perhaps one institution, looking at, for example, the post-18 destinations of male and female students in one college of further education; or pupils' performance in SATS in one primary school.

Surveys collect data at a specific point in time in order to explain current phenomena and make comparisons between them. The most commonly used method for this approach is a structured tool such as questionnaires, using the same questionnaire content and format for all subjects. These questionnaires gather data which are numerical or can easily be converted into numerical values making them suitable for statistical analysis. Surveys sometimes gather qualitative data too, but this is usually confined to a few open ended questions at the end of the questionnaire seeking a response in the form of a statement. Traditionally large-scale surveys are carried out by administering question-naires with a set number of questions in a certain sequence which do not vary during the process of data collection. Surveys carried out on small samples cannot claim generalizability. Although this presents a somewhat narrow view of surveys, this method has conventionally been used to investigate large samples resulting in generalizable findings.

In the field of education, this approach can be used to examine the achieve-ment of primary school pupils; minority ethnic students' completion of higher education courses; and boys' attainment in mathematics at GCSE. For example, a Local Authority (LA) wants to find out whether a particular government initiative is proving effective in its primary schools. It will employ a researcher to conduct a survey involving its 45 primary schools. This will entail adminis-tering questionnaires to a large representative sample from schools including headteachers, coordinators, teachers, teaching assistants, governors and parents. The survey will report findings which will be generalizable.

Structured interviews and structured observations, as well as questionnaires are quite popular for student projects using the survey approach. The common principle in these methods is that the questions asked to gather data are predetermined with no leeway to reformulate the questions or to introduce new themes. Researchers are tempted to conduct surveys using semi-structured interviews or unstructured observations, but this leads to data collection which is extremely time consuming, not to mention data analysis which is messy and unmanageable. Researchers, therefore, need to think carefully about the approaches and methods used in their research. While a survey is suitable to gather data of a biographical, factual and attitudinal nature from large samples, it is not the most appropriate approach to gather in-depth data from small number of respondents about perceptions, feelings and viewpoints.

Surveys can be carried out in a number of ways. Postal surveys are the traditional and most widely used approach. Other ways of conducting surveys is through structured face-to-ace interviews, by telephone, on the internet, and through structured observation.

Research spotlight

Croll (2008) examined young people's occupational choices at the age of 15 with regard to their educational attainment, parental occupation, and the young people's actual occupations when they were in their early 20s. He used data from the British Household Panel Survey over 5 to 10 years, which made longitudinal and intergenerational analysis possible. He found that choice was heavily constrained for many young people.

Research spotlight

Lambert et al. (2008) investigated bullying in schools by carrying out a survey of over 26,000 children aged 11–16. They asked questions about being bullied and being a bully, and explored risks and protection for young people. A significant relationship was found between behaviour and attitudes and being a bully. There was a strong relationship between being a bully and being bullied.

Postal survey

Postal surveys can access a large portion of the population and collect data quickly and cost effectively in a confidential manner. They can cover a wide geographical area and can reach people who would otherwise be difficult to access. They can be completed in respondents' own time, at their convenience in a place of their choice. Such surveys are not likely to be affected by researcher bias.

However, postal surveys have a poor return and response rate. Unlike interview surveys, the intended sample in postal surveys is unlikely to be the achieved sample; i.e. a large percentage of the questionnaires may not be returned. It is quite common to have a 20 per cent–40 per cent response rate in such surveys. Potential respondents may not wish to spend time completing a survey in which they have no interest. As they are usually anonymous, it is difficult to ascertain if the sample is truly representative of the population being studied. Respondents may return a partially completed questionnaire leaving some of the questions unanswered because of lack of comprehension or lack of interest.

Punch (2003) recommends planning ahead for a poor response rate by increasing the sample size. Other factors that can help with improving the response rate include sending stamped addressed envelopes with the questionnaire for its return, including a covering letter to introduce the researcher and to explain the purpose of the research, offering incentives for return of questionnaires, sending a reminder in case of nonresponse by the required date, and making the questionnaire simple and appealing.

Face-to-face interview survey

In face–to-face interview surveys the researcher can build a rapport with the respondents and clarify points raised by them, which facilitate a fuller response. This is a better method for looking at the views of people who cannot complete a questionnaire because of a disability or literacy problems. While it uses the standardized format, the interviewer can rephrase the questions or change the order in which they are asked depending on the information imparted by the respondent. Further, the researcher knows that the questions are being answered by the person whom they want to target; something which cannot be checked in case of a postal survey.

However, because of the flexibility in interview surveys, there may be problems of consistency and reliability. Researchers' bias such as their age, gender, social status, ethnicity, personality, appearance, dress, speech and so forth may influence the outcome. While these may be advantageous in some situations and help to develop a rapport between the researcher and the researched, and improve the quality of the responses, in other cases, these may be a hindrance and the respondents may want to withhold some of the information or give a response which they may think the researcher wants to hear. Interview surveys are time consuming as the researcher needs to physically get to the respondent, which may involve long distance travel in some cases which can be costly. People who work are not available during the day and may need to be approached in the evening or at weekends. This can be tricky; researchers may not feel safe going into certain areas when it is getting dark, and potential participants may not want to give up their free time if they have been at work all day.

Telephone survey

Telephone surveys help the researchers to save time and travel costs. A telephone call does not cost as much as actually travelling to the respondent and if the time is unsuitable, then the researcher can call back at a time convenient to the respondent. In case the persons called are not interested in participating, others with similar attributes can be approached.

Telephone surveys are more feasible if the telephone numbers of people are available. Some potential respondents may be ex-directory; others may not have a telephone. For example, if we want to conduct a survey on poverty and education to see how many young people from poor families go into further education, we may find that many of them do not have telephones and have to be approached by a different method. On the other hand, technological advancement has enabled affluent people to filter incoming calls by using answering machines, nonacceptance of unknown numbers and caller ID displayed on telephone apparatuses. This inconsistency in participant selection may lead to a skewed sample. Further, researchers may find that they have to repeat some questions, especially those that are asking for ranking or rating of categories, as such questions may not be understood properly on the telephone.

Internet surveys

In this technological age, the computer and the internet are proving to be great assets to researchers. We use them to search the literature, download and save the literature, word process our writing, gather data and analyse data.

Survey respondents can be directed to a website to complete the questionnaire. Potential respondents can be initially contacted by email, and also reminded by email in case of nonresponse. If email is used to send the questionnaire, then the file should be kept simple and should not contain graphics or it will become too big and might overload participants' mailboxes. Like paper questionnaires, the font should be of a reasonable size and not too intricate. Attachments should be avoided as potential participants may be reluctant to open files from an unknown source unless they have been alerted prior to the survey.

Internet surveys cost less, save time, are easy to administer, and data collected through web-based surveys can be processed automatically. However, internet surveys are mainly suitable for use with educated participants and younger participants who are more adept at using the internet.

Experimental design

Experiments can bring a degree of objectivity to the research as researchers can remain relatively aloof from the participants (Robson, 2002). Education and other social sciences have adopted this model from scientific research traditions. Undertaking an experiment means creating an artificial environment to test hypotheses. It entails making a change in the value of one variable, i.e. the independent variable, and observing the effect of that change on another variable, i.e. the dependent variable. In this approach, researchers intentionally control and manipulate situations and events which they wish to study. They may do so by introducing an intervention and subsequently measuring the difference made by it.

Experimental research can be:

- *Confirmatory*, when it uses a fixed design and supports or rejects a null hypothesis;
- *Exploratory*, when it discovers the effect of specific variables.

For example, we want to look at the development of the reading ability of 30 children in Year 4 in a primary school. These children have been in the same primary school for 3 years. They can be roughly divided into three groups of 10 pupils each according to their previous reading performance. We want to ascertain if using teaching assistants in the classroom will make a noticeable difference in their reading ability. We divide each of the three groups of

10 children into two, with 5 children in each subgroup. The whole class is then taught the same reading curriculum for one term. One half of each of the three groups, with 5 pupils each, does not get any additional treatment and represents the control group. Each child in the other half of the three groups works with a teaching assistant who listens to them read for 15 minutes every day. At the end of the experiment we find that the control group's reading has developed as much as was expected, but there is a marked improvement in the reading performance of the experimental group when the whole class is given a reading test. We can conclude that since the whole class got the same treatment, it was the teaching assistant who made a difference to the development of the experimental group.

Experimental research is based on the hypothetic-deductive model. It can show the relationship between cause and effect. In large-scale experiments, groups need to be matched for age, gender, social class, ethnic origin and so forth. However, this is difficult in smaller experimental studies undertaken by students for a higher degree. Most educational research using experiments is quasi-experimental rather than experimental. Gorard (2003) contends:

> In many ways, the experiment is seen as the 'flagship' or gold standard of research designs. The basic advantage of this approach over any other is its more convincing claim to be testing for cause and effect, via the manipulation of otherwise identical groups, rather than simply observing an unspecified relationship between two variables. In addition, some experiments will allow the size of any effect to be measured. It has been argued that only experiments are thus able to produce secure and uncontested knowledge about the truth of propositions. Their design is flexible, allowing for any number of different groups and variables, and the outcome measures taken can be of any kind (including qualitative observations), although they are normally converted to a coded numeric form. The design is actually so powerful that it requires smaller numbers of participants as a minimum than would be normal for a survey, for example. The analysis of the results is also generally easier than when using other designs. (p. 161)

In educational research, researcher and participant bias can be reduced by making the experiments blind or double blind. In blind experiments, participants do not know they are in the experimental or the control group, though the researcher is aware of which group each participant belongs to. In double blind experiments, even the researcher does not know who is in the experimental group and who is in the control group; this information is held by a third party, for example the class teacher. Sometimes it is necessary not to tell the participants that they are in an experiment. While this may be seen as deception, a debrief session to explain the reasons need to follow the experiment (see Chapter 3).

Gorard (2003: 163) summarizes the steps involved in a basic experiment:

1. Formulate a hypothesis (which is confirmatory/disconfirmatory rather than exploratory)
2. Randomly assign cases to the intervention or control groups (so that any nonexperimental differences are due solely to chance.
3. Measure the dependent variable (as a pre-test, but note that this step is not always used)
4. Introduce the treatment or independent variable.
5. Measure the dependent variable again (as a post-test).
6. Calculate the significance of the differences between the groups (or the effect size).

Experiments can be of two main kinds:

1. The true experiment

The true or the controlled experiment, is carried out in laboratory conditions on two or more groups, and where the variables are isolated, controlled and manipulated. There is at least one experimental group and at least one control group, which are allocated at random. The independent variables are isolated, controlled and manipulated, a pre-test is carried out, at least one intervention takes place, and a post-test is conducted to see the effects of the dependent variable.

2. The quasi-experiment

The quasi-experiment or the field experiment, is carried out in the same way as a controlled experiment, but in a natural setting, by isolating, controlling and manipulating the variables. However, it does not include all the elements of the true experiment stated above. In particular, the experimental and the control groups are not exactly matched for age, gender, ethnic origin and so on, as it is quite difficult to get perfectly corresponding features between groups in natural settings.

Cresswell (2003) suggests that:

> In experimental studies, investigators need to collect data so that all participants, and not only an experimental group, benefit from the treatments. This issue may require providing *some* treatment to all groups or staging the treatment so that ultimately all groups receive the beneficial treatment. (p. 65)

There can be a number of threats to the validity of experiments as noted by Gorard (2003: 164–168), citing Campbell and Stanley (1963); and Cook and Campbell (1979):

1. *History:* Participants may undergo other experiences during the study which are beyond their control that affect their recorded measurement, e.g. a child feeling sleepy during an experiment.

2. *Maturation:* We need time to ascertain if the experiment has been successful as only an immediate change in behaviour may be apparent, e.g. did the children become interested in reading for pleasure only for a week after an experiment introducing them to new books? Researchers also need to beware of the Hawthorne effect (see Chapter 3).

3. *Testing:* Participants may become used to testing or measurement and may respond to questions unthinkingly in the post-test. The experimenter effect is a serious threat to validity in testing as the researchers may convey their expectations of the experiment to the participants or sway the results in another way, such as by wrongly recording or analysing the findings of the test.

4. *Instrumentation:* Even when both groups appear to be treated equally, if the instrument used, the measurement taken, or the characteristics of the researchers change during the experiment, then it may influence the results.

5. *Regression:* Researchers are usually mainly concerned with aggregate scores in an experiment. Aggregate scores close to an extreme value tend to regress towards the mean score over time, regardless of whether they are slightly higher or lower than the mean, or the treatment they have received.

6. *Selection:* If subjective judgement or nonrandom methods of sample selection have been used, then the results will be biased. This problem can be solved to a large extent by randomly selecting the sample, and also allocating it randomly to the experimental group and the control group.

7. *Mortality:* Participant dropout or subject mortality can affect the validity of the experiment as participants who drop out may be quite different in their characteristics from those who continue with the experiment, or the nature of the experiment itself may cause a particular group to drop out.

8. *Diffusion:* The potential diffusion of treatments between groups can be the greatest threat to experiments. This can happen when the treatment cannot be confined to the experimental group and infects the control group, e.g. a new method of learning to spell may be told to participants in the control group by their friends in the experimental group in an attempt to help them with their spelling homework.

Gorard (2003) observes that because of the above threats and other potential limitations, perhaps the experimental design is not ideal after all and leaves room for doubt. He, nevertheless, argues that through our basic study design we can take steps to counter possible bias in experiments; and the experimental design is still the most theorized and understood approach in social science research, because our familiarity with this design brings an awareness of its shortcomings.

Research spotlight

Marsden (2007) writes about two experiments carried out in two secondary schools in England to investigate two different ways of teaching French verb agreements and auxiliaries to 13–14 year old students in top sets of Year 9. She argues that despite the limitations of small-scale educational experiments, experimental designs which combine a range of methods are able to generate new and useful substantive knowledge.

Designing the Project: preparing the groundwork

2

Chapter Outline

The purpose of the research dictates how to design and carry out our study. Whatever paradigm we select, the methodology we choose, the approach we take and the methods we apply in our research, all need to have fitness for purpose, i.e. all of the above have to be suitable for examining the construct under scrutiny and answering our research questions or testing our hypotheses. This chapter will discuss the different steps in project design. It will look at the role of theory, searching and reviewing the literature, choosing the hypotheses or research questions, and selecting the sample.

The trajectory of a researcher follows the life cycle of a research project. Certain tasks have to be completed before others can be engaged in, and specific matters have to be considered and tackled. The framework for designing a project will depend on the nature of the research and will be different for different projects. Yet, carrying out a research project entails addressing certain issues and taking specific steps which are common to all studies. These include choosing an issue to investigate; reading around the subject; devising our research questions or hypotheses; identifying the aims and objectives of the research; contemplating the paradigms, methodologies, approaches and methods to choose the most suitable one for our purposes; formulating research instruments; thinking about data analysis; considering issues of validity and reliability; taking steps to ensure ethical practice in research; conducting the pilot and gathering data for the main study; contemplating our audience and method of reporting and dissemination.

It is useful for researchers to produce a timetable, at the research design stage, of what they see as the key phases of research and present these in the form of a GANTT chart or critical path analysis, which shows not only the sequence and duration of activities, but also where certain elements are dependent on the completion of others. For example, sampling and fieldwork are dependent on having negotiated access.

The role of theory

Theory is 'a set of interconnected propositions that have the same referent – the subject of the theory' (Argyris and Schon, 1974: 4–5). Theory is an assumption, a concept, or a philosophy about a certain phenomenon or about the relationship between specific phenomena in a social setting. It explains what these assumptions are and presents an argument to inform us what the theory entails and how it was formulated. Theory enlightens us about what is known about and written about a particular issue, and thus provides a helpful backdrop to our research. Further, it provides explanations of the social world which are open to criticism and modification by future researchers. Silver (1983) maintains that theory is a unique way of perceiving reality and is an expression of profound insight into an aspect of nature. In congruence with other social sciences, research in education draws on theories from various disciplines such as anthropology, economics, political science, psychology and sociology.

Kerlinger (1986) defines theory as:

> A set of interrelated constructs, definitions and propositions that presents a systematic view of phenomena by specifying relations among variables with the purpose of explaining and predicting phenomena. (p. 9)

Hitchcock and Hughes (1995) contend that theory is concerned with the development of systematic construction of knowledge of the social world. They believe that in this way theory employs concepts, systems, models, structures, beliefs, ideas and hypotheses to make statements about actions, events and activities to analyse their causes and outcomes. O'Brien (1993) views theory as a kaleidoscope which brings into view new colours, shapes and patterns whenever it is shifted. Similarly, when we shift our theoretical perspectives, the way we perceive the social world and carry out research about it also change. A useful theory is one that tells an enlightening story about some phenomenon; a story that gives us new insights and broadens our understanding of the phenomenon (Anfara and Mertz, 2006: xvii).

Hopkins (2008: 72) uses the term theory in two distinct senses:

1. A set of personal assumptions, beliefs or presuppositions that we hold, including our view of the world and our individual construction of reality.
2. The more traditional or grand definition, referring to a coherent set of assumptions, which purport to explain, predict, and be used as a guide to practice.

McMillan and Schumacher (2001) insist that in order to help in the development of scientific knowledge, a theory needs to meet certain criteria. These are:

- To provide a simple explanation of the observed relations relevant to a phenomenon.
- To be consistent with both the observed relations and an already established body of knowledge.
- To be considered a tentative explanation and provide means for verification and revision.
- To stimulate further research in areas that require investigation.

Theory can be used in two different ways in a research project:

1. The research can start with theory and can be based on a theoretical or conceptual framework. This can help us to formulate our hypotheses and research questions and tell us how to proceed with our research.
2. The research can generate theory grounded in the data. Here, we need not necessarily rely on a theory to guide us from the outset. Instead, we develop a theory which emanates from our own data (see Chapter 9).

Punch (2005) distinguishes between the above two modes as theory-first research and theory-after research and proceeds to explain the distinction as follows:

> In theory-first research, we start with a theory, deduce hypotheses from it, and design a study to test these hypotheses. This is theory verification. In theory-after research, we do not start with a theory. Instead the aim is to end up with a theory, developed systematically from the data we have collected. This is theory-generation. (p. 16)

However, a theory is not sacrosanct. Every theory can be developed, modified or refuted as well as acceded to. This can be done by undertaking high quality research or by presenting convincing theoretical arguments. In fact, it is a rare theory which has not come under scrutiny. Theories which originated decades or even centuries ago are still being discussed today. Einstein's theory of Relativity, Newton's theory of Gravity and Darwin's theory of Evolution are classic examples of such theories. Also, Structuralism, Marxism, Postmodernism and Feminism illustrate theories that are used as frameworks for empirical research. Research in education draws on various theories such as theories of Learning and theories of Leadership. Below are examples of significant theories that are constantly debated and employed by educational researchers and those in other social sciences:

- Piaget's theory of Cognitive Development
- Vygotsky's theory of Zone of Proximal Development
- Bruner's theory of Scaffolding
- Herzberg's theory of Hygiene Factors
- Maslow's theory of Hierarchy of Needs
- Tajfel's theory of Social Identity
- Bourdieu's theory of Habitus
- Coleman's theory of Social Capital
- Bloom's theory (Taxonomy) of Educational Objectives
- Bernstein's theory of Sociolinguistics

Maslow's original theory of Hierarchy of Needs (Maslow, 1954) below (Figure 2.1) is a typical example of a theory that has been thoroughly debated and critiqued over the years.

Researchers need to decide at the beginning of their research, at the design stage, what role theory will play in their study. Sometimes the research issue is a familiar one and there are several theoretical frameworks to choose from.

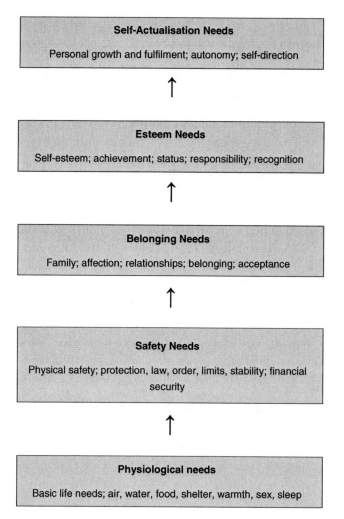

Figure 2.1 Maslow's Hierarchy of Needs

In such cases, it is helpful to use one of these theories as the conceptual framework for our research. Miles and Huberman (1994) note:

> A conceptual framework explains, either graphically or in narrative form, the main things to be studied – the key factors, constructs or variables – and the presumed relationships among them. Frameworks can be rudimentary or elaborate, theory-driven or commonsensical, descriptive or casual. (p. 18)

Selecting a theory to fit our research issue can be a complex process. Sometimes, several theories need to be considered before a theory apposite to our study is discovered. On the other hand, we may not wish to base our empirical research on an existing theory and may want to develop theory grounded in data collected for our research. Both these approaches are perfectly legitimate as long as we are clear in our mind about theorizing, and that the way theory is being employed or generated fits the purpose of our research. Mercer (1991: 42) points to the dual function of theories:

1. To set agendas for research by generating certain kinds of questions that the research will aim to answer.
2. To provide an environment of discourse within which research findings can be explained and discussed.

LeCompte and Preissle (1993: 239) note that theorizing is 'simply the cognitive process of discovering or manipulating abstract categories and the relationships among these categories'. Still, it is not straightforward to develop a theory from empirical research or to link an existing theory to practice by using it as the basis of our research. Hopkins (2008: 72) argues that in many cases, the gap between theory and practice is so big that no useful connection can be made between the two. This happens because theories are either not sufficiently precise or the propositions that they hold are not readily generalized to specific situations.

Understanding theory and its relationship to research, therefore, requires effort and the development of appropriate skills to do so. However, once we have grasped a theory, it can seem pretty straightforward. Anfara and Mertz (2006: xiv) argue that understanding a theory can involve:

- Travelling into someone else's mind and being able to perceive reality as they do.
- Experiencing a shift in our mental structure and discovering a different way of thinking.
- Wondering why we never saw before what seems to have been so obvious all along.
- Stretching our mind to grasp the theorist's meaning.

It is argued that it would be difficult to imagine a study without a theoretical and conceptual framework to guide us and act as a structure, scaffolding and frame of our research (Merriam, 1998: 45–46). Even if we do not use a theoretical framework, we need to be cognizant of what research has been undertaken previously on the topic that we have chosen for our study. This necessitates a literature search followed by a critical review of the relevant literature.

Searching and reviewing the literature

Searching

No research study can be undertaken without an understanding of the context to which it is related and what previous researchers have found when investigating a topic similar to the one we have chosen to study. We need to engage with previous literature as one day our research will become part of this wider body of literature. Such a review is crucial for all dissertations and theses reporting projects conducted for higher degrees, and for post doctoral studies. Sometimes there is no literature, which is directly pertinent to our area of research, if no research has been carried out on that issue. In that case researchers have to look at the literature which is somewhat linked to the topic they are examining and consider how it relates to their own research. However, it is unlikely that a researcher studying for a higher degree will choose an unresearched area as it will be time consuming to search for literature for such a study.

Conversely, and more frequently, there may be a great deal which has already been written about our chosen subject. In this case, we need to question our choice of topic, whether more research is required in this area unless we can bring in a new angle or choose a sub-theme which has been overlooked so far. If we have an abundance of literature to draw on, then we ought to look carefully at what we are reviewing and how it relates to our research focus.

There are a number of sources that we can search for to access the literature on a particular subject. These include the following:

- Books
- Refereed academic journals
- Practitioner journals
- Conference papers
- Newspapers and magazines
- Websites
- Government reports
- Government policies
- Government white and green papers
- Photographs, slides, videos and DVDs
- Transcripts of interviews and fieldnotes
- Diaries, logs and journals
- Statistics
- Drawings
- Tables, bar charts, histograms

- Archives
- Theses written by former students
- Unpublished documents

Wallace and Wray (2006: 80) divide frontline literature into four types. These are as follows:

1. *Theoretical* literature, which presents models and theories for interpreting and explaining patterns in practice.

2. *Research* literature, which describes systematic enquiries into policy and practice.

3. *Practice* literature, written by informed professionals who evaluate others' practice, and by practitioners who evaluate their own practice.

4. *Policy* literature, which proposes changes in practice that are desired by policy makers, thereby implying a negative evaluation of present practice.

A decade and a half ago, researchers used microfische and card indices to search for sources of literature. Now the internet has made searching extremely swift and easy. All we need to do is to put the search term or keyword in a search engine to find books, journal articles, reports and so forth. We can try several different keywords to access the appropriate literature. We may need to use synonyms and words spelt differently such as organisation/organization and behaviour/behavior.

Most university libraries are up-to-date and well-stocked with books and journals. Increasingly, libraries are subscribing to electronic versions of journals instead of the hard copies. Books can be accessed easily through the libraries' online catalogues. Journal articles can be found through search engines such as the British Education Index (BREI), the Educational Resources Information Centre (ERIC) and the Australian Education Index (AUEI).

It is always a good idea to look at the abstract first to check if the paper is useful for us. The full text of most journal articles can then be downloaded to our computer, if our university library subscribes to the journal. If not, then we can either buy the paper, which can be expensive, get it through inter-library loan, or approach the author to request a copy. Once we become familiar with the name of an author who has written about issues similar to those that we are investigating, we can put the name of the author in the search engine, specifying the year that we want to go back to, and it will display all the papers published by that author starting from that year to date.

Rather than searching to build up a comprehensive list of literature sources, it is better to start reviewing the literature as soon as we have identified a few sources, while continuing with the search. It is always helpful to look at recent sources first as reference lists at the end of journal papers and books provide other invaluable sources that researchers can look at.

Reading

Taylor (1989) maintains that:

> Critical interpretation and evaluation such as we use for writing essays feeds on the half-formed images and experiences of general reading. Critical reading must respond to details. (p. 55)

Perusing the literature in a critical fashion is a skill that all researchers need to develop. We have to constantly question what we are reading instead of taking everything at face value. Rather than reading everything that we come across which has a vague connection to what we propose to do, it is important to be selective in what we read. Researchers always need to have their working title and their research questions or hypotheses in mind when reading for their study.

Fairbairn and Winch (1991: 12–13) suggest that critical reading is a process that involves the following:

- *Reorganizing* what we have read by selecting what is important in each of the sources and putting together what we have learned in a way that is coherent and relevant to our particular concerns.
- *Inferring* from what we have read that there is a possibility that there is more to what the authors wish to communicate than what they have stated.
- *Evaluating* the worth of what we read by appraising the arguments, evidence and assertions; assessing if the views expressed are consistent with one another; and checking the veracity of facts by differentiating between facts and opinions.

As stated above, abstracts of papers will inform us if a paper is useful for our purposes. Researchers can also look at the Conclusions of journal papers, books and theses to find out whether they need to read the preceding sections. It is not always necessary to read the entire book because sometimes only specific chapters and sections are pertinent to our research. On the other hand, if we are aware of a seminal publication on our subject which is much cited, then we ought to read it fully. *The Discovery of Grounded Theory* by Glaser and Strauss (1967); *Learning to Labour* by Willis (1977); *Orientalism* by Said (1978); and *Fifteen Thousand Hours* by Rutter et al. (1979) are examples of such publications. Reading not only tells us what to write, but also teaches us how to write in a critical fashion, as we learn to develop our style of writing by looking at the way other researchers have written about their work.

Wallace and Wray (2006: 31–32) state five critical synopsis questions that researchers need to ask themselves when reading a text:

1. Why am I reading this?
2. What are the authors trying to do in writing this?
3. What are the authors saying which is relevant to what I want to find out?
4. How convincing is what the authors are saying?
5. In conclusion, what use can I make of this?

Researchers need to get into the habit of making notes and summaries of their readings early on. Key points of a paper, chapter or report can be written with full reference to the source in the form in which it will go in the reference list. This can be done on cards, if the researcher finds it easier, or on the computer. Most people find it useful to work on their laptop in the library or in their office and make notes as they read. This has the advantage of research-ers being able to cut and paste when the Literature Review chapter is being written. Categorizing the literature according to themes as we make notes in a Word document can save time later when writing up the review of literature, as the chapter can be organized using some of these themes as subheadings. Hart (2005: 177) suggests using spider diagrams and tables that show the main themes of the literature. Software programmes such as Endnote and Refworks are particularly helpful in keeping a record of the references.

Marshall and Rossman (2006: 26) maintain that a careful reading of the related literature serves two purposes:

1. It provides evidence for the significance of the study for practice and policy and for its contribution to the ongoing discourse about the topic (often referred to as contributing to 'knowledge').
2. It identifies the important intellectual traditions that guide the study, thereby develop-ing a conceptual framework and refining an important and viable research question.

Reviewing and writing

Once we have searched the literature for our study, have read it and recorded it in some way, we need to start writing a critical review of the literature pertinent to our research. Richardson (1994) views writing itself as a method of inquiry and argues that it is:

A way of finding out about yourself and your topic. Although we usually think about writing as a mode of 'telling' about the social world, writing is not just a mopping-up activity at the end of a research project. Writing is also a way of 'knowing' – a method of discovery and analysis. By writing in different ways, we discover new aspects of our topic and our relationship to it. (p. 516)

This suggests that writing is a continuing process during a research study. Researchers need to ensure that the review of literature is critical, evaluative and dialogic, and not descriptive. We are not required to merely describe and replicate what someone has written, but have a dialogue with what is known and written about the specific subject and offer a critique of it. This does not mean that we look at someone's work and criticize it in a negative or disparaging way. Critique means analysing something to look at its strengths and weaknesses, offering arguments in favour of or against it, in the light of our own standpoint on the subject. Hart (1998) maintains that a literature review involves:

The selection of available documents (both published and unpublished) on the topic, which contain information, ideas, data and evidence written from a particular standpoint, to fulfil certain aims, or express certain views on the nature of the topic and how it is to be investigated, and the effective evaluation of these documents in relation to the research being proposed. (p. 13)

It is important to remember that whatever literature is reviewed is succinct, relates to our research issues, and answers our research questions or test our hypotheses. It has to be closely linked to the story that we want to tell about our research. It is a fallacy that once we have reviewed the literature at the beginning of our study and written a chapter on Review of Literature, that part of our study is finished. Though it is extremely important to review the literature at the onset in order to gain an insight into our chosen area of research, to develop our research questions and hypotheses, and to formulate our research instruments, yet literature review is an ongoing process which will be updated a few times during our research. It ends with the completion of our study because new and unthought-of themes are likely to emanate during the research process and compel us to return to the literature to look for comparisons with our research. While it is not always possible, but we may also need to take into account pertinent research by others that is published during the course of our own study.

Sometimes researchers choose to review the literature on their topic and analyse their findings together under a number of themes. Though this method is unconventional, it makes perfect sense and tells the reader about previous and current research, comparing and contrasting them at the same time (for an example, see Basit, 1995), while telling a coherent story about the issue that has been examined, using an academic style of writing.

However, learning to write in an academic style is not easy and is a skill that needs to be developed over a period of time. Like most skills, the more we do it the better we get. This is assuming that we read and reflect on what we have written, and receive regular feedback from others, such as supervisors, critical friends, editors and peer reviewers on how we can improve our style. Holliday (2007) points to the mixed messages given to researchers. He maintains that:

> A major factor which makes the conventions of academic writing in English problematic for the novice is that there are conflicting signals. At first sight, a major criterion for 'acceptable' writing seems to be that there should be a huge amount of reference to other people, leaving very little room for the ideas and experience of the writer. (p. 118)

We need to achieve a balance between what, who and how much is cited from previous literature and how much analytical commentary of our own is included in the discussion. It is vital that researchers appropriately cite the sources of literature that they review. Failure to do so, even inadvertently, is tantamount to plagiarism.

Researchers do not just need to review the literature on the substantive area of their study, but have to read and review the literature on research methods as well. This is fundamental to research as we need to convince our audience which research methods we have considered before designing our own project and why the way we have planned and executed our research is the most appropriate design for a study of this kind. This discussion needs to be presented in a chapter or section on Research Design, interweaving our argument with abundant references to the research methods literature to justify our stance.

Formulating the hypotheses or research questions

Developing a hypothesis

Devising a hypothesis is similar to developing research questions for a qualitative study and will entail reading around the subject and about the research conducted in the field by other researchers. A hypothesis is a statement formulated by researchers that they want to test when undertaking a quantitative study. It is a hunch or idea that a researcher has about relationships between specific variables. Hypotheses are formulated for quantitative studies, during the course of which they are proven or unproven.

Kerlinger (1986) views a hypothesis as a conjectural statement or an educated guess about the relations between two or more variables. He argues that hypotheses are significant research tools because:

1. They organize the efforts of the researchers by enabling them to understand the problem and providing them with a framework for gathering and analysing the data.
2. They are the working instruments of theory and can be deduced from theory or from other hypotheses.
3. They can be tested empirically or experimentally resulting in their confirmation or rejection.
4. They are powerful tools for the advancement of knowledge.

Cohen et al. (2007: 82–83) note that a 'good' hypothesis has the following features:

1. It is clear on whether it is directional – stating the kind or direction of difference or relationship between two conditions or groups; or nondirectional – simply predicting that there will be a difference or relationship between two conditions or groups.
2. It is written in a testable form, in a way that makes it clear how the researcher will design an experiment or survey to test it.
3. It is written in a form that can yield measurable results.

Testing hypotheses will involve looking at two or more variables to prove or disprove a statement, such as the following:

- Final year students studying for a Bachelor in Education attain higher grades when taught by a combination of lectures and seminars than just by lectures (i.e. there is a relationship between final year students' attainment and teaching by lectures and seminars).
- Year 6 primary pupils find Science lessons more interesting and comprehensible when given the chance to conduct experiments themselves rather than just observing demonstrations by the teacher (i.e. there is a relationship between primary pupils' science comprehension and hands-on experience of the subject).

Or they can be stated simply as:

- People who are intrinsically motivated make better teachers.
- There is no relationship between social class and entry to grammar school.
- Ethnicity and gender do not play a part in getting into higher education.

The two main types of hypotheses are the null hypothesis and the alternative hypothesis. The null hypothesis (written as H_0) shows no relationship or difference between variables. The alternative hypothesis (written as H_1) shows a correlation between variables. In testing the hypotheses, if one of them is supported, then the other is unsupported.

Devising research questions

Research questions are the qualitative equivalent of hypotheses: a quantitative study tests hypotheses and a qualitative study addresses research questions. Miles and Huberman (1994) maintain a flexible approach to the development of research questions in a research study:

> The formulation of research questions may precede or follow the development of a conceptual framework. The questions represent the facets of an empirical domain that the researcher most wants to explore. Research questions may be general or particular, descriptive or explanatory. They may be formulated at the outset or later on, and may be refined or reformulated in the course of the fieldwork. (p. 23)

Research questions are directly relevant to the working title and aims and objectives of the study. They represent a breakdown of the working title, splitting it into questions which the research project will seek to tackle. These questions tell us what we can, and cannot, explore through our research. Punch (2005: 37) regards the role of research questions as:

- Organizing the project and giving it direction and coherence.
- Delimiting the project and showing its boundaries.
- Keeping the researcher focused.
- Pointing to the methods and data that will be needed.
- Providing a framework for writing up the research.

We may have a notion of what questions we need to ask of our research, but it is a mistake to finalize our research questions prematurely. These questions ought to be devised after a thorough review of the literature on the issue under investigation. This will help us to determine what research has already been carried out in the area and what gaps exist in the field. To some extent, the process is iterative, as we may need to modify our research questions in light of what we discover in further readings, and even during our pilot study. Cresswell (2003) contends:

> Expect the research questions to evolve and to change during the study in a manner consistent with the assumptions of an emerging design. Often in *qualitative*

studies, the questions are under continual review and reformulation (as in a grounded theory study). (p. 107)

Most doctoral studies will have 3–4 primary research questions and each of these will have 2–3 secondary research questions. These are the wide questions that our research will address, not the specific questions that we will actually ask in interviews and questionnaires. Gorard (2003: 117) notes that novice researchers 'become confused between their research questions, which define what they are trying to find out, and the questions they use in an investigation to answer those research questions'.

Once we are fairly certain about the research questions that we want to ask, we can consider the methods of gathering data for our study that will be suitable for addressing these research questions, and develop appropriate instruments for this purpose. Research questions form the foundation for developing research instruments. Questions asked in questionnaires and interview schedules, and statements in observation checklists will have a clear linkage with our primary and secondary research questions. Ultimately, our analysis of data needs to refer back to the research questions to demonstrate that these questions have been addressed through our research.

Selecting the sample

Researchers cannot study the entire population of the group – for example, primary school children or female lecturers – that they want to investigate because of constraints of time, access and expenditure. They, therefore, have to choose a subset of that population. This subset is called the sample. Cohen et al. (2007) maintain that questions of sampling arise directly out of the issue of defining the population on which the research will focus and researchers must take sampling decisions early in the overall planning of a piece of research. According to Oppenheim (1992: 38), 'the term sample is used to indicate a smaller group, which is usually, though not always, a representative of a population'. Gorard (2003) maintains:

The main reason that the samples are used is to save time and money for the researcher. Sampling is a useful shortcut, leading to results that can be almost as accurate as those for a full census of the population being studied, but for a fraction of the cost . . . A second reason for using a sample is that many methods of formal data analysis are based explicitly on sampling theory. Most notably, all the statistical tests of significance . . . assume that the data was collected from a sample drawn independently and randomly from a previously defined population. (p. 57)

There are two main sampling strategies, probability sampling and non-probability sampling. Educational researchers can choose from a number of sampling methods below which are related to these two main strategies:

Probability sampling

In this sampling strategy the researcher has equal access to each participant in the population from which the sample is drawn, such as a college of further education, and each participant has a similar chance of being selected for the sample. This is our sampling frame. This kind of sampling is viewed as representative of the entire population because of the way the sample is selected. It is believed that there is less risk of bias when using probability sampling and the findings are seen as generalizable.

Random sampling

In simple terms, it can be done by picking participants' names out of a hat. Researchers can also use a statistical package for a random number generator. In this sampling method, each member of the population under study has an equal chance of being selected and the probability of a member of the population being selected is unaffected by the selection of other members of the population. The sample needs to have participants with characteristics similar to the population as a whole, for example, old and young; male and female; tall and short; ethnic majority and ethnic minority; rich and poor; fit and disabled and so forth. The exact proportion of these subgroups in relation to the wider population is however difficult to achieve because a complete list of the wider population is rarely available.

Systematic sampling

This method is similar to random sampling except that the sample is selected in a systematic manner rather than randomly. Researchers can select random numbers from a list of names in the same sequence depending on how big a sample they want to select. For example, if we want to choose 60 respondents from a population of 300, we will pick every fifth name from a list of 300 primary school children. Researchers should randomly decide the point in the list at which the selection should start because if a list is alphabetical, then the first person will have a higher chance of being selected than the others.

To avoid selecting a skewed sample, the initial listing has to be chosen randomly too.

Stratified sampling

If we need to choose research participants with different traits, such as male, female; young, mature; ethnic minority, ethnic majority; then we need to split the sampling frame into different lists of homogeneous groups with similar characteristics, though in order to do that we will need to have this information, which could be obtained prior to choosing the sample. So, if we want to examine how many students complete Masters courses in higher education institutions (HEIs) in a particular geographical area of England, such as the North West, we will need to decide whether we are interested in looking at gender, ethnicity or age of the students, or to find out whether they are studying for a Masters in science, humanities or social sciences, and compile our sampling frames accordingly before selecting the sample. In our sample, group one can contain young students – aged under 25, and group two can include mature students – aged 25 and over. To obtain a sample representative of the whole population in terms of age, a random selection of participants from group one and group two has to be taken. If possible, the exact proportion of young and mature students in the entire population of Masters students in the North west of England can be reflected in the sample.

Cluster sampling

This means choosing our sample from a cluster or area which is geographically convenient for the researcher to approach. This can be pupils in primary schools within the same local authority (LA) or in the same part of a city. This sampling strategy is used to avoid logistical and administrative problems when investigating a widely distributed population. For example, if we want to look at the use of the Internet amongst secondary school children, we can select a sample of secondary schools within a radius of 20 miles in the city where we live. This will not only make it easy to negotiate access, but also save time and expense when carrying out the fieldwork. This method is popular in small-scale research.

Stage sampling

This is an extension of cluster sampling whereby the sample is chosen in a number of stages. For example, if we want a national sample of mature students in higher education, we can create a sample of HEIs in different geographical areas within the country, then different schools within these HEIs, then students within these schools, assuming the schools have students' ages on their databases.

Nonprobability sampling

This sampling strategy is used when we do not have the need or ability to draw on a sampling frame, or where none is available, mainly when we are working within an interpretive paradigm using a qualitative methodology. In this, some members of the wider population definitely will be excluded and others definitely included, i.e. every member of the wider population does not have an equal chance of being included in the sample because we have deliberately chosen a particular section of the wider population. This happens when we are conducting a small-scale study. In this case, we are not concerned about the generalizability of our findings and are willing to work with a small sample. The sample is not representative of the wider population: it only represents itself. This sampling strategy is used in research approaches such as case study, ethnography and action research.

Convenience (or opportunity) sampling

This method of sampling is used to select what is easily accessible to the researcher. The sample drawn by this method does not claim to be representative of the wider population, nor can it claim generalizability, and this is something that we should make very clear when reporting our research. Nevertheless, it does not mean choosing just about anybody we know. For example, if we want to examine the views of parents regarding the teaching of mathematics at primary school level, we will need to have participants who have children in primary schools, though we may access parents personally known to us, parents who have children at our local primary school, or at the few primary schools nearby.

Purposive (or judgemental) sampling

In this method of sampling, we use our discretion, knowledge or experience to choose the sample which we think suits the purposes of our study. The researcher needs to make it clear in the study that the sample is selective and does not seek to represent the wider population or claim generalization. This method is useful for small-scale studies in which the researcher knows exactly what kind of sample is required and how it can be accessed. For example, a group of trainee teachers in an HEI is selected because it dropped out of teacher training courses, or a group of minority ethnic pupils in a secondary school is chosen because it has been a victim of racism.

Quota sampling

This nonprobability method of sampling which is used in qualitative studies is the equivalent of stratified sampling, which is a type of probability sampling. After determining the sample size, the researcher can allocate quotas for numbers to be included in each category of the final sample, trying to ensure that the proportion of participants in each group are similar to those in the population from which they are drawn.

Dimensional sampling

This is an extension of quota sampling where quotas are set for two or more characteristics in a group. For example, if we have set a quota for university lecturers below the age of 30, then we may set a quota on the basis of not just their age, but also their subject specialism, gender and so forth. A table showing these dimensions can have the lecturers' age horizontally along the top, and their gender, qualifications, subject and so forth vertically along the side.

Snowball sampling

This sampling method is used when it is difficult to obtain the desired sample at the outset. The researchers may only be able to approach a couple of participants with the required characteristics. These participants can then be requested to refer the researchers to others with similar attributes, who can then in turn direct the researchers to similar others. Thus, like a snowball, the researchers have a sample that keeps getting bigger and bigger. It has also got the advantage of giving credibility to the researchers as they are introduced to further participants by someone with whom these new participants are usually well acquainted. This method is particularly useful when examining sensitive issues such as bullying in primary schools or the gang culture in a particular LA. It is also beneficial in studies in which the sample cannot be easily traced, for example, students who withdrew from Bachelor courses at HEIs in the last five years.

The choice of the sampling method is dependent on a number of factors. Significantly, we need to determine what statements we want to make on the basis of our data. For generalizable national surveys, this would involve hundreds and thousands of respondents. If we want to make generalizations from our data that we have collected for a master's or doctoral project, then we will need to use a large sample of at least 100 subjects. However, if our purpose is to illuminate a phenomenon or elucidate a specific case, then we need to do an in-depth investigation of a small sample.

The size of the sample will also be determined by what kind of data we want to collect. If we want to gather information which is factual, biographical, or relates to people's attitudes, and are sure of the questions that we need to ask, then we can use a large sample, using a quantitative methodology, working within a positivist paradigm. On the other hand, if we are seeking in-depth data, based on people's perceptions and feelings, and want to keep ourselves open to addressing issues raised by the research participants during data collection, then we will choose a small sample, using a qualitative methodology working within an interpretive paradigm. Most importantly, the size of the sample needs to be based on the time and other resources available for that particular research project.

Issues in Research: moral, authentic and trustworthy investigations

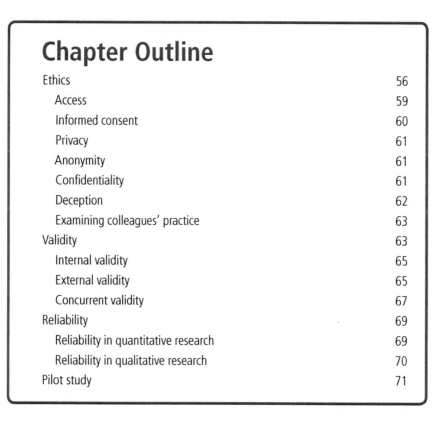

There are a number of issues that researchers have to take into consideration during their study. This chapter will discuss matters that need to be remembered and dealt with when designing, conducting and reporting research. These include research ethics, validity and reliability.

Ethics

'Ethics is concerned with the attempt to formulate codes and principles of moral behaviour' (May, 2001: 59). Simons (1995: 436) defines ethics as the 'search for rules of conduct that enable us to operate defensibly in the political contexts in which we have to conduct educational research'. Ethical considerations are extremely important in educational research and researchers need to ensure that research is conducted in an ethical manner. This entails going for one option when another option is available, or when several other options are available, making our choice on the basis of moral and ethical reasoning. This must be kept in mind throughout the study – at design stage, in gaining access to the sample, in collecting and analysing the data, in writing up the report, and in disseminating the research findings. Care needs to be taken to conduct the study with sensitivity, preserve the dignity of the participants, and not to harm or hurt them in any way during the research process, while still being able to undertake quality research. The data collected and the findings reported must not be falsified to make them socially acceptable or to appease a specific audience.

Pring (2004: 142–145) notes that the word ethics is often used loosely and interchangeably with morals, and that moral judgements require substantial deliberation because of the multitude of factors that have to be considered. He distinguishes between moral considerations which relate to general 'principles of action' and those which relate to the dispositions and character of the researcher. He also draws attention to 'principles', which one appeals to in justifying an action; and 'rules', which are more specific and less open to interpretation. He, nevertheless, argues that while principles have the logic of general rules, they embody the values appealed to in the establishment of the rules, or in questioning the appropriateness of the rules on various occasions. He refers to two principles which seem particularly important to educational research, but are often irreconcilable: the principle requiring respect for the dignity and confidentiality of the 'objects' of research; and the principle reflecting the purpose of research, i.e. the pursuit of truth. He highlights the dilemma faced by researchers when he advocates respect for the dignity and privacy of research participants on the one hand, and the pursuit of truth and the right of society to know on the other.

'Some of the most intractable ethical problems arise from conflicts among principles and the necessity of trading one against the other. The balancing of such principles in concrete situations is the ultimate ethical act' (House, 1993: 168). Gorard (2003) argues that:

> Ethically, the first responsibility of all research should be to quality and rigour. If it is decided that the best answer to a specific research question is likely to be obtained via an experimental design, for example, then this is at least part of the justification in ethical terms for its use. In this case, the experiment may be the *most* ethical approach even where it runs a slightly greater risk of 'endangering' participants than another less appropriate design. (p. 173)

Other considerations involve the manner in which researchers communicate with the research participants and the way the findings are conveyed to an audience. We need to demonstrate acute sensitivity regarding the participants' gender, race/ethnicity, social class, disability and so forth when interacting with them. We should also be careful in the way we address issues pertaining to these constructs even if they do not directly relate to the participants. The language used by the researchers while asking questions or reporting the findings must not be sexist. It is better to use s/he, or he or she; him/her, or him or her; or use plurals if possible, such as they, them, their. Also, the language must not be racist and researchers should not use terms for different ethnic groups which are viewed as derogatory, such as Nigger, Paki, Wog. However, if sexist or racist terminology is used by the participants during data collection, then researchers need to report it as such in their writings, referring to the discriminatory nature of the terms. As I have noted elsewhere, we also need to create a nonhierarchical relationship with our research participants, and dress appropriately for the fieldwork, which does not necessarily mean dressing in the same way as the participants (Basit, 1995).

Researchers ought to show due consideration for the equipment and buildings in the field too. Cresswell (2003) argues that during data collection:

> Researchers need to respect research sites so that sites are left undisturbed after a research study. This requires that inquirers, especially in qualitative studies involving prolonged observation or interviewing at a site, be cognisant of their impact and minimise their disruption of the physical setting. For example, they might time visits so that they intrude little on the flow of activities of participants. (p. 65)

Organizations such as the British Educational Research Association (BERA), the British Sociological Association (BSA) and the Economic and Social

Research Council (ESRC) have their own ethical guidelines to advise research-ers how to conduct research. BERA (2004) recommends that:

> Educational researchers should operate within an ethic of respect for any persons involved directly or indirectly in the research they are undertaking, regardless of age, sex, race, religion, political beliefs and lifestyle, or any other significant differ-ence between such persons and the researchers themselves or other participants in the research. (p. 6)

Similarly, the ESRC (2005) states six key principles of ethical research that it expects to be addressed:

- Research should be designed, reviewed and undertaken to ensure integrity and quality.
- Research staff and subjects must be informed fully about the purpose, methods and intended possible uses of the research, what their participation in the research entails and what risks, if any, are involved (though some variation is allowed in exceptional contexts).
- The confidentiality of information supplied by research subjects and the anonymity of respondents must be respected.
- Research participants must participate in a voluntary way, free from any coercion.
- Harm to research participants must be avoided.
- The independence of research must be clear, and any conflicts of interest or partiality must be explicit. (p. 1)

Universities now operate university-wide Ethics Committees, and such committees within each school/department as well. Researchers have to obtain approval from the relevant ethics committee before they start their research. A detailed proposal needs to be submitted by researchers, when they seek the consent of their institution, specifying how they will conduct their research in an ethical manner. Subsequent sections of this chapter will discuss matters concerning research ethics regarding access, informed consent, privacy, anonymity, confidentiality and deception.

Activity

You are designing a research project. This involves carrying out a **qualitative** study. Explain briefly what your research is about and then write down in detail what ethical considerations will impinge on your research.

> ### Activity
>
> You are designing a research project. This involves carrying out a ***quantitative*** study. Explain briefly what your research is about and then write down in detail what ethical considerations will impinge on your research.

Access

Gaining access to the kind of sample that we require for our research is not always easy. Our potential participants may be busy, uninterested, or have already had too many demands on their time by researchers. Sometimes access needs to be negotiated in stages. For example, if we want to look at the way Information and Communication Technology (ICT) is taught in secondary schools in a particular LA, we will need to approach someone in the LA to get a list of primary schools and contact details of the headteachers. Then we will contact the headteachers and ask them if they are willing to let us observe ICT lessons and interview the teachers and pupils. Some headteachers may be willing, but some of the teachers in their schools may be unwilling to participate. At every stage, we will need to explain who we are and why we are capable of conducting this research, what our research is about, and what its likely benefits are, to seek the acceptance of the gatekeepers i.e. the LA officer and the headteachers; and the participants, i.e. the teachers and the pupils. We will also need to assure them that the research will be carried out in an ethical manner, explaining to them the ways in which it will be done.

For interviewing young children in infant or primary schools, parents' permission will also be required to gain access to their children. It is always a good idea to negotiate access for all aspects of the fieldwork at the onset. Otherwise, we may find that we have been given permission to observe the lessons, but when we get to the interviewing phase, the teachers declare they are too busy to be interviewed. Researchers need to be sensitive to the working milieu and the timetable of the institutions in which they want to gather data. For example, it will be inconsiderate to request access for fieldwork at a time when teachers at a secondary school are about to undergo an Ofsted inspection, or when students at an FE college are preparing to sit their final examination. When carrying out fieldwork in schools, Burgess (1984) advises researchers to take note of the three-term cycle in British schools and its influence upon timetable and related activities.

Walford (1991) gives an account of the ways in which he successfully negotiated access to carry out research in a City Technology College, and notes that researchers' persistent attempts to gain access to the research sites can be viewed by some as perseverance, but by others as unwarranted harassment. Woods (1998) observes that sometimes researchers themselves can create barriers to access:

> Access involves movement on the part of the researcher, but that cannot always be taken for granted. We can set up our own blocks through sloth, ennui, tiredness, failing spirit, bad choices where accepting one line of access stops more promising others. (pp. 43–44)

He, however, notes that, conversely, serendipity can sometimes play a part and something occurs to redeem the situation and reveal new possibilities providing new inspiration for the researcher.

Informed consent

Obtaining the informed consent of participants means that they agree to take part in the research project after they have been fully informed of the facts pertaining to the research. This includes the kind of involvement expected by them, what will be done with the data, and if there are any risks involved. The researcher ought to tell the participants as much as possible about the study. Informed consent assumes that the participants are capable of making a decision about participating or not participating, i.e. they are of a sound mind and are old enough to understand what is involved. They need to make this decision voluntarily and not under any kind of duress.

In gaining access to young children, their parents' informed consent is needed, since young children do not have the cognitive abilities to understand the research process and the role of a researcher to give their informed consent. The researcher will, however, need to be accepted by the children themselves in order to observe and interview them. A gentle and friendly demeanour is therefore important so that the children do not become distressed during data collection. Also, an adult working with the children, such as the class teacher, will need to explain beforehand that an outsider will be present in the classroom, or will talk to them. Researchers also need to inform the participants that participants have the right to withdraw at any point in the research if they wish. David et al. (2001) write about the distinctly educational strategies that they used to inform the child participants about their research project, which included the use of leaflets and classroom activities, to enable the children to make choices about participation.

Privacy

Privacy denotes individuals' concern and entitlement to control the access of other people to themselves. Persons who agree to take part in a project put themselves in a vulnerable position and to some extent are at the mercy of the researchers to guard their privacy. Ethical research respects the participants' right to privacy not just during the study, but forever after. Even if participants voluntarily waive their right to privacy, the data obtained from them have to remain separate from their names and other identifiers. Further, researchers need to anticipate the possibility of harmful information being revealed during the data collection process. For example, a student may mention parental abuse or a teacher may disclose instances of bullying from senior management. In these situations, the ethical code for researchers is to protect the privacy of the participants, though they should also seek guidance from their institution's ethics committee without revealing the name of the participant involved.

Anonymity

Anonymizing the participants means that the data gathered are not linked to the participants and the identity of the participants is not disclosed to anyone by the researcher. The institutions where they are working or studying need to be anonymized too. In this way the participants' privacy is assured. It is easy to keep questionnaires anonymous and use numbers or letters of the alphabet to identify the responses. Interview participants' anonymity can be safeguarded by using pseudonyms when reporting data from interviews. Researchers, however, need to be aware of the participants' identity. Even if questionnaires are used for data collection to begin with, the researcher may want to contact the participants for follow up interviews, or to send them a copy of the final report.

Confidentiality

This is linked to privacy and anonymity. If the research participants are anonymized, then no matter how confidential or sensitive the data are, these data will not lead to any harm or anguish to the participants. Nevertheless, in order to keep the data confidential, researchers ought to ensure that they do not name the participants' place of study or work and their job title. Another way of keeping the data confidential is not to name the institution and use terms such as 'a university in the Midlands'. Data generated in empirical research must be kept in a safe place, such as a locked cabinet. If they are in electronic form, then they should be in password protected files.

Deception

Sometimes we need to use deception in research when it is not possible to obtain informed consent. This can be the case in some experimental studies when telling the participants about the nature of the experiment will change their behaviour and consequently the result of the experiment will be affected. Similarly, it can be used in ethnographic studies that require covert observation. It can also be done in case study and action research when the researcher either hides the purpose of the research from the participants or deliberately misinforms them. Researchers may also hide their identity and simply not inform the participants that they are in a specific setting for research purposes.

This strategy is sometimes necessary as without a measure of deception it will be impossible to carry out studies on sensitive issues of considerable significance such as racism, bullying, abuse and professional misconduct. No one will be willing to take part in a study if it is revealed to them beforehand that we are aiming to examine one of these areas. It can be argued that this practice is ethical as long as no harm is done to the participants. Researchers can counteract the use of deception by having a debrief session with the participants, explaining to them candidly the purpose of data collection and why it was essential not to inform them, or indeed misinform them, prior to the fieldwork (For an example, see Al-Saadi, 2009).

Activity

You have been informed by a former colleague that the FE college in which he teaches seems to have a high incidence of drug-taking by students, resulting in failure and drop-outs. The college principal has tried to tackle the problem, but has been unsuccessful, and now simply ignores it. How can you design a project to find out what is happening without compromising your security and the integrity of the participants?

Examining colleagues' practice

Researchers need to be especially vigilant when they are carrying out an investigation in their own institution and observing or interviewing their colleagues. Hopkins (2008: 202–203,), discusses the ethical procedures in action research and argues that researchers have to go beyond the usual concerns for confidentiality and respect for research participants. Citing Kemmis and McTaggart (1982), he outlines the following principles that researchers need to adhere to when undertaking action research:

- Observe protocol by informing, consulting and gaining permission from relevant committees and personnel
- Involve participants by encouraging them to shape the form of research
- Negotiate with participants to take into account their responsibilities and wishes
- Report progress by keeping the work visible and being open to suggestions
- Obtain explicit authorization from colleagues and others whom you wish to observe
- Obtain explicit authorization to examine and copy documentation
- Check descriptions by allowing those whose work you are describing to challenge the fairness, relevance and accuracy of your accounts
- Verify accounts by allowing participants in interviews, meetings or document writing to suggest amendments if they enhance fairness, relevance and accuracy
- Obtain explicit authorization from participants before using extracts from interviews, observation and documents
- Negotiate reports for various levels of release such as a verbal report to colleagues, a written report to a full staff meeting, and a journal article
- Accept responsibility for maintaining confidentiality of the data
- Retain the right to report your work to a wider audience, provided those involved view it as relevant, fair and accurate
- Make your principles of procedure binding and known to the participants so that they agree with your responsibilities as a researcher and their rights as participants.

Validity

Traditionally, validity signifies that the research actually measures or describes the phenomena it set out to measure or describe. Hart (2005) argues that:

> Validity is about ensuring that you build into your research sufficient robustness to have the confidence to make generalizations . . . It is about carefully constructing definitions of your concepts, hypotheses or propositions, so that they can be translated clearly and predictably into detailed operational methods, down to the

level of specific questions and observations. It is about ensuring that there are strong transparent relationships between the conceptual or theoretical part of your research, the phenomenon you have identified for investigation and the method you intend to use to get access to that phenomenon. Your methods operationalise your concepts and so provide a bridge to 'reality' . . . If you correctly integrate these elements, which include appropriate sample construction, you will have the basis for making generalizations beyond the sample of subjects you have researched. (pp. 334, 338)

Nevertheless, the notion of validity is complex and there are different kinds of validity which can be dealt with in different ways. No research is totally valid as threats to validity cannot be completely removed in a research project, though they can be minimized. We have to accept a measure of standard error in quantitative research and participants' subjectivity in qualitative research. We cannot expect the same kind of validity in qualitative and quantitative research because they seek to meet quite different criteria. For example, a qualitative study does not claim generalizabilty, yet it cannot be considered invalid on these grounds.

Validity is connected with the functioning of concepts, which means that the researchers ought to show that their concepts can be identified and measured in the way they have claimed. Validity is a vital element of effective research because if a particular study is invalid, then it is worthless. Validity is therefore a requirement for both quantitative and qualitative research. However, in addition to dealing with validity in a conventional manner, it can be addressed in other ways. For example, in qualitative research, validity can be addressed through the honesty, depth, richness and scope of the data achieved, the participants approached, and the use of triangulation. In quantitative research, validity can be dealt with through paying meticulous attention to sampling, development of instruments and statistical analyses.

Two concepts which relate to validity and which the researchers ought to be wary of, are the 'Hawthorne Effect' and the 'Halo Effect'.

The Hawthorne effect

This relates to the following:

- Initial improvements in participants' performance as a consequence of a recently introduced change. Researchers therefore need to be cautious when evaluating a new initiative.
- Reactivity on the part of the participants as the presence of the researcher alters the situation. Participants may wish to avoid, impress, influence or reject the researcher. Remaining in the research field for some time before and after the data collection phase can counter this effect.

- Realization by the participants that they are part of an experiment can change their behaviour or performance in a test or experiment. To avoid this, researchers do not tell the participants beforehand what exactly the experiment or test is seeking to measure, and provide this information in a feedback session afterwards.

The Halo effect

This indicates that the researchers' knowledge of the participants, or knowledge of other existing data about participants or situations, can affect the researchers' judgement. This can consequently cause them to be selective in the way they gather data, analyse their data, and report their findings. Triangulation can counterbalance this effect.

There are several types of validity. However, not all are relevant to small-scale projects. Some of the most common kinds that concern individual researchers working on masters, doctoral or post doctoral research are as follows:

Internal validity

Internal validity demonstrates the degree to which findings correctly map the phenomena in question (Denzin and Lincoln, 1998: 186). This kind of validity is particularly relevant to qualitative research and shows that the way specific phenomena or perceptions have been described can indeed be upheld by the data. Hammersley (1992: 71) maintains that qualitative researchers can ensure internal validity by paying attention to:

- The plausibility and credibility of the research
- The evidence required – the greater the claim being made, the more convincing the evidence has to be
- Clarity on the kinds of claim made from the research – whether the researcher is defining, describing, explaining or generating theory.

External validity

External validity, commonly associated with quantitative research, denotes the extent to which the results can be generalized to the wider population, groups or contexts.

Generalizability

Generalizability is a necessary end product of quantitative research. All studies that are conducted within a positivist paradigm need to have generalizable findings. Qualitative research, as a rule, does not seek to generalize to the wider population, so does not meet the requirements of external validity. Lincoln and Guba (1985: 300) observe that there are a number of threats to external validity in qualitative research. These are as follows:

- Selection effects – constructs selected are only relevant to a certain group
- Setting effects – results are largely a function of their context
- History effects – situations arrived at by unique circumstances, and thus not comparable
- Construct effects – constructs being used are peculiar to a certain group.

In qualitative research comparability and transferability are the equivalent of generalizability. The description presented in qualitative research needs to be sufficiently detailed so that the audience can determine the extent to which findings from an individual research project are generalizable to another situation and can be transferred to another context. Bassey (1999: 12) differentiates between statistical and fuzzy generalizations found in quantitative and qualitative studies respectively:

- *Statistical generalization* arises from samples of population and typically claims that there is an *x* per cent or *y* per cent chance that what was found in the sample will also be found throughout the population: it is a quantitative measure.
- *Fuzzy generalization* arises from studies of singularities and typically claims that it is possible, or likely, or unlikely, that what was found in the singularity will be found in similar situations elsewhere: it is a qualitative measure.

Mason (2002: 195) maintains that generalization can be considered in two distinct ways:

- *Empirical generalization* is mainly claimed in quantitative studies, whereby researchers are able to make generalizations from an analysis of one empirical population (e.g. their sample) to another, wider, population (e.g. all adults in Britain) on the basis that the population in their study was statistically representative of that wider population.
- *Theoretical generalization* is mainly claimed in qualitative studies. It does not represent a standard form of generalizing, but instead comprises a range of approaches based on diverse ways of thinking, some of which may

seem to be more theoretical than others. Significantly, all of them should be grounded in the empirical part of the research. Researchers making these kinds of generalizations need to consider that in the context of their own research, what kinds of theoretical generalizations they can make and what are the basis on which they can make these generalizations.

Concurrent validity

Concurrent validity signifies that data collected from one source correlates, or concurs, with those collected from another source. This enables the researchers to show greater confidence in their findings, or in other words, claim that the data and findings are valid.

Triangulation

Triangulation is a strategy that is used to establish concurrent validity in research by looking at the same issue from different perspectives. Converging data from different sources can offer an enhanced portrayal of the social world. Lin (1976) argues in favour of triangulation by stating that exclusive reliance on one method may bias or distort the researcher's view of the specific part of the social world being investigated. However, this is not strictly true as the depth or breadth of data generated by one method can portray a fuller picture without having to rely on triangulation. Fielding and Fielding (1986) maintain that methodological triangulation does not necessarily increase validity, reduce bias or bring objectivity to research. Hammersley and Atkinson (1983: 199) caution that researchers 'should not adopt a naively optimistic view that the aggregation of data from different sources will unproblematically add up to produce a more complete picture'. Nevertheless, triangulation is a helpful strategy to check not just the validity but also the reliability of data. The two main types of triangulation that concern an individual small-scale researcher are the following:

- *Methodological triangulation:* The same phenomena are investigated by using two or more methods of data collection such as questionnaires and observation, or interviews and documents. Or the researcher can work within different methodologies to ascertain if the data collected are indeed valid. For example, quantitative data in the form of questionnaire responses can be followed up by gathering qualitative data through semi-structured interviews.

- *Sample triangulation:* The same issues are examined by interrogating different groups of participants such as students and teachers, or teachers and parents. Again, this can be used to allow the researchers to assert that their findings are valid. Conversely, this strategy can also be used to check the mismatch between the views of two groups of participants, as discussed later in the chapter.

Cohen et al. (2007: 144–145) suggest a number of ways in which researchers can minimize threats to validity throughout their research projects. For example, at the following stages:

Design stage
By using an appropriate timescale; adequate resources; appropriate methodology to answer research questions; suitable instruments to gather data; appropriate sample; demonstration of validity and reliability.

Data collection stage
By reducing the Hawthorne effect; minimizing reactivity effects; avoiding participant dropout rates; taking steps to avoid nonreturn of questionnaires; avoiding too long or too short an interval between pre-tests and post-tests; matching control and experimental groups fairly; addressing factors concerning researcher identity.

Data analysis stage
By avoiding subjective interpretation of data; reducing the halo effect; using appropriate statistical treatments for the level of data; recognizing spurious correlations and extraneous factors affecting data; avoiding poor coding of data; avoiding making inferences and generalizations beyond the capability of data; avoiding selective use of data; avoiding unfair aggregation of data.

Data reporting stage
By stating the context and parameters of the research in the data collection and treatment, a degree of confidence in the results, a degree of context-freedom or context-boundedness of data; presenting the data without misrepresenting their message; making claims which are sustainable by the data; avoiding inaccurate reporting of data; ensuring that the research questions are answered; releasing research results neither too soon, nor too late.

Reliability

Reliability denotes that the research process can be repeated at another time on similar participants in a similar context with the same results. The data collection methods and the way the research is carried out have to remain uninfluenced by the difference in the sample and setting. If it does not, then it is unreliable. Reliability is a necessary prerequisite to validity. Research which is valid is always reliable. Nevertheless, reliable research is not necessarily valid. Reliability can be ensured in different ways in quantitative and qualitative research. In quantitative research, it can be achieved through the standardization of research instruments, by crosschecking the data, and by using different instruments to examine the same thing. Qualitative researchers do not use standardized methods to ensure reliability, yet need to consider carefully the methods and tools used in their research.

Reliability in quantitative research

When working with a quantitative methodology, consistency and replicability over time, instruments and participants serve the purposes of reliability. This kind of reliability entails precision and accuracy. For example, a question seeking biographical or factual data need to elicit the same response on all occasions if the sample and context are similar. Following are the three main types of reliability in quantitative research:

Stability means that a reliable instrument will generate similar data from similar participants over time. For example, in surveys and experiments, a test and a re-test carried out within an adequate period of time will yield similar results. Further, a test or questionnaire administered to two closely matched groups will produce similar results.

Equivalence involves using equivalent or alternative forms of a test, experiment or questionnaire. If they generate similar results, then the test, experiment or questionnaire is reliable. Equivalence also relates to inter-rater reliability, which means that if more than one researcher is taking part in the same research project, then they all need to code the data in the same way. However, this does not relate to an individual researcher conducting research for a higher degree and is more likely to be relevant to researchers undertaking projects for post-doctoral work involving multiple researchers.

Internal consistency requires that, as opposed to the two types of reliability measures stated above, the tests, experiments or questionnaires have to be administered only once through the split-half method. For this purpose the items or questions will be divided equally into two parts and matched in difficulty and ease of content, i.e. half the questions or items in part one can be as easy as half of them in part two; and half the questions or items in part one can be as difficult as half of them in part two. Each half is marked separately and indicates split-half reliability if the result obtained on one half matches or shows a high correlation with the result of the other half.

Reliability in qualitative research

Unlike quantitative studies, there is little possibility of replication by using similar participants, similar contexts, and the same methods in qualitative research carried out by small-scale researchers. The latter type of research is unique and particular to a setting, and does not seek duplication to claim reliability. Instead, it includes trustworthiness, honesty, distinctiveness of context, authenticity, comprehensiveness, detail and depth of response, and significance of the research to the participants. Qualitative researchers ought to illustrate to their audience that their entire research procedure, including data collection and analysis, has been scrupulous, honest and precise, and has addressed their research questions. This will involve stating that they have not falsified their data or have been careless in the analysis of the data. Kirk and Miller (1986: 72) maintain that it is incumbent on qualitative researchers to document their research procedure in detail for reliability to be calculated.

Two qualitative researchers examining the same issues in the same setting may yield different data and findings, which may still be reliable because they will interpret the data and report the findings in their own unique and idiosyncratic ways. For example, a teaching assistant may be viewed as being extremely helpful to the pupils she is working with by one observer, whereas another observer may regard her help as doctrinaire and stifling the children's creativity. Lincoln and Guba (1985) reject the term reliability in qualitative research and suggest substituting it with concepts such as credibility, neutrality, confirmability, dependability, consistency, applicability, trustworthiness, and transferability. Bogdan and Biklen (1992: 48) argue that in qualitative research, reliability can be regarded as a fit between what researchers record as data and what actually occurs in the natural setting that is being researched, i.e. a degree of accuracy and comprehensiveness of coverage.

I have discussed triangulation above with reference to validity. Triangulation is also an effective technique to check the reliability of the data by drawing on the perceptions of more than one group of participants and/or using more than one method of data collection. If a group of students convey something during interviews which we find implausible, then we can utilize sample triangulation and check it by interviewing their teachers. This may convince us that what the students have told us is indeed true. On the other hand, if interviews with teachers generate data which are contrary to the data obtained from the students, then we can use another way to check the reliability of the data, by using methodological triangulation by conducting observation or perusing documents.

Another way of verifying the reliability of data is participant validation. Sending the interview transcripts to the interviewees to check whether the transcript matches their recollection of the interview can ensure that the data are reliable. However, this is a risky strategy as sometimes research participants delete some of the comments that they have made during the interview, especially if what they have said seems negative or outrageous on paper. This can be the case with sexist or racist remarks or if they have criticized a colleague or the institution that they work in, and seeing it all in the form of a transcript has illustrated the gravity of the remarks. Thus in an attempt to check the reliability of their research, the researchers may lose valuable data.

Pilot study

In order to enhance the validity and reliability of the research, we need to conduct a pilot study. A pilot study is a prelude to the main study, and before embarking on our actual research project, it is imperative that we carry out a pilot. The sample for the pilot should be representative of the sample of the main study, and the approach, methodology and methods used in the pilot ought to be reflected in the actual study later on. There are a number of advantages attached to a pilot study. It allows the researchers to:

- Illustrate their ability to conduct and manage a study and lends credence to their claims
- Verify the reliability of the research in general
- Experience the mechanics of research, i.e. gaining access to the sample, gathering data, and analysing data
- Focus on a smaller sample to carry out research, using the same procedures that will be used in the main study, thereby gaining confidence as a researcher

- Ascertain the validity and reliability of the data by concentrating on a few participants
- Learn how to conduct research in an ethical manner
- Test the research instruments, for example, the interview schedule, the questionnaire and the observation checklist
- Obtain feedback on the possible ways in which the research instruments can be improved
- Modify the research instruments to eliminate any ambiguous, leading, insensitive offensive, or superfluous questions or statements
- Revise the research instruments to include any significant questions that have been omitted
- Determine the time required to complete the data collection and data analysis phases in the actual study
- Highlight gaps and wastage in data collection
- Predict research problems and establish the feasibility of the main study
- Identify any other issues that may be detrimental to the actual study such as researcher safety.

(Source: Oppenheim, 1992; Wragg, 1999; Marshall and Rossman, 2006; Cohen et al., 2007).

Both beginner and experienced researchers can be overconfident about how many lessons can be observed or how many participants can be interviewed. Therefore observing and interviewing even one or two participants will reveal the viability of the process. Sometimes the main study is too ambitious. We may have decided to interview too many participants, observe several lessons, or design a rather elaborate experiment. A pilot study will give us a taster of what will be involved in the actual study and help us to scale down our objectives. This is made clear by Tizard and Hughes (1991: 23) who designed a study to compare the same children at home and at nursery school, and compare children from a working-class background with children from a middle-class background. They wanted a sufficient number of children in each group to be able to use statistical tests to compare the groups. They also wanted, initially, to have equal numbers of boys and girls in each group to look at gender differences, and proposed a sample of 60 children, 30 of whom would be working class and 30 would be middle class, of whom 30 would be boys and 30 would be girls. All of whom were to be observed at home and at school. However, they found that:

> When we tried to put this design into practice, we soon realized that we would have to reduce the size of this sample. Our pilot studies made it very clear that the

process of recording and transcribing children's conversations was much more time-consuming than we had anticipated. Clearly the social class dimension was crucial to the aims of the study, so the only way to restrict the sample size was to omit the boys. (Tizard and Hughes, 1991: 23)

As the social class aspect was important, Tizard and Hughes (1991) chose to disregard the gender factor in their research for the following reasons:

There were two main justifications for the decision. First, at this age, girls tend to talk more and articulate more clearly than boys – using only girls would thus make the task of transcribing the conversations less difficult. Second, it reflected our wider concern with general issues – in a society dominated by men, there was something attractive about the idea of studying girls, their mothers and their female nursery teachers. (p. 23)

Thus, overall, a pilot study helps us to design a realistic and logical project of the kind that we want to conduct within our time frame. It not only helps with the wording of questions, but also with procedures such as the covering letter, the sequence of the questions and how to minimize nonresponse rates. Further, the questions or items in the research instruments may have been phrased in a way that do not lend themselves easily to analysis, and piloting will allow us to formulate the questions and items in a way that make them suitable for analysis.

The practice of analysing the data in the pilot study gives the researchers a different perspective on the questions asked, and warns them that such questions need adjustment or they might cause problems at the analysis stage. It is necessary to pilot every question, the sequence of questions, and the statements and scales in an instrument. Also, researchers should pilot the question layout on the page, the instructions given to the respondents, the sections and numbering in the questionnaire. If the piloting indicates that the interview schedule or questionnaire needs to be modified, then the improved version needs to be piloted too.

Researchers ought to ensure that the participants included in the pilot study are not part of the main study as they will have prior knowledge of the issues raised, which may sensitize them to the questions asked, and cause them to provide ready-made answers. They may be inclined to offer socially acceptable answers in the actual study and may also have discussed these issues with other participants of the pilot study. Further, data gathered in the pilot study should not be used in the main study. While researchers may be tempted to include these data in their main study, as it will mean fewer interviews or observations in the main study, the purpose of data collection in the pilot study is to inform the main study. Researchers should be allowed to make mistakes and experiment with the process and the outcome of the research in the pilot study to learn from it rather than see it as a component of the main study.

Part 2
Gathering Data

Questionnaires: the strength of numbers

4

Chapter Outline

A common misapprehension is that questionnaires offer an easy way to gather a great deal of information in a relatively short time and anyone who can write can formulate a questionnaire. Nevertheless, questionnaires, like other research methods and instruments of data collection, need to be carefully formulated, piloted and administered, keeping in mind at all times how we are going to analyse the oodles of gathered data and make sense of them. As Oppenheim (1992: 47) points out, 'Questionnaires do not emerge fully-fledged. They have to be created or adapted, fashioned and developed to maturity.' A poorly devised questionnaire can make the task of data analysis extremely difficult and time-consuming. In fact, researchers need to contemplate how they will analyse the data while they are preparing the questionnaire as this will inform the content and design of the questionnaire.

Questionnaires are mainly designed to gather numerical data or data that can easily be converted into numerical values. They offer a standardized method of data collection in large-scale surveys when the main purpose is to collect a considerable amount of data from a wide ranging population and make generalizations from the findings. The national Census is a good example of this. An individual researcher, carrying out a small-scale study, may also want to choose this method to gather qualitative data from a number of respondents who cannot be accessed in any other way. Further, researchers sometimes use questionnaires in an attempt to gather both qualitative and quantitative data from a wide-ranging sample which they cannot reach in any other way. However, this strategy may result in a low response rate as respondents do not like writing detailed answers to questions and may not return the questionnaire or send it back in a partially completed form.

Questionnaires can be used in a small survey, case study, action research and in research studies with an experimental design. However, they are primarily used when we are certain that working within a positivist paradigm, with a quantitative methodology, and using a questionnaire to generate mainly numerical data is the most appropriate approach for our research. Walker (1985) points to the advantages and disadvantages of questionnaires:

> The questionnaire is like interviewing-by-numbers; and like painting-by-numbers, it suffers from some of the same problems of mass production and lack of interpretive opportunity. On the other hand, it offers considerable advantages in administration. It presents an even stimulus, potentially to large numbers of people simultaneously, and provides the investigator with an easy accumulation of data. (p. 91)

The ontological and epistemological stance of the researchers determine how, why and with whom we use questionnaires. For example, if we view the world as a hard reality, which can be scrutinized in an unproblematic way, then we will use highly structured methods of data collection to produce what we believe are objective and generalizable data and findings. The possible reasons due to which researchers use questionnaires with closed questions as a method of data collection are the following:

- Their *ontological* perspective sees the social world as a hard reality, external to humans, in which data on attitudes and behaviours can be conveyed by actors without the close involvement of a researcher.
- Their *epistemological* perspective suggests that knowledge and evidence of the social world can be generated superficially by asking participants to respond to questions as interpreted by them.
- The researchers' view of the ways in which *social explanations* can be constructed lays emphasis on large numbers, breadth and surface analysis of broad patterns.
- Researchers may conceptualize themselves as carrying out research in the tradition of the natural sciences where all data must be *statistically* analysed.
- Researchers may feel that *ethical* research means they have to be distant from the participants in order to gather data which are objective, valid and reliable.

Woods (1986: 114) notes that ethnographers tend not to use question-naires as they view them as belonging to research traditions with assumptions which are totally opposed to ethnographic practices. These assumptions include the belief that researchers can measure social reality in the same way as they measure natural phenomena. He nevertheless observes that while questionnaires are not popular with ethnographers as the sole method of data collection, they are used by them for triangulation purposes, or to reach a larger sample initially to be followed up by the collection of qualitative data. He (Woods, 1979) used questionnaires in an earlier school-based ethno-graphic study to gather data from parents as it was problematic to interview them on various occasions. He also used questionnaires in the same study to gather data from staff.

Formulating the questionnaires

Devising a questionnaire is time consuming and will need several attempts. It is advisable to spend a great deal of time initially on this exercise. Once we have a reasonable draft, we need to pilot it to ensure that it is fit for the pur-poses of our research (see Chapter 3 for Piloting). Following the pilot, the questionnaire will be revised and then administered. Piloting the question-naire will also tell us if the data collected through the questionnaire will lend themselves easily to analyses, particularly if we are aiming to analyse them by using a statistical method of analysis. A carefully formulated questionnaire will save time at data analysis stage. Gorard (2003) contends:

> Good question design is the key to easy survey analysis. You do not commit your-self to any particular form of analysis just by thinking about it before designing your questions, but you do restrict the kind of analysis available to you by the design of your instrument. Therefore, . . . consideration of analysis is more like the first rather than the last stage of research design. You do not want to ask any questions that you cannot analyse. (p. 102)

Content

The content of the questionnaire will be linked to our research topic, its aims and objectives, and the primary and secondary research questions or hypotheses. It will also be informed by the review of literature and previous research on the subject. If it is a relatively under-researched topic, then we may wish to have informal discussions with informed professionals and practitioners to generate ideas for questions and carry out a pre-pilot to check if these questions work. It is vital that the questions and statements in the questionnaire generate data that address our research questions or prove or disprove our hypotheses.

Respondents ought to be given clear instructions at the beginning of a questionnaire about completing it. Furthermore, whenever a different type of question is posed (see below), they have to be advised how to answer that particular question, i.e. whether they have to tick once, tick as many times as applies, write a number, circle a number, write a one word answer, or write a detailed answer. Detailed guidance about completion is crucial if the questionnaire is administered by post or is likely to be completed in the absence of the researcher.

Researchers need to ensure that the questions asked are not ambiguous, complex, leading, insensitive, threatening or offensive. Double negatives should be avoided, and information relating to only one item should be sought in any one question. This can be checked by trying out the questions on friends and colleagues and by piloting the questionnaire (see Chapter 3). It is important that the language and vocabulary used is commensurate with the reading and writing ability of the respondents. For example, if a questionnaire is designed for primary school children, then the language has to be simple. For older respondents too, sophisticated terminology ought to be avoided unless we are absolutely sure that they will be familiar with the jargon, for example if it relates to a particular profession and the questionnaire respondents belong to that profession.

Although this will be noted in the covering letter accompanying the questionnaire (see below), we need to include a statement at the beginning of the questionnaire to assure the questionnaire respondents about anonymity and confidentiality, even when we will have their contact details for follow-up interviews. This additional assurance will be useful in case they have lost the covering letter and are hesitant to answer questions of a personal nature. Another statement thanking the respondents for their time, and asking them to tick a box and insert their contact details if they want a synopsis of the major findings at the completion of the study, should be included at the end of the questionnaire.

Types of questions

Closed questions

For large samples, it is better to use closed questions only. Such questions are mainly used to gather data of a biographical or factual nature, and to examine attitudes and behaviour. They yield responses which can easily be converted into numerical values for analysis. Ideally a combination of different kinds of closed questions will make up a questionnaire. Some commonly used types of closed questions are noted below. Different types of questions will be preceded by instructions about how the respondents should record their response:

Dichotomous:

In this kind of question, the respondents are simply required to tick one of the two options:

(Please tick one of the two options)

Do you teach full time: Yes ☐   No ☐

Do you teach in a: State school ☐   Independent school ☐

Multiple choice, single response (or Category):

In this the respondents are asked to choose one of the responses. The responses offered need to be mutually exclusive and offer the full range of possible responses:

(Please tick one of the responses)

How old are you?

Under 26 years ☐
26–30 ☐
31–35 ☐
36–40 ☐
41–45 ☐
46–50 ☐
51–55 ☐
Over 55 ☐

Multiple choice, multiple response (or List):

Multiple choice questions can also ask the respondents to choose as many responses as apply:

(Please tick all responses that apply)

At the FE college where I teach:
The senior management team is supportive ☐
The majority of colleagues are friendly ☐
The majority of students are well-behaved ☐
The majority of students are unmotivated ☐
I have easy access to all the resources ☐
There are no opportunities for career development ☐

Ranking:

This kind of question asks the respondents to prioritize their responses in order of importance:

(Please indicate your priority by putting a number in the box – 5 for the highest priority; 4 for the second highest priority; and so on. Please do not use the same number twice.)

What features of the Research Methods module that you have recently completed were useful?

Lectures ☐
Recommended readings ☐
Handouts ☐
One-to-one tutorials ☐
Discussion with peers ☐

Rating:

These show the differentiation between the responses in a numerical form. A widely used example is the Likert Scale:

(Please tick only one box)

All organizations employing more than 25 people should provide a free crèche for their employees' children:

1. Strongly disagree ☐
2. Disagree ☐
3. No opinion ☐
4. Agree ☐
5. Strongly agree ☐

Rating:

This asks the respondents to circle a number on a continuum from 1 to 10, with 1 being very poor and 10 being excellent.

(Please circle only one number for each statement to indicate your response about your son's/daughter's school). The lowest number indicates very poor and the highest number means excellent:

	Very poor								Excellent	
The quality of teaching	1	2	3	4	5	6	7	8	9	10
Accessibility of teachers	1	2	3	4	5	6	7	8	9	10
Feedback on progress	1	2	3	4	5	6	7	8	9	10
Resources – Library and books	1	2	3	4	5	6	7	8	9	10
Resources – ICT facilities	1	2	3	4	5	6	7	8	9	10
Sports facilities	1	2	3	4	5	6	7	8	9	10
School atmosphere	1	2	3	4	5	6	7	8	9	10
School buildings	1	2	3	4	5	6	7	8	9	10
School lunches	1	2	3	4	5	6	7	8	9	10

Matrix or Grid:

A Likert Scale can also be inserted in a questionnaire in the form of a matrix which includes a number of statements relating to the same question.

(Please respond to the following question by ticking in only one column for every statement when the numbers of the column correspond to the following responses: 1 = Strongly disagree; 2 = Disagree; 3 = Don't know; 4 = Agree; 5 = Strongly agree.)

Do you think that in your child's primary school:	1	2	3	4	5
The teachers are supportive?					
The quality of teaching is good?					
There is a wide range of extracurricular activities?					
The school library is well-resourced?					
There are frequent opportunities to go on field trips?					
The pupils are well-behaved?					
The standard of discipline is outstanding?					
All pupils are able to read fluently when they leave school?					

Quantity:

This type of question requires the respondents to insert their own response to the question in the form of a numeral. The response can also be zero.

(Please answer the following question in the form of a number which you estimate is the closest to the exact figure, which may be a zero.)

How many qualified teachers are there in your school? ——
How many full time teaching assistants are there in your school? ——
How many pupils do you have in your class? ——
How many pupils have special education needs? ——
How many pupils' parents attended the parents' evening last term? ——
How many pupils went on the school trip to the Natural History Museum last month? ——

Open ended questions

These can be used for small surveys, but we ought to be sure that we want to use questionnaires for collecting data which are likely to be qualitative. Interviews may be a better option. If face-to-face interviews are not possible, then telephone interviews can be used. Questionnaires with too many open ended questions have a poor response rate, mainly because participants prefer talking to writing. Open ended questions enable research participants to write a free flowing account in their own words, to explain and justify their responses without the constraints of pre-set categories of responses. Nevertheless, they can also generate irrelevant and superfluous data as they may be too open ended for the respondent to know what kind of data are being sought. Such questions make the questionnaire appear long and off-putting, require a longer time from the respondents to insert a response, and may lead to incomplete questionnaires.

If open ended questions must be used in a questionnaire, then they can be used in combination with closed questions. The combination which is popular in educational research is a questionnaire which has a majority of closed questions and one or two open ended questions at the end seeking qualitative data. Open ended questions need to give the respondent as much guidance on answering the question as possible because the researcher is usually not present to explain it to the respondent. These questions are very difficult to convert into numerical data and ought to be analysed as textual qualitative data.

Open ended questions in questionnaires can be in the form of a statement asking to explain something:

Please describe what it is like to be a newly qualified teacher as opposed to a trainee teacher.

Or as a question to answer in a descriptive way:

How do you see your career developing and where do you see yourself in ten years?

Or in the form of a sentence to be completed by the respondent:

The defining features of a successful secondary school are:

....

Design

The sequence in which the questions are asked in a questionnaire needs to be given careful thought. As Oppenheim (1992: 121) observes, 'a covert function' of each question is to 'motivate the respondent to continue to cooperate'. The questionnaire should be arranged in such a way as to maximize the chances of completion. This can be done, for example, by intermingling questions of general interest, attitude questions, and questions about behaviour throughout the questionnaire. Such questions reduce monotony and frustration, yet provide valuable data.

Questions which are straightforward and can be readily answered are usually at the beginning, such as those of a factual or biographical nature. This makes the respondent confident and interested in proceeding to complete the rest of the questionnaire. However, depending on the nature of the study, sometimes it may be better to ask personal questions at the end. Sapsford and Jupp (1996) argue:

> It is better to put demographic questions, i.e. those on age, marital status, occupation etc. towards the end. This is partly because they are uninteresting and partly, being sensitive, they may be resented. (p. 105)

Questions related to similar themes need to be asked in tandem. To avoid ennui, researchers should use the different types of closed questions noted above in a varied format, rather than a series of the same type of questions. Using the same questions in succession may sensitize the respondents and they may tick or circle items in the same rows or columns without paying much attention to the questions. Changing the format of the questions frequently will retain their interest in the exercise. If open ended questions are asked, they should be kept to a minimum, one or two at the most, and to be put at the end of the questionnaire. A respondent who has almost completed the whole questionnaire is more likely to write a detailed answer to a question or two at the end.

The questionnaire should be designed to attract, not to intimidate, the respondents. It must be appealing and must not be cluttered. The questions should be clearly laid out with appropriate margins and gaps. If possible, the questionnaire should be divided into sections rather than asking question after question without any break. This kind of format will make the questionnaire more manageable and will encourage the respondents to complete one section and move to the next. Questionnaire design should be attractive to the group that will complete it, for example, 'fun' fonts and pictures can be used if questionnaires are to be used with children.

The questionnaire has to be of a reasonable length. If it is a precursor to an interview, then a two-page questionnaire printed on both sides of an A4 paper will suffice, with a short section at the end of page 2 asking for respondents' contact details if they are willing to be interviewed. If it is the only instrument being used to collect data, then it should not exceed 8 pages, printed on both sides of 4 sheets of paper. Researchers need to consider the time it will take the respondents to complete the questionnaire. Again, piloting the penultimate draft of the questionnaire will give an indication of the time required for completion. If the completion time is too long, then the researchers should consider condensing the questions or eliminating some of the questions. Very long questionnaires are viewed as tedious and are not likely to be returned, or may be sent back in a partially completed form.

The paper on which the questionnaire is printed must be of a reasonably good quality. The pages should be clearly numbered, and securely stapled if more than one page is used. The font used should not be too intricate. Times New Roman or Arial are the most commonly used fonts. A font size of 11 or 12 is viewed as suitable for a questionnaire, with bigger and emboldened fonts for headings and subheadings. However, if the questionnaire is likely to be completed by respondents with sensory disabilities, then a font size of at least 14 ought to be used.

Below is an edited version of a questionnaire, used in a national study in which I was involved, which employs different types of questions discussed above. We were given specific instructions by the funder not to use a 'Don't know' or 'Not sure' category, as it was believed that the respondents would then be encouraged to tick one of the other responses. We were unable to determine if the respondents ticked another category because of the nonavailability of a 'Don't know' response, or would have chosen that category anyway.

Questionnaire for Minority Ethnic and Majority Ethnic withdrawers from teacher training courses

Please tick or fill in as appropriate

Section 1: Entering training

1. What motivated you to go into teacher training?
   ....

2. Did your family support your decision to embark on a teacher training course?
   If yes, in what ways?..
   If no, for what reasons?...

3. How long had you been considering a career in teaching before you began the course?
   10+ years ☐   5–9 years ☐   1–4 years ☐   Less than 1 year ☐   Not sure ☐

4. Were you able to get into your first choice institution?   Yes ☐   No ☐
   If no, then please state what difference you believe this made to your studies ....

5. Which region did you train in?
   London ☐   South East ☐   South West ☐   West Midlands ☐
   East Midlands ☐   North West ☐   North East ☐   Yorkshire & the Humber ☐

6. Did you have to move house when you started the course?   Yes ☐   No ☐

7. Did you move to another region when you started the course?   Yes ☐   No ☐

8. Where did you mainly live during the course? (Tick only one)
   Parental home ☐   Own home (mortgaged) ☐   Own home (rented) ☐
   Halls of residence ☐   Shared accommodation ☐

9. Did you come to teacher training: (Tick as many as necessary)
   Straight after college/university? ☐   After a career change? ☐
   After working in schools in another capacity? ☐   After bringing up a family? ☐   Other? ☐ (Please specify) ....

10. Were you on a flexible/part time/modular route into teaching? Yes ☐   No ☐
    If yes, please provide details of the course ....

1   ⇨

11. Which, if any, of the following services did you use before registering on the course?
Teaching Information Line ☐   Subject Knowledge Booster Course ☐
Taster courses ☐   Open school visits ☐   Teacher Advocate ☐   Others ☐
(Please specify) ....

12. Were you engaged in paid work while you were on the course? Yes ☐   No ☐
If yes, please indicate the:
Nature of the job ....Average hours worked
per week........

13. Did you have to care for a family member while you were on the course?
Yes ☐   No ☐
If yes, please give details...

14. Which course were you on? Postgraduate ☐ Undergraduate ☐

15. Which age range(s) were you training to teach?
Early Years ☐   Key Stage 1 ☐   Key Stage 2 ☐
Key Stage 3 ☐   Key Stage 4 ☐   Post-16 ☐

16. Were you trained as a subject specialist teacher? Yes ☐   No ☐
If yes, what was your main curriculum specialism? ....

17. How long were you on the course before you withdrew?
Less than a full week ☐   1–4 weeks ☐   1–2 months ☐
Less than a semester ☐   One year ☐   2 years ☐   3 years ☐

18. Did you withdraw:
Before your first teaching placement? ☐
During/ or immediately after your first teaching placement? ☐
During/ or immediately after your second teaching placement? ☐
Just before one of the Skills Tests: Literacy ☐   Numeracy ☐   ICT ☐

Section 2: Your ITT provider and the course content

19. Please rate your training in relation to the following statements by ticking
the scale: 1 = Poor; 2 = Adequate; 3 = Good   4; = Very Good.

How good was your training in:	1	2	3	4
Helping you to understand the National Curriculum?				
Providing you with knowledge and skills to teach your specialist subject?				
Providing you with knowledge and skills to use ICT in subject teaching?				
Preparing you adequately for the skills' tests?				
Helping you to plan your teaching for progression in pupil learning?				

Preparing you to monitor, assess, record and report pupils' progress?				
Helping you to establish and maintain a good standard of discipline?				
Helping you to develop effective teaching methods?				
Helping you to use teaching methods which promote pupils' learning?				
Preparing you to teach pupils of different abilities?				
Preparing you to teach pupils from minority ethnic backgrounds?				
Preparing you to work with children with English as an additional language?				
Preparing you to work with children with special education needs?				
Providing you with relevant skills to work with colleagues?				
Providing you with relevant skills to work with parents?				

20. Please rate your ITT institution in relation to the following statements by ticking the scale: 1 = Strongly Disagree; 2 = Disagree; 3 = Agree; 4 = Strongly Agree.

Do you think that in your training institution:	1	2	3	4
The vast majority of your tutors/lecturers were supportive?				
The quality of teaching was in the main good?				
There was too much to do and you had no time to relax?				
Most other trainees on the course were supportive?				
Most other trainees on the course were friendly?				
You felt isolated during the course?				

Section 3: Your placement school and teaching experience

21. Did your placement school have:
    (i) a large minority ethnic student population? No ☐ Yes ☐
    (ii) a predominantly white student population? No ☐ Yes ☐
    (iii) some minority ethnic teachers? No ☐ Yes ☐ How many?..............
    (iv) some minority ethnic classroom assistants? No ☐ Yes ☐
    How many? ....
    (v) other minority ethnic school staff? No ☐ Yes ☐
    Position?...........................

⇨

3

22. Please rate your placement school in relation to the following statements by ticking the scale: 1 = Strongly Disagree; 2 = Disagree; 3 = Agree; 4 = Strongly Agree

Do you believe that in your placement school:	1	2	3	4
The senior management had a good understanding of minority ethnic issues?				
You made a connection with the pupils?				
You had a supportive mentor with whom you had a good rapport?				
Your mentor provided regular feedback?				
The teaching staff were supportive?				
You had easy access to all the resources?				
Preparing for teaching was too time-consuming?				
You were easily able to maintain discipline in the class?				
You did not possess enough subject knowledge to teach?				
You were not sure if you were teaching effectively?				

Section 4: Assessment

23. Please rate your feelings in relation to the following statements by ticking the scale: 1 = Strongly Disagree; 2 = Disagree; 3 = Agree; 4 = Strongly Agree

Was it the case that during your training:	1	2	3	4
You were not anxious about taking the Skills Tests?				
You were apprehensive about writing assignments?				
Completing assignments and other tasks was very time-consuming?				
It was difficult to complete the tasks on time because of family commitments?				
It was difficult to complete the tasks on time because of work commitments?				
You did not mind being observed in your classroom?				

Section 5: Finances

24. Was your financial situation such that:
  (i) It was hard to manage with the £6,000 training salary? Yes ☐   No ☐   N/A ☐
  (ii) You did not get into debt? Yes ☐   No ☐
  (iii) You had too many financial responsibilities Yes ☐   No ☐
  (iv) You would have managed financially on a teacher's salary? Yes ☐   No ☐
  (v) You withdrew and moved straight into paid employment? Yes ☐   No ☐

⇨

Section 6: Discrimination

25. Do you believe you were a victim of deliberate racial harassment in your ITT institution?
Yes ☐ No ☐
If yes, did you report it? Yes ☐ No ☐ If yes, was action taken?
Yes ☐ No ☐
Who were the perpetrators?..

26. Do you believe you were a victim of unwitting racism in your ITT institution?
Yes ☐ No ☐
If yes, please provide details ....
....
....
....

27. Do you believe you were a victim of deliberate racial harassment in placement schools? Yes ☐ No ☐
If yes, did you report it? Yes ☐ No ☐ If yes, was action taken? Yes ☐ No ☐
Who were the perpetrators?..

28. Do you believe you were a victim of unwitting racism in placement schools?
Yes ☐ No ☐
If yes, please provide details ....
....
....
....

Section 7: Withdrawal

29. What was the most significant deciding factor that caused you to withdraw from the course?
....
....

30. Please rank the following factors as influences from 1–5 with 5 as the most important:
Personal..........   Family ....
Performance on Skills Tests ....   Financial ....
ITT Provider ....

31. Was your decision to withdraw discussed with: (Tick as many as necessary)
Family? ☐ Colleagues? ☐ School mentor?☐ ITT provider? ☐

32. Do you regret your decision to withdraw? Yes ☐ No ☐

33. What are you doing now?..

34. Would you consider returning to teacher training in the future? Yes ☐ No ☐

35. What could have been done by your ITT provider to prevent you from leaving?
....
....

36. What could have been done by your placement school to prevent you from leaving?
....
....

37. How can the government help more trainees to successfully complete teacher training courses?
....
....
....

Section 8: About you

38. Your gender: Male ☐   Female ☐

39. Your age: Under 25 ☐   25–34 ☐   35–44 ☐   45 & over ☐

40. In which country were you born?..

41. If born outside the UK, how long had you lived in Britain before starting the course? ....years

42. Is English your first language? Yes ☐   No ☐

43. Which other languages can you:
Speak?..
Read?..
Write?...

44. What do you consider to be your ethnic origin?
White ☐   White British ☐
White Irish ☐   White other ☐
Black Caribbean ☐   Black African ☐
Black other ☐   Asian Indian ☐
Asian Pakistani ☐   Asian Bangladeshi ☐
Chinese ☐   Asian other ☐
Mixed White & Caribbean ☐   Mixed White & African ☐
Mixed White & Asian ☐
Other mixed background ☐   (Please state)......................................
Other ethnic background ☐   (Please state)......................................

Thank you very much for your help. We want to follow up this questionnaire with some focus group interviews. The interview will be carried out at a place and time convenient to you. Please indicate if you are willing to be interviewed. If yes, then please give the telephone number and email address on which you can be contacted so that a member of the research team can arrange a time to interview you.

I am willing/not willing to be interviewed

Telephone number:..
Email address...

6

Administering the questionnaires

Compared to other methods of data collection, questionnaires have a poor response rate. The response to postal questionnaires is between 20 per cent–40 per cent. However, this can be increased substantially with careful planning and by conveying the right message. Most people are too busy to sit and complete questionnaires unless a clear purpose is evident and they view themselves as having an expert opinion on the issues being addressed in the questionnaire. Still, most potential respondents, including professionals, can be wary of requests to complete questionnaires. We therefore need to convey to them how important their views are and how the study is likely to contribute towards generating knowledge, or improving policy and practice.

Covering letter

It is important to include a covering letter with the questionnaire that is not being completed in the presence of the researcher. If a researcher is present, then the contents of the cover letter can be conveyed to the respondents verbally before distributing the questionnaires. Where the names of the potential respondents are available to the researcher, the covering letter should address them by name. The researchers should then introduce themselves, stating their name; designation; course, if any, for which the research is being carried out; and the name of the institution to which they are affiliated.

This should be followed by the working title of the research study, its purpose, the methods of data collection, the kinds of participants being approached, and why it is important that the study be carried out at this time. We also need to tell the participants why they have been chosen to take part in the study, who has recommended the group to which they belong, how they were selected from that group, and from where we obtained their contact details. The researchers should provide their own contact details at the end of the letter and ask the respondents to get in touch if they require further information before completing the questionnaire.

The cover letter should contain sufficient detail to encourage the reader that they should complete and return the questionnaire. Respondents must be assured of their anonymity and the confidentiality of the data that they provide, when the findings of the research are reported. They need to be convinced that this will apply even if they provide their contact details in case of follow-up interviews. If possible, the typical time required to complete the questionnaire can be indicated, such as 15 minutes or half an hour. A return date should be specified, and a stamped addressed envelope should be included with the covering letter and the questionnaire for return of the questionnaire. This should be noted at the end of the cover letter.

Questionnaires for large-scale studies are usually administered by post. This is assuming that the researcher has acquired the postal addresses of potential respondents. For small-scale projects carried out by researchers for Masters, Doctorates or Post-doctoral studies, any one of the following methods of questionnaire administration can be used.

Postal

The researchers can send the questionnaires by post in the conventional manner. This is a cost-effective way of administering questionnaires. If the field-work is being carried out in an organization, such as a primary school or a university, then a letter from the headteacher or the head of department accompanying the questionnaire will be useful and will give credence to the research. The researcher will need to assure the respondent that the data will remain anonymous and the research will be confidential, i.e. their names will not be linked to any data reported widely, nor will their names be revealed to anyone in the school or the university, including the headteacher or head of department, or indeed outside.

If postal questionnaires are not returned by the due date, then researchers should make a follow-up phone call or send a letter or email, politely reminding the respondents to return the questionnaire. They should also re-emphasize the importance of the research and the respondent's participation. Reminders usually result in more returned questionnaires. It is up to individual researchers to decide if they have time to send a second and a third reminder and if more returns will make a great deal of difference. A stamped addressed envelope should be sent with every reminder, as well as with the initial questionnaire.

Self-administered to be completed independently or in the teacher's presence

The researchers can hand out the questionnaires to the respondents and ask them to return them to the researchers in person or by post. This method of administration can be used at conferences, staff meetings, professional development workshops, parents' evenings, school fêtes and so on. If the data are being collected from the researcher's own institution, then the questionnaires can be put in colleagues' pigeonholes, after alerting them to the fact by email beforehand when they will be put there. These can then be returned to the researcher's pigeonhole by a specified date. Researchers can also request teachers to administer questionnaires on their behalf when the teachers have a class of students in one place. The added benefit is that data can be collected from a number of respondents in a short time. The questionnaire will need a covering letter, similar to the one sent with questionnaires administered by post to describe the project. The teachers will of course need to be given clear instructions by the researchers in case the students raise queries about particular questions. The teachers can administer, supervise the completion, and collect, the questionnaires, thus saving the researchers a considerable amount of time, and this strategy is likely to result in a 100 per cent response rate.

Research spotlight

Colley and Comber (2003) conducted a research study to examine the gender gap in computer use. They gathered data from students in five secondary schools through questionnaires, which were administered and completed in the presence of the teachers. The participants included 144 female and 220 male students aged 11–12 years; and 273 female and 302 male students aged 15–16 years. Each teacher was provided with an instruction sheet to ensure common administration procedures.

Self-administered to be completed in the researcher's presence

This, too, needs to be organized at a time when potential respondents are likely to be in one place. They will of course need to be notified beforehand that a researcher will approach them after a meeting or during a conference to ask if they wish to participate in a research project, so that a group of respondents can be gathered in one place. The occasions stated above, when the questionnaires are self-administered but completed later, are pertinent to this method as well. Other possibilities are a class of students whose teacher has allowed the researcher to use the period, such as a Personal, Social and Health Education (PSHE) lesson, for this purpose. The biggest advantage of getting the questionnaire completed in the researcher's presence is that the researcher is at hand to explain if a respondent cannot understand a question. The possibility of partially completed questionnaires is thus eliminated as the researcher is able to check each questionnaire before the respondents leave the premises. This results in a 100 per cent response rate.

Self-completed face-to-face

This is similar to a structured interview (see Chapter 5). If the sample is in the researcher's own place of work, or is fairly local, then the questionnaire can be completed swiftly by the researcher who asks the questions and inserts the answers given by the respondents into the questionnaire. This method is helpful when the respondents are young children or older infirm people. It can also be used to collect data from people gathered in one place at a particular time, such as parents' evenings or seminars and conferences.

Self-completed by telephone

Like the face-to-face self-completed questionnaire above, the questionnaire can be completed over the phone. The researcher will need to obtain the telephone numbers of the respondents and have a prior agreement with them to call them at a certain time to complete the questionnaire.

By email

If potential respondents' email addresses are available, then this is a method of administering and retrieving the completed questionnaire without incurring any costs. If the questionnaire is short, then it can be sent as email text, preceded by a covering letter. Longer questionnaires can be sent as an attached file with the covering letter as email text. It is advisable to approach the respondents by email first to introduce the project and inform them that they will be receiving the questionnaire shortly as an email attachment. This will ensure that respondents do not delete the file, as people usually delete unsolicited emails with attachments because of fear of viruses.

On the web

For large projects, the questionnaire can be put on the web. The respondents are sent the web address to access the questionnaire and they complete it on the web and submit it. Even an individual researcher with limited resources can use an online survey software, such as the SurveyMonkey (http://www.surveymonkey.com) for this purpose. There are several benefits attached to this method. There are no postal costs, it is easy to use, and some versions offer instant descriptive statistics, and allow the researchers to export the data into a spreadsheet.

Activity

Questionnaires appear to be the most appropriate method of data collection for the research project that you are undertaking. Look at the different ways of administering questionnaires above and state which of these will be the most suitable for your study and why.

Validity and reliability

Oppenheim (1992) maintains that we should think of questions as measures. Each question has a job to do, that is the measurement of a specific variable, as set down in the questionnaire specification. He explains the concepts of reliability and validity when using questionnaires:

> Reliability refers to the purity and consistency of a measure, to repeatability, to the probability of obtaining the same results again if the measure were to be duplicated. Validity on the other hand tells us whether the question, item or score measures what it is supposed to measure . . . The degree of reliability (consistency) sets limits to the degree of validity possible: validity cannot rise above a certain point if the measure is inconsistent to some degree. On the other hand, if we find that a measure has excellent validity, then it must also be reliable. (pp. 144–145)

Woods (1986: 115) argues that when questionnaires are used in ethnographic research, they are seen as subordinate to interpretive techniques and their use will need further qualitative work. This will involve checking that all the participants had interpreted questionnaire items in the same way, as this will go somewhat further than the traditional reliability checks used. He observes that the fact that questionnaires lack the sense of process, flux, inconsistency and contradiction, which are essential features of ethnographic research, can be seen as an advantage. They can offer insights into structures and patterns related to social life which may not be possible through interviews or observation.

Ethical considerations

The ethical considerations discussed in Chapter 3 are relevant to all research methods. Questionnaires encroach on respondents' time as they have to set aside a period of time to complete them. However, respondents cannot be forced into completing the questionnaire and may well decide to discard it. It is therefore important to choose the sample with care, and make a case for the research in the cover letter. The respondents are more likely to complete the questionnaire if it is relevant and comprehensible to them, and if they view it as a tool to improve the status quo.

We need to ensure that respondents are not exposed to questions which are threatening, insensitive or offensive. Oppenheim (1992: 122) suggests that we should structure questions in a way that they 'avoid humiliating respondents, baffling them with terminology, patronizing them or making them feel in the wrong'. Guarantees of anonymity of the respondents and confidentiality of the data are also vital. These ought to be stated in the covering letter and again at the beginning of the questionnaires. Researchers must adhere to these promises and should never reveal the identity of their sample, even years later.

Interviews: the beauty of verbal interaction

An interview is a conversation, but it is different from the conversations that we have in everyday life. 'It is both private and public; formal and informal; lived in the present, but preserved for the future' (Brown and Gilligan, 1992: 25). It allows the interviewee to 'move back and forth in time to reconstruct the past, interpret the present, and predict the future' (Lincoln and Guba, 1985: 273). The long interview gives us the opportunity to step into the mind of another person to see and experience the world as they do themselves (McCracken, 1988). Interviews are the most popular method of gathering data for researchers working within an interpretive paradigm using a qualitative methodology. A research interview is different from the interviews that we participate in for other reasons, such as to seek a job. While all interviews are conducted for a purpose, a research interview is specifically designed to collect research-relevant data on a particular issue and to illuminate certain phenomena. Interviewing is a highly eclectic method of data collection and is commonly used in case study, ethnography and action research. It can even be used in small-scale surveys; and in experimental design for pre-test and post-test purposes.

The fundamentals of interviewing comprise generating and maintaining conversations with participants on specific subjects, and the way the data obtained are interpreted by researchers (May, 2001: 120). An interview is an interaction between two people. It is not a one way communication with the interviewer asking the questions and the interviewee answering them. A successful interview provides the interviewee with the opportunity to ask various questions as well. These can be for the purpose of clarification, or even asking the researchers to explain their view on something, or to narrate their own experience of what they are asking the interviewees. This interactive approach enhances the quality of the data collected from the interviewee. Kvale (1996: 14) sees an 'inter-view as an interchange of views between two or more people on a topic of mutual interest', and Walford (2001: 90) observes that 'interviewers and interviewees co-construct the interview'.

Interviews are embedded in human experience and flagrantly draw on the participants' subjectivities. They seek the participants' perceptions of the social world as it is experienced and lived by them and those around them. These are highly personalized portrayals of social phenomena. For this reason, this method of data collection is not concerned with generalizing from the findings. Tuckman (1994: 216) maintains that both interviews and questionnaires provide access to what is inside a person's head and make it possible to measure:

- What a person knows: knowledge or information
- What a person likes or dislikes: values and preferences
- What a person thinks: attitudes and beliefs.

Interviews have a clear advantage when in-depth data are sought. Yin (2009: 106) views interviews as one of the most important sources of information in a case study which are guided conversations rather than structured queries, indicating fluidity instead of rigidity. He notes that the researchers have two tasks during the interview:

1. To follow their own line of inquiry, as reflected by their case study protocol.
2. To ask their actual questions in an unbiased manner, which will also serve the needs of their line of inquiry.

There are several advantages to interviews. Interviewing provides the researchers with the opportunity to build a rapport with the participants, so that there is a relationship of trust between the two participants in the interview situation, i.e. the interviewer and the interviewee, which encourages the interviewees to respond to the questions with candour. Oppenheim (1992: 89) views rapport as an 'elusive quality which keeps the respondent motivated and interested in answering the questions truthfully'. This method of data collection also enables the researchers to explain a question if the interviewees have not understood it the first time. The response rate is 100 per cent as the interviews are conducted either face-to-face, by telephone, by email or on the internet with participants who have agreed to be interviewed. Interviewing has also got some disadvantages. It is time consuming as data collection takes a long time and data analysis even longer. It can be expensive in terms of travel costs and transcribing costs.

Types of interviews

Once the researcher has decided on the issue to be investigated, reviewed previous literature on the subject, formulated the research questions and contemplated the paradigm, methodology and approach for the research, it is time to make a decision about the main method to be used to gather data. Usually by this stage, we have a fair idea of the method that will be appropriate for our purpose, and we may deduce that it is interviewing. This may be used in isolation or in combination with other methods for the purposes of triangulation (see Chapter 3).

There are many kinds of interviews, and the three main types which are likely to be used by individual small-scale researchers are the structured, semi-structured, and unstructured interviews, which are discussed below. The various kinds of interviews differ in their openness of purpose, degree of structure, the extent to which they are exploratory or hypothesis-testing, whether they are seeking description or interpretation, or if they are cognitive-focused or emotion-focused (Kvale, 1996: 126). Interviews can be seen on a continuum, on the one end of which are highly structured interviews with closed questions, and on the other end are interviews which are totally unstructured. Lincoln and Guba (1985: 269) make an interesting distinction between structured and unstructured interviews. They observe that the structured interview is useful when researchers are aware of what they do not know and pose questions to seek the required information. On the other hand, the unstructured interview is useful when researchers are not aware of what they do not know and have to rely on the interviewees to tell them. Whichever type of interview is chosen, the researchers need to pay due consideration to the way the sample is selected to ensure that the participants will have sufficient insight into the issues to be discussed in the interview.

Structured interview

This kind of interview is very similar to a questionnaire in which closed questions are asked. The only difference is that rather than asking the respondent to insert the response, the interviewers write the answers themselves or audio-record the answers to the questions. The questions asked have been formulated in advance and the sequence in which they will be asked is also decided before the interview. Bailey (1996) observes that the structured interview is expected to take a specific amount of time, and the same questions are asked of all those being interviewed, with the interviewer controlling the order and pace of the questions and keeping the respondent on track.

A typical example of structured interview is the market research interview which is rapidly conducted by researchers in shopping centres or from door to door whereby they record the responses of the interviewees on a pro forma stuck to a clipboard, and more recently in an electronic form on a laptop. While this kind of interviewing is mainly conducted to gather data on trends that influence the retail market, it has an obvious function in educational research, especially to gather preliminary data in preparation of, for example, a focus group or observation.

A structured interview is used mainly to ask questions of a biographical and factual nature or to examine attitudes and behaviour. The format for questions suggested for questionnaires (see Chapter 4) can be used for structured interview schedules too. While the data collected are basic, the method has a patent advantage over questionnaires. Instead of waiting for questionnaires to be

returned, the researchers can collect data from a number of peopl
days. Also, while questionnaires might be returned partially answ
tured interview is more likely to elicit a response to each questi
collected can be analysed as qualitative data, or converted int
values and analysed as quantitative data. As long as the participant
based, travel costs are minimal.

Unstructured interview

This is the other extreme which is an open situation. Nevertheless, it does not
mean that we can carry out this kind of interview without any preparation.
It has to be planned as carefully as any other type of interview and the themes
discussed must relate to our research objectives and research questions. This
form of interview can be conducted informally and is quite useful to gather
data on topical issues from informed participants who can shed light on recent
developments, for example a new educational policy, something that has yet to
be critiqued in the literature.

The researchers go into the unstructured interview situation with some
notions or questions, but are amenable to constructs introduced by the interviewee during the interview. These are then turned into questions as the interview progresses, and an in-depth discussion ensues, the outcome of which are
rich, illuminating data. While most of the discussion may be useful, the
researcher will need to ensure that the interviewees focus on the research issues
by asking a pertinent question if the participants are going off on a tangent.

Semi-structured interview

This is the most favoured type of interview in educational research. Researchers using this kind of interview for data collection are usually aware of the
constructs that need to be addressed in the interview. They formulate various
questions that they will ask in the interview. However, they are also prepared
to pose a number of supplementary questions that they will devise during the
interview. The supplementary questions will be linked to the interviewees'
responses to earlier, pre-formulated, questions for the purpose of achieving a
more elaborate, in-depth response.

So while there is some structure to the interview in that some of the same
questions will be asked of all the interviewees, not all the same questions will

be asked of all participants. Further, the supplementary questions asked of various interviewees may be different depending on how they have responded to some of the earlier questions. In this type of interview, the questions need not necessarily be asked in the sequence in which they are written in the interview schedule. Also, not all questions may have to be asked. The interviewees may be answering a question and in giving a detailed response to that question they may answer one of the subsequent question as well, in which case the latter question will become redundant. The beauty of a semi-structured interview is that, unlike a questionnaire or a structured interview, there is no need for equivalence or asking the same questions of all participants. It is however important that all the questions asked relate to, and seek to address, our research questions.

Focus group

This is a kind of interview which is conducted by researchers with a group of participants. A focus group is not an ordinary group interview in which the researchers ask questions and one of the participants responds. This type of interview commences with the researchers explaining what the purposes of the research and the focus group are, and thereafter acting as facilitators of a discussion between the participants, interjecting occasionally with a question or remark for clarification or summing up. A focus group is particularly helpful when the researchers do not know what issues are involved in a particular research situation, and want to generate ideas to ask questions in questionnaires or individual interviews, or items for observation checklists.

The participants chosen for the focus group are assumed to have an insight into, and experience of, the issues discussed, and it is the interaction between the participants that supplies the researchers with the data that they seek. The intention is to gather data which comprise congruent and contradictory views on the same issues from people gathered in the same place. It is a cost effective way of gathering data from a number of people. Morgan (1988) recommends between four and twelve people to make up a focus group. Researchers have to ensure that all participants have the opportunity to contribute to the discussion without asking focus group members directly to do so. There is a danger that dominant personalities in the group will participate more and shy people will stay quiet. Also, if some participants want to state something which is different from the view expressed by the majority of participants, then they are likely to remain silent. The researcher can avoid this by summarizing the discussion a few times during the focus group and checking if all participants agree with what is being deduced from the interaction.

Life history/Narrative

A biography or life history explores the chronology of life against a thematic network, i.e. a set of issues, dealing mainly with one phase of life (Stake, 1995: 96). Life history is a verbal narrative and is very much like an unstructured interview. The interviewees have considerable leeway to choose the course of the interview. It involves empowering the participants to recall significant events in their lives and narrate them in their own way without too much direction by the researcher. Life history relates to charting a journey of some sort, such as becoming a headteacher, or turning round a failing school, and can enable participants to examine change over a period of time and express it to the researcher in their own words.

Elliott (2005: 6) notes some of the common themes related to narrative research which show that the researchers involved in this kind of interview have:

- An interest in people's lived experiences and an appreciation of the temporal nature of that experience
- A desire to empower research participants and allow them to contribute to determining the most salient themes in an area of research
- An interest in process and change over time
- An interest in self and the representations of self
- An awareness that researchers are narrators too.

Life history is basically narrating the story of our lives in a sequential and meaningful way to someone who is usually not aware of it. While the participants have substantial control over what they say, it is not uncommon for them to reveal considerably more to the researchers than they had intended while reflecting on their lives, which may have implications for the confidentiality of the data. The participants' stories are then retold by researchers who interweave their own reflection on, and analysis of, the participants' narrative. Stronach and MacLure (1997), writing about action research, observe:

> On the whole, in these life interviews, both interviewee and interviewer are engaged in a joint mission to *explain*. We act on a set of common assumptions: that a life story will be linear, directional, cumulative, coherent and developmental; that the past will help to explain the present (and not vice versa). (p. 127)

Research spotlight

Smith (2007) examined the life histories of 40 female secondary school teachers to explore their perceptions of the factors affecting their career decisions. Life history interviews were conducted with 10 newly qualified teachers, 20 experienced teachers, and 10 headteachers, as this method was seen as allowing the participants to define the factors of significance for them in the context of their lives, rather than responding to the researcher's agenda. Three spheres of influence on women's career decisions were discernible in the narratives: societal factors – including women's maternal and relational roles and specifically the impact of motherhood on career; institutional factors – including endemic sexism and discrimination in the educational workplace; and personal factors – including the women's values and motivation, aspirations and perceptions of school leadership, and personal agency. Two types of narrative were identifiable: some women saw their careers as defined largely by factors external to themselves, while others positioned themselves as agent in the narrative, seeing their careers as self-defined and self-powered.

This method can also be advantageous when we want to gather data on participants' experiences over a period of time, for example, of discrimination or harassment in their educational institution or workplace because of their race, gender or disability. An abundance of data are generated in life history and narrative research, the analysis of which is very time consuming, yet highly illuminating.

Telephone interview

In correspondence with the email and electronic interview, this kind of interview is less intrusive than a face-to-face interview. It is specifically useful for interviewing participants who live at a considerable distance. It is also safer to interview someone living or working in an unsafe area by telephone, rather than actually going there. There is no travelling involved and even an half an hour telephone interview costs little, assuming the participants have a telephone, and we have their telephone number. It can be conducted after office hours when professionals or parents are relatively free to talk at length on the telephone in a quiet room. Telephone interviews must be arranged in advance so that participants can indicate a convenient time for this purpose. It is not always possible to interview someone on the telephone when we call them for the first time; they may simply hang up. A preliminary letter, email or phone call should provide the participant with the kind of information sent in a covering letter with questionnaires (see Chapter 4).

A telephone interview has got most of the advantages of a face-to-face interview for the researchers except that there is less opportunity to develop a rapport with the interviewees, and no prospect of observing nonverbal communication. If we have the interviewees' permission to record the interview, then a telephone interview can be recorded easily by using an audio-recording device, the one end of which can be put into the telephone and the other end into the audio-recorder. (See Basit et al., 2006 for an example of telephone interviewing).

Email/electronic interview

Like the telephone interview, email and electronic interview is useful in reaching a widely dispersed population in different geographical areas, and even in other countries. If the researchers' institutions have internet access, then they do not incur any expenses when they use email interviewing for data collection, but we can only interview those people by this method who have access to the internet. If it is a structured interview, then the interview schedule can simply be emailed to the interviewees who send their responses to the questions.

Nevertheless, this type of interview can also generate in-depth data. It can be conducted by a series of emails when the researchers approach the interviewees sending them one question at a time. The interviewees reply to the question by email. The interviewers look at the response and email the next question which may be part of the initial interview schedule or a supplementary question composed after looking at the interviewees' response. This kind of interview can be conducted within a day or over a few days when the interviewers and interviewees are also involved in other work and do not have to set aside time for the specific purpose of interviewing, as long as they check their emails at regular intervals, and ask or answer the next question. There is also the advantage that data generated by email interviewing is already in the form of a transcript (See Basit et al., 2006 for an example of email interviewing). The other method of electronic interviewing, which is quicker, is similar to an internet chat whereby the researchers type a question and the interviewees reply by typing their response. This form of interview can be completed in one sitting at a prearranged time. While this method is more spontaneous than email interview, it is still safeguarded in the sense that the interviewees are able to read their response before they send it to the interviewer.

This kind of interviewing is particularly helpful in gathering data from busy professionals who may wish to be approached in the evening after office hours. For example, James (2007) used email interviewing in her research to generate online narratives to understand how academics construct their identities, and notes that the method increased reflexivity and created an arena in which the academic self could be articulated and explored by the participants, and studied and understood by the researcher. This method is favoured by teenagers and young adults who enjoy this kind of interaction. Further, it can be used to interview participants who do not wish to speak to the researcher in case they are persuaded to reveal more information than intended. It is beneficial for interviewing participants who are shy and diffident and can write better than they can speak, or who need to contemplate the question carefully before they respond to it. This, however, means that the researchers need to consider how valuable the spontaneity of responses given in a verbal interview is, and whether an email interview serves their research purposes.

Activity

You are undertaking qualitative research and interviewing seems to be the most suitable method of data collection for your study. Consider the different types of interviews above and state which one of these you will use for your research. Give reasons for your answer.

Formulating the instruments

When interviewing, the vast majority of researchers work with an interview schedule. This is a set of questions that will be asked in the interview. With the exception of the structured interview, there is considerable flexibility in how this schedule is to be used. Most interview schedules will have a number of core questions that will guide the interaction between the interviewer and the interviewee. In addition, the researchers will formulate supplementary questions during the course of the interview depending on what the interviewees have said in response to an earlier question or whether the interviewers want to move the discussion to another area. The interviewers will also use appropriate probes when the interviewees are taciturn or at a loss. All interview schedules should be piloted, ideally with participants similar to those who will take part in the main study. Researchers should be prepared to revise them in light of the pilot. The data gathered through the pilot study should be analysed to ensure if they are addressing the questions they need to address.

Below is an example of a semi-structured interview schedule used in a study on newly qualified teachers (NQTs) in which I was involved. In this research, which was conducted in the North West of England, 500 questionnaires were administered to NQTs, followed by in-depth interviews with 30 NQTs. The interview schedule does not show the prompts used or the supplementary questions asked of the participants.

Interview schedule for NQTs

1. What made you decide to be a teacher?

2. How well did your teacher training course prepare you for your first teaching post?

3. How does it feel to be a newly qualified teacher?

4. How is being an NQT different from being a trainee teacher?

5. Are you conversant with the Induction Standards?

6. What kind of formal and informal induction has your school provided for you?

7. To what extent have you been able to work successfully with other adults during the year?

8. Have you found the termly assessments helpful?

9. How would you evaluate your induction activities?

10. What would you keep, change, drop and bring in to assist NQTs during their induction year?

11. How would you put together a support package for inducting NQTs?

12. Has your first year as a teacher met your expectations of it?

13. What do you think are your main achievements during your first year as a teacher?

14. How do you see your career developing?

15. You note in your questionnaire that during your teacher training...... Would you please say some more on this?

16. You note in your questionnaire that at your present school......... Would you like to elaborate on it?

Interviewers' role and perspective

The ontological and epistemological stance of the researchers determine whom and how we interview. If we see the world as consisting of human interactions and perceptions, influenced by human subjectivities, then we will conduct unstructured or semi-structured interviews to generate in-depth qualitative data and nongeneralizable findings, which are pertinent to a specific context, though they can be replicable or transferable to another situation.

Mason (2002: 63–64) notes some of the possible reasons due to which researchers use qualitative interviews as a method of data collection:

- Their *ontological* perspective suggests that people's knowledge, views, understandings, interpretations, experiences and interaction are meaningful properties of the social reality.
- Their *epistemological* perspective suggests that a legitimate way to generate data on these ontological properties is to interact with people, to talk to them, to listen to them, and to gain access to their accounts and articulations.
- The researchers' view of the ways in which *social explanations* can be constructed lays emphasis on depth, complexity and roundness in data rather than surface analysis of broad patterns.
- Researchers may conceptualize themselves as *active and reflexive* in the research process rather than as a neutral data collector.
- The data researchers want may not be feasibly *available* in any other form.
- Researchers' particular view of research *ethics and politics* may suggest giving the participants more freedom in, and control of, the interview situation than is possible in structured approaches.

The role of the researcher as interviewer is extremely important. The interview situation has a number of benefits for the researchers. They hone their interviewing skills as they progress through the interviewing phase. They learn from their own mistakes and every interview is better than the previous one. They have the opportunity to develop a rapport with the interviewees and gather detailed data on various issues while continuing to probe deeper by asking more questions. Interviews allow the researchers to collect data which are both verbal and nonverbal.

In-depth interviews are particularly suitable for case study and ethnographic research as they offer a multitude of opportunities to researchers to achieve depth; a *sine qua non* for these two research approaches, and something that no other method can accomplish. Woods (1986: 63–65) notes the following attributes of ethnographers as interviewers:

- **Trust:** A relationship between the interviewer and interviewee, which transcends the research and promotes a bond of friendship, a feeling of togetherness, and joint pursuit of a common mission rising above personal egos.
- **Curiosity:** A desire to know, to learn people's views and perceptions of the facts, hear their stories, discover their feelings, and overcome the difficulties involved in setting up and conducting successful interviews.
- **Naturalness:** The aim to secure what is within the minds of interviewees, uncoloured and unaffected by the interviewer.

Oppenheim (1992) notes the significance of interpersonal skills and researchers' identity:

> The interview, unlike most other techniques, requires interpersonal skills of a high order (putting the respondents at ease, asking questions in an interested manner, noting down the responses without upsetting the conversational flow, giving support without introducing bias); at the same time, the interviewer is either limited or helped by his or her own sex, apparent age and background, skin colour, accent etc. When taken seriously, interviewing is a task of daunting complexity. (p. 65)

Although they will already have done it in an initial letter or phone call when they contacted the interviewee, it is good practice for researchers to introduce themselves to the interviewee at the beginning of the interview; tell them how long the interview is expected to last; reiterate the topic and purpose of the research; how many participants are involved; and what they hope to achieve by carrying out the study, for example generate knowledge, contribute to policy, and/or improve practice. They should ask the interviewee again if it is all right to record the interview. This is something that they will also have checked with the interviewee before the day of the interview. Before starting the interview, the researchers should ask the interviewees if they want to ask any questions. Most interviewees want to know more about the research project and the researchers' background. It is vital to develop a rapport with the interviewees before starting the interview. At the end of the interview, researchers should ask the interviewees again if they have any questions or if they want to add anything to what they have said in the interview.

Research spotlight

I carried out an ethnographic case study in which I used semi-structured interviewing as the main method to gather data for my research. I interviewed adolescent British Muslim girls, their parents and their teachers to examine the girls' educational, social and career aspirations. I used an interactive style of interviewing whereby I allowed the participants to ask me questions before, during and after the interview. A total of 99 in-depth interviews were carried out during the two phases of data collection. Documentary evidence was used to verify the mismatch between some of the views of the participants (see Basit, 1997).

The interview is not a situation of an equal power relationship. Ostensibly, the interviewers are in a position of power as they possess sufficient cognition of the research issue and are in a role in which they are asking the questions. However, the interviewees have a power status too. They are the ones who hold all the information that the interviewer is seeking in the hope to comprehend the way the interviewees view their social world. The interviewees may decide to withhold that information, or provide just a glimpse of it, or choose to mis-inform or lie about their perceptions of various phenomena. The researchers therefore have to conduct the interview in a manner that ensures the collection of data which are spontaneous, candid, rich and profound. Still, sometimes, it is difficult to convince people in power to agree to be interviewed, such as headteachers, vice chancellors, policy makers and politicians. This means that the choice of subjects for research in which data need to be collected through interviews is constrained by whom the researchers can interview.

A successful interview requires the correct degree of rapport between the participants. Nevertheless, Hammersley and Atkinson (1983) point to the notion of over-rapport, which they view as problematic, and McCracken (1988) advocates unambiguous social distance between the researcher and the participants which he sees as necessary when asking tough questions and undertaking delicate analyses. Oppenheim (1992) considers both extremes:

> There can be too much or too little rapport, and either would be undesirable. If the interviewer creates too little rapport, or fails to sustain good rapport, then the respondent will be resistant, will start guessing or joking, will not take the task seriously, and will try to cut the interview short. If rapport is too good, then the interviewer will find herself cast in the role of a helper or a social worker or a personal friend, the interview schedule may have to be abandoned half-way through, and the interview becomes unduly prolonged and difficult to terminate. (pp. 89–90)

However, sometimes the best interviews are those in which the interviewers are as willing to answer the interviewees' questions as the interviewees are to respond to the interviewers' questions. This interactive style of interviewing generates rich, illuminating data which may not be possible otherwise (see Basit, 1997). The interviewers cannot hope to get an honest response from the interviewees if they refuse to engage in a dialogue with them about issues which, though personal to the interviewer, may help to inform and illuminate the interviewees' responses. Oakley (1981) argues against the disengagement of researchers conducting social research, particularly feminist research, which aims to give a voice to women's experiences and issues. In her interviews with 233 women, she answered their questions about her own experiences as well as asking them questions about their experiences. Finch (1984) notes her female research participants' willingness to talk to her, which she attributes to her own identity as a female researcher interviewing female participants, and the fact that women are more willing to talk to a sympathetic listener.

An interview is a particular medium for enacting or displaying people's knowledge of cultural forms since questions are not neutral, but are couched in the cultural repertoires of participants (Barker and Johnson, 1998: 230). These cultural forms are more nuanced when examining cross-cultural contexts with respect to race, ethnicity and religion. It is noted by Shah (2004) that the risk in cross-cultural interviewing is that the efforts to understand or explain cultural phenomena, particularly those which do not fit an accepted standpoint, may lead researchers to make false assumptions, or perceive difference as a peculiarity. She maintains that this may misdirect the interview procedure, distort the data gathered, and the interpretations of those data. This means that researchers who have insiders' knowledge of particular cultures are better able to elucidate those cultures. Further, those who do not possess such insights need to be mindful of the nuances in different cultures that they are studying and must not use conventional or stereotypical perspectives to interpret these cultures. Similar caution should be exercised in relation to the social class, gender and age of the researchers and the participants.

Recording the interview

If audio-recording of the interview is possible, then the researcher will have a verbatim record. However, if the interviewee has not agreed to recording the interview, then notes will need to be taken. This will mean jotting down the key points which must be turned into detailed notes straight after the interview while the researchers can still recall the vital aspects of the interaction.

Fieldnotes constitute an important part of research. If the interview is being recorded, the researchers may not wish to write notes and want to concentrate on the interview process so that they can actively listen to what the interviewees are saying and ask relevant supplementary questions at the appropriate time. They can also pay more attention to nonverbal communication.

However, writing a few words during the interview may not be difficult, especially making a quick record of nonverbal communication relating to body language, whether the respondent frowned, laughed, was reluctant to answer, thought for some time before answering, or was taciturn and needed several probes to provide a response. We can also note the paralinguistic aspects of the interview, for example, the interviewees' tone of voice; whether they were shy, reticent, hostile, angry, enthusiastic or confident. These minor signs are easily forgotten once the interview is over.

Interviews can also be video-recorded, which is an excellent way of recording nonverbal communication. Again, we will need the interviewee's permission. As video recording of interviews is time consuming and usually beyond the resources available to a small-scale individual researcher, we need to ensure that video recording is adding value to our data collection in ways that is not possible through audio-recording.

Transcribing the interview

Ideally all interviews should be audio-recorded and transcribed verbatim. This provides us with in-depth perceptions of the interviewees which can never be captured by note-taking during the interviews. If we are transcribing the interviews ourselves, then we should start transcribing as soon as we have completed the first interview, possibly the day after. This will mean that we will still be able to recall what the interviewee said even if some words cannot be heard properly in case of the poor quality of recording. Also, it will prevent us from accumulating tapes and having to transcribe all of them together which can be extremely tedious. All audio tapes and transcripts should have the pseudonym of the interviewee and the date and time of the interview for future reference.

Transcribing is a time consuming activity. One hour of clearly audible interview usually takes about four hours to transcribe if we do it ourselves, and is expensive if we employ a professional transcriber to do it. A small-scale researcher may not have the resources to transcribe all the interviews. Nevertheless, if the interviewees have granted us permission to record the interviews, then we must do so, while making notes at the same time. The audio-recording can then be used as a backup to listen to if we have missed part of a specifically enlightening remark or if we want to check something which seems inaccurate in our notes. We can also undertake a partial or selective transcription of our interviews to transcribe only particularly illuminating quotations that we want to analyse and include in our writings.

While computer software for transcribing is now available, it has problems with voice recognition and a great deal of time needs to be spent to prepare the software to recognize the different voices of the interviewer and the interviewees. Still, mistakes are inevitable and the researchers need to spend a lot of their time in checking the transcripts to see if they match the audio-recording. However, further development of this particular software would undoubtedly be welcomed by researchers who spend several weeks, even months, in transcribing their interviews manually.

Validity and reliability

The process of interviewing is a subjective experience for the interviewer and the interviewee. There is a huge possibility of bias, both in the way the questions are asked and the way they are answered. The researchers may have preconceived notions about the interviewees and may be inclined to ask the questions in a particular way. The interviewees may be impressed by the researchers' personality, or may want to impress them, thereby giving socially acceptable answers. Conversely, the interviewees may view the interview as an exercise in futility, and respond to questions in a mechanical and impulsive manner.

While eliminating bias in interviews is not entirely possible, skilful researchers are able to minimize bias by different means, for example, by keeping an open mind about what kind of data will be generated from the interviewees. They can also ask the interviewees to explain their response or to give an example. Furthermore, they can ask other questions to check the validity and reliability of earlier responses. Sample or methodological triangulation can also be used for this purpose (see Chapter 3). It is also important that researchers are aware of their own biases when they carry out the interviews.

May (2001: 127) points to the tension between subjectivity and objectivity during interviewing and notes that though interviews are thought to elicit knowledge free of bias, yet we are required to let the interview flow regardless of how the interviewees express their perceptions. This means that there is a need for the interviewer and the interviewee to establish an inter-subjective understanding, while at the same time maintaining a distance to situate the interviewees' perceptions objectively within the social setting.

Some researchers think that they must take the interview transcripts back to the participants for validation. This is unnecessary and does not make the research more valid. These researchers feel that the data belong to the participants, but this is an erroneous assumption. The data belong to the researchers as they will have gained permission from the participants prior to the collection of those data to use them in their writings anonymously. Unless the researchers have designed the project in a way that participation is required by those involved in research, in which case such participation should be sought at every step, i.e. formulation of instruments, data collection, analysis and reporting, then involving the participants to confirm what they have said is pointless. As long as researchers have recorded the interview, and have not invented, falsified or distorted the data, their research is valid and ethical. Inexperienced researchers wanting to gain participant validation are at risk of losing important data. Interviewees sometimes do not like to see the strong and critical views in print which they had readily expressed in interviews, and may want them to be deleted from the transcript. They may also have articulated something in the interview and contradicted themselves later in the same interview. This is a significant finding, but they may find it embarrassing and may want one of the statements removed.

Ethical considerations

Research ethics discussed in Chapter 3 should be kept in mind during interviewing. The need for confidentiality and anonymity is more acute as we actually know the names and identity of the participants, talk to them and even see them if we conduct face-to-face interviews. The manner in which the interview is conducted by the researcher should be courteous and cheerful. It is important to convey to the interviewee that we are grateful for their time and value what they are saying.

Oppenheim (1992: 64–65) advises researchers to be aware of the ethical problems in interviewing and the resultant biases and distortions that may be created by these problems. He mentions some ethical issues linked with the way interviewees react to interviews. On the one hand:

- They resent the intrusion by a complete stranger.
- They do not want to be too accurate or attentive in their responses.

- They want to share in the control of the interview and ask questions of the interviewer.
- They fear the potential use to which their responses might be put.

And conversely:

- They may feel enormously flattered at being interviewed at all.
- They may engage in elaborate displays of friendship and hospitality.
- They may involve the interviewers in personal or family matters.
- They may seek to strike up a lasting relationship.

The interview must be conducted with acute sensitivity and finesse. We must not harm or hurt our research participants through word or action. At no point before, during or after the interview should we suggest that we disagree with what the interviewees have said. We must not be judgemental; we are interviewing them to discover their perceptions of the social world, not to impose our own views on them. Ultimately, we have to recognize that what the interviewees say is individual to them; it may be biased and subjective, but if it is their view of the social world, whether rational, blinkered, pompous or naïve, then it should be accepted.

Activity

Problems of validity and reliability and the need for ethical considerations are greater in research using interviewing for gathering data. How will you deal with these issues in the research project that you are undertaking in which interviewing is the main method of data collection?

6 Observation: the charm of gathering data *in situ*

Chapter Outline

Observing the behaviour of others is a natural phenomenon. In all social situations, human beings deliberately or reflexively observe what others around them are doing. As we do it anyway, do we really need to learn about observation? The answer is yes, because we may look, but may not see. Research observation requires us to *see* what is happening, rather than what we *want* to happen, or *think* is happening. Gathering data *in situ* is an appealing prospect. However, this means that we need to train ourselves to observe as a researcher and look at the underlying factors in a situation. Also, observation in research is done for a purpose, i.e. to gather data on a specific subject. Therefore we cannot afford to be haphazard or sloppy, but have to observe in a systematic way, and attention to detail is crucial. Delamont (1992: 115) believes that choosing where to look and when to look is a matter of systematic, principled, reflexive decision-making. Muijs (2004: 55) argues that in research studies using observation for data collection, researchers 'are not just sampling respondents or settings, but slices of time (or occasions) as well'.

Cohen et al. (2007) note that observation can be of:

- *Facts* – such as the number of books and students in a class, or the number of students who visit the library in a certain period.
- *Events* – such as what happens in a situation, the amount of communication between teacher and pupils, the amount of off-task talk, or the amount of group work undertaken.
- *Behaviours or qualities* – such as the friendliness of the teacher, or the extent of aggressive or unsociable behaviour amongst pupils.

Observation is common practice in most professions, such as the Law, where trainees learn by observing their mentors or colleagues advise a client or conduct a court case; Medicine, in which they observe how patients are examined and the news about their illness imparted to them; and Surgery, in which they observe a new operating procedure undertaken by a senior colleague to learn about it, before assisting with and then carrying out such an operation themselves. Similarly, apprentices in different skilled and semi-skilled occupations learn by observing their instructor. Many trainees learn merely by shadowing and observing senior members of their profession. This method can also be used by researchers aiming to investigate, for example, how headteachers in effective schools carry out their day-to-day activities.

In educational contexts, observation can be employed for appraisal and evaluation. Trainee teachers are observed by their mentors and tutors and given feedback on their teaching practice. Teachers in schools, further education and higher education institutions are also periodically observed by Ofsted inspectors to determine the quality of teaching and learning in an educational establishment. Peer observation of colleagues by teachers and lecturers is also becoming common and is indeed mandatory in certain institutions. The biggest advantage of observation is that it allows us to gather data from participants who cannot be interviewed or cannot complete questionnaires, for example, young children, and the disabled.

Tuckman (1994: 378) contends that observation is looking; though not totally unstructured looking, but looking for something, mainly the following:

1. Relationships between the behaviours of the various participants, for example, do students work together or alone?
2. Motives or intentions behind the behaviour, for example, is the behaviour spontaneous or teacher directed?
3. Effect of the behaviour on outcomes or subsequent events, for example, do they play together later on in the playground or work together in other classes?

A major advantage of direct observation is that it provides here and now experience in depth (Lincoln and Guba, 1985: 273). Naturally, observation needs to take place in a setting where we are likely to gather the kind of data that we are seeking from the kind of participants we wish to observe. It, therefore, requires us to be present in the research field, overtly or covertly, and record what is happening. For this reason researchers using observation insist that this method of data collection is better than any other as they are able to observe behaviour directly and gather data *in situ*, rather than relying on secondhand accounts of participants' perceptions of their own or other people's behaviour. This method of collecting data is popular with researchers adopting an ethnographic approach, though its use is also prevalent in case study and action research. In addition to using observation as the principal method of data collection, researchers can use it to triangulate the data collected by other methods. For example, we can check through observation if research participants actually do what they say they do in interviews or on questionnaires.

Muijs (2004: 52), too, points to the advantages of observation as a method of data collection. He notes, for example, that teachers' own reports of their behaviours and teaching styles may not be accurate and may conflict with reports from external observers and students. This may be because they are not able to reflect on their own practice, compare their teaching with that of colleagues, or are motivated to give a response to a question in an interview or questionnaire which conforms to a government policy. An outside observer observing the teaching of these teachers may be able to portray a more accurate picture of their teaching styles. Muijs (2004: 53) also considers the disadvantages of observation, which include the need to observe the same people in the same setting a few times, to ascertain if the behaviour observed is typical or uncharacteristic of the participants, in order to gather reliable data.

Yin (2009: 109) discusses the use of observation in case study research and maintains that as case study takes place in the natural setting of the case, it creates the opportunity for direct observation, which can range from formal to casual data collection activities, and the researchers may assess, for example, the occurrence of particular kinds of behaviours during specific periods of time. Hopkins (2008: 77) notes that there are three main skills involved in observation:

1. Guarding against the natural tendency to move too quickly into judgement by having a clear focus for the observation and agreeing the ground rules beforehand.
2. Employing interpersonal skills when invading someone's space by creating a sense of trust so that the observed does not feel threatened.
3. Designing schedules that will allow the collection of appropriate data.

In educational research, observation is mainly used in the classroom to look at teaching and learning, student behaviour, teacher–pupil interaction and so forth. Additionally, playground dynamics, learning at home, power relations in the staffroom and committee meetings, racism, bullying, gender and ethnic relations are all areas that can be investigated using observation as a method of data collection. This method of gathering data can be more exhausting than any other method. It requires the researchers to concentrate for long periods and make on the spot judgements about which behaviour to observe and record and which to omit. There is no time for distraction and respite as significant activities of participants may be missed out if researchers are not attentive and focused.

Research spotlight

See *Hightown Grammar* by Lacey (1970) for an example of classroom observation.

See *Young Children Learning: Talking and Thinking at Home and at School* by Tizard and Hughes (1984) for an example of observation of nursery school children at school and at home.

The ontological and epistemological stance of the researchers determine how and what they observe. For example, if we view the world as a hard reality, external to the humans, which can be observed in an unproblematic way, then we will carry out structured observation to produce objective and generalizable data and findings. Conversely, if we see the world as consisting of human interactions and perceptions, influenced by human subjectivities, then we will conduct unstructured observation to generate in-depth data and nongeneralizable findings, which are pertinent to a specific context, though they can be replicable or transferable to another situation.

Mason (2002: 85–86) notes some of the possible reasons due to which researchers use observation as a method of data collection:

- Their *ontological* perspective sees actions, interactions and behaviours, and the way people interpret these and act on them, as central.
- Their *epistemological* perspective suggests that knowledge and evidence of the social world can be generated by observing, or participating in, or experiencing, natural or real life settings and interactive situations.
- The researchers' view of the ways in which *social explanations* can be constructed lays emphasis on depth, complexity and roundness in data rather than surface analysis of broad patterns.
- Researchers may conceptualize themselves as *active and reflexive* in the research process because of the premium placed on the experiential nature of this form of data collection.
- The data researchers want may not be feasibly *available* in any other form.
- Researchers may feel it is more ethical to enter into and become *involved* in the social world of those they research to gain understandings than to stand outside and use other methods.

Observation of a particular setting can be conducted by more than one person, for example, a student, a teacher and an independent observer, to gain three different perspectives on the same situation. A secondary school teacher may think that most students interacted with her during a geography lesson, but observation might reveal that out of a class of 30, the same 10 students asked or answered questions or made a comment. Wragg (1999) argues:

> In order to determine and record how often or to what degree something happens, it is usually necessary to have decided in advance what is to be quantified. The main strength of this rational *a prori* view is that it allows the observer to concentrate on elements of classroom life according to procedures carefully worked out in advance. The weakness is that it is less easy to respond to the unexpected, or to retain the flexibility to follow one's judgement about what is important in the lesson in the light of actual events. (p. 21)

Observation as a method of data collection has a specific charm for researchers because we are physically present in the context where social interaction is occurring, and are able to see and record it first hand. Nevertheless, we need to be sure that observation is the most suitable method for data collection for our project. In writing about research conducted with colleagues (Edwards and Mercer, 1987) on classroom discourse, Mercer (1991) justifies their decision to use observation:

> We knew from the earliest stages of planning the research that we would use observational rather than experimental methods. We had begun this whole line of research in a state of disenchantment with experimental approaches to the study of cognitive development and reasoning . . . We also knew that we would be making a qualitative, rather than a quantitative, analysis of our observations. We could not pursue our interests by conducting a large-scale, statistical analysis of classroom interactions in which only a relatively superficial consideration of the exchange of meanings would be possible. (p. 42)

In congruence with other methods of data collection such as interviews and questionnaires, it is usually difficult for the researcher to observe an entire group and generate meaningful data. It is therefore advisable to choose a small group to focus on. For example, if observing in a primary school, we can choose 4–6 pupils and concentrate on them. Depending on the nature of the study, these pupils can be selected because of their gender, ethnicity, ability or other characteristics.

Researchers need to recognize when they have sufficient data and when they should cease observing. Adler and Adler (1994: 380) suggest that we stop observing when theoretical saturation has been reached. In other words, if subsequent observations are replicating the data that have been collected in earlier observations, then we should not carry on. Nevertheless, if it is important to look at the most frequent or least frequent behaviour or activity, then we should continue to observe.

Research spotlight

Galton, Simon and Croll (1980) carried out the renowned ORACLE study, reported in *Inside the Primary Classroom*. This was followed by another study two decades later, by Galton, Hargreaves, Comber, Wall and Pell (1999), reported in *Inside the Primary Classroom: Twenty Years on*. The studies were based on classroom observation. The second study was carried out in some of the same primary schools which were included in the first study, using the same kind of observation and giving the pupils the same attainment tests.

Kinds of observation

Flick (1998: 137) argues that observation needs to be considered along the following five opposing facets:

Participant	Nonparticipant,
Structured, systematic, quantitative	Unstructured, unsystematic, qualitative
Overt	Covert
In natural settings	In artificial settings
Self-observation	Observation of others

Depending on the research questions and the design of the project, observation can be undertaken as a participant observer or a nonparticipant observer.

Participant observation

Participant observation is a special form of observation in which the researchers are not merely passive observers, but assume a variety of roles and participate in the events being examined (Yin, 2009: 111). A participant observer is someone who is usually present in a setting on a regular basis and wants to observe and improve their own practice, which can be the case in action research. Nevertheless, an outsider can also act as a participant observer. For example, a researcher examining the National Numeracy Strategy may decide to teach a few mathematics lessons to a group of secondary students and carry out an observation of the lessons at the same time. These researchers immerse themselves into the activities and culture of the group they are observing to gain insights into that particular setting.

While it is not totally avoidable, participant observers need to be careful not to approach the observation milieu with their preconceived ideas based on prior knowledge and experience of the situation. In any case, they need be prepared to look beneath the surface and refine their judgements as a result of the observation. On the other hand, the insider perspective that they bring to participant observation is an asset and can enable them to comprehend complex phenomena, which a nonparticipant outsider may overlook. Participant observers usually do not have the opportunity to make fieldnotes during the observation and it is advisable to do so straight after the observation and before carrying out another observation. It is also useful to audio- or video-record the observation.

Participant observation can generate several categories of data. These include information about:

- Specific acts
- Longer activities and events
- Timing and sequence of acts, activities and events
- Research settings
- Artefacts and objects in various settings
- People in research settings
- Relationships between people in various contexts
- Participants' involvement in various activities
- Participants' goals and how they achieve them
- People's feelings and how they express them
- Participants' explanation of meanings, causes and purposes of events or actions.

(Source: Lofland, 1971; Spradley, 1980)

However, participant observation can be criticized because the researchers are too closely involved in the research setting and the research participants. As the data generated are mainly qualitative, they are viewed as subjective, biased, unquantifiable and nongeneralizable. By going native, participant researchers may lose their perspective and may not be able to recognize the nuances in a setting.

Nonparticipant observation

Nonparticipant observers usually sit unobtrusively at the back of a classroom or in a corner of a meeting room, trying not to talk or make eye contact with the observed. They appear to be emotionally detached from the research environment. However, they need to do their homework before they observe a setting. In most cases, they will be familiar with the issues under investigation, but they need to know the background of the particular context and group to be observed in order to make relevant and meaningful inferences from the observation. A nonparticipant observer is viewed as an unbiased researcher open to interpreting a situation without prejudice. Fieldnotes offer a very useful record of the observation and the advantage of being a nonparticipant observer is that observation and note taking can be undertaken contemporaneously.

> **Activity**
>
> Choose a topic that you want to investigate using observation as a method of data collection. Would you want to be a participant or a nonparticipant observer?
>
> Give two reasons in favour of participant and two in favour of nonparticipant observation.
>
> Give two reasons against using participant and two against using nonparticipant observation.

Using observation with different methodologies

Observation is a method of data collection that can be used in both quantitative and qualitative research. Quantitative methodology requires us to undertake structured observation and in qualitative methodology unstructured observation is carried out. Nevertheless, the two types of observation need not be in conflict, but can complement each other in a research project to gather different kinds of data. Researchers may choose to use a combination of the two methods and carry out a semi-structured observation to meet their research objectives. Semi-structured observation also means that the researcher has some ideas about what to observe, but need not stick to an agenda and has the flexibility to record other interesting and pertinent phenomena.

Structured observation

This kind of observation requires the observer to have predetermined checklists indicating areas and issues to be investigated. These can be in the form of rating or ranking scales which can be ticked off by the researcher as things happen. Yes and No answers can also be written in front of statements or a category system can be used. Observation data can also be used to prove or refute pre-formulated hypotheses. Structured observation generates the kinds of data which can be turned into numerical values and can be analysed statistically.

This kind of observation is very helpful when the frequency of occurrences is being studied. For example, a primary teacher may want to know how many pupils use the computer during the week, and what they choose to do on the computer. A tutor may want to record how many times a trainee teacher engages primary school pupils by asking them questions or letting them make a comment, and whether she involves more boys or more girls or about the same. Such observation is particularly useful when a large number of groups have to be observed, for example, if researchers want to investigate how history is taught in Year 7 at secondary schools in an LA, then they can carry out structured observation of several history lessons in that year group in different secondary schools and are able to generalize from their findings.

A popular framework used in structured observation in the classroom is the Flanders Interaction Analysis Category (FIAC) system (Flanders, 1970), which is a 10-category system and has been widely used in its original form and has subsequently been refined and modified by others. Its application is not difficult though it is demanding as the observer needs to tally every 3 seconds. It is therefore helpful to observe for short periods of 15–30 minutes followed by intervals.

Flander's Interaction Analysis Categories (FIAC)

Below are the 10 categories developed by Flanders. These are not hierarchical and the numbers next to the categories do not denote a ranking or rating scale; these are just numbers listing the categories:

1. **Accepts feeling**: accepts and clarifies the feeling tone of the pupils in a non-threatening manner. Feelings may be positive or negative. Predicting and recalling feelings are included.
2. **Praises or encourages**: praises or encourages pupil action or behaviour, jokes that release tension, not at the expense of another individual, nodding head or saying 'uh uh' or 'go on' are included.
3. **Accepts or uses ideas of student**: clarifying, building or developing ideas or suggestions by a pupil. As teacher brings more of his or her own ideas into play, shift to category 5.
4. **Asks question**: asking a question about content or procedure with the intent that a pupil should answer.
5. **Lectures**: giving facts or opinions about content or procedure; expressing own ideas; asking rhetorical questions.
6. **Gives directions**: directions, commands or orders with which a pupil is expected to comply.
7. **Criticizes or justifies authority**: statements, intended to change pupil behaviour from nonacceptable to acceptable pattern, bawling someone out; stating why the teacher is doing what he or she is doing; extreme self-reference.

⇨

8. *Student talk-response*: talk by pupils in response to teacher. Teacher initiates the contact or solicits pupil statement.
9. *Student talk-initiation*: talk by pupils which they initiate. If 'calling on' pupils is only to indicate who may talk next, observer must decide whether pupil wanted to talk. If pupil did, use this category.
10. *Silence or confusion*: pauses, short periods of silence and periods of confusion in which communication cannot be understood by the observer.

Hopkins (2008: 102) notes that the two main advantages of the FIAC are that it is easy to learn and apply, and the 10 categories describe behaviours that are important such as teachers' use of praise and criticism, and pupils' solicited and unsolicited talk. Further, tallying events every 3 seconds generates a great deal of data. However, he also points to the disadvantages of the system, as much data are lost, particularly nonverbal communication. Further, some of the 10 categories are too broad or discriminate insufficiently. For example, category 5 does not discriminate between giving correct or incorrect information.

Wragg (1999) discusses another method of recording observation, which is the Exeter Primary Class Management Schedule. He differentiates between an observation system which notes categories every time they occur – a Category System; and an observation system which ticks a category only once regardless of how many times it occurs – a Sign System. The Category system will record all instances that take place in a period of say 10 minutes; whereas the Sign system will tally once in two 5-minute segments.

A carefully devised structured observation schedule takes a long time to prepare, but will make the analysis easier. Piloting the checklist is crucial as the categories need to be robust and mutually exclusive. Piloting will also enable the researcher to introduce new categories to the observation schedule that they had not anticipated and to decide if the observation slot should be longer.

Unstructured observation

As discussed above, there are a number of ways in which researchers can quantify observation data. However, not all features of field activity can be quantified and researchers need to take detailed fieldnotes to capture other aspects of interaction in a situation, particularly those they want to examine in depth. This requires unstructured observation. This kind of observation is especially valuable for recording nonverbal and sensory data. Furthermore, it is useful if the researchers know what they want to investigate, but are not sure about the precise focus of the study. Unstructured observation can expose them to a whole array of scenarios and enable them to ultimately concentrate on one area.

However, unstructured observation of areas such as teaching and learning in the classroom is not a method that can be easily learned. Researchers' fieldnotes may be viewed as subjective by others because of their own biases and preconceived ideas about quality and effectiveness of teaching and learning; and classroom processes including how a lesson should be taught, how the teacher should interact with the pupils and how the pupils should behave and respond. There is also a possibility that the same event observed by two researchers may be interpreted in different ways by them, one reporting it in a positive light and the other explaining it in a negative way. For example, a teacher severely reprimanding a pupil for misbehaving may be seen by one researcher as insensitive and by the other as someone with an ability to control the class.

Wragg (1999: 65–66) recommends that researchers undertaking qualitative observation keep some points in mind. Nevertheless, his suggestions mainly pertain to observation for evaluation of teaching, and I add to his recommendations by looking at these points from a researcher's perspective too:

1. The purpose of the observation has to be made clear to the teacher being observed. To avoid confusion, the teacher needs to be aware whether the researcher is there to evaluate the teaching, offer advice, or gather data for a research project to be analysed later. However, in case of a research project, the teacher will already have been informed about the purpose of the observation and his/her permission will have been obtained before the commencement of the observation.

2. Researchers carrying out unstructured observation need to reflect on the nature of quality and effectiveness and be cognizant that, in addition to their own views, there are several definitions of effectiveness and quality. In research projects, before the researchers label a teacher's teaching effective or of high quality, or vice versa, they need to look at how effective teaching and learning is defined in the literature and how many different versions exist of high and low quality teaching.

3. If providing feedback to the teacher, researchers need to determine which aspects should be discussed, how the discussion should be structured, and who should take the lead. Nevertheless, researchers undertaking unstructured observation for a research project may not wish to discuss their initial thoughts with the teacher and may want to leave it until they have had time to analyse the data properly.

4. Researchers have to decide how to record the observation and who should be the focus of the notes: specific events, teacher, pupils or all. One way is to make detailed notes as and when events occur; the other is to write under predetermined

headings such as teaching style or pupil response. Researchers working on a specific project will either focus on pre-identified areas or go into the field with an open mind to record, for example, what happens in biology lessons in a secondary school. Initial observations of this context will help them to focus on particular areas in subsequent observations.

Activity

Design a research study using observation as the main method of data collection. You can carry out this study by using

Structured observation
Unstructured observation
Semi-structured observation

Give a rationale for your choice to state why your chosen type of observation is the most appropriate method of data collection for your project and why the other kinds of observation are not suitable.

Observer effect

An observer watching closely what people do over a period of time may be annoying. On the other hand, some research participants may prefer to be observed while carrying on with their day-to-day work rather than having to sit and complete a questionnaire or be interviewed. The presence of an outsider, however unobtrusive, in the classroom or any other milieu to be observed can change the dynamics of that situation. Also, it can change the behaviour of the observed, as they may want to please, impress or irritate the observer. This may be the result of the observer's age, gender, ethnicity, social or professional status, attire, speech, or just because they are a welcome distraction or an unwelcome intrusion. Woods (1986) notes the need for researchers to be unobtrusive in order to witness events as they are, untainted by researchers' presence and actions.

Observer effect cannot be totally removed but can be minimized. The researchers can explain to the group being observed what the purpose of the observation is and what they are going to focus on. Nevertheless, sometimes the nature of the issues to be investigated makes it necessary not to brief the participants beforehand. For example, researchers examining disruptive behaviour in the classroom or bullying in the playground will not want to inform the participants what kind of behaviour they are observing (see Chapter 3 on Ethics). Researchers can also practise habituation whereby they stay in the research setting for a long time. In this way, the research participants become accustomed to the presence of an outsider and behave normally. However, this option is usually not available to researchers studying for a higher degree as they have limited time available for fieldwork. Still, Tuckman (1994: 378) notes that the more observations researchers make and the more unobtrusive they remain, the less likely they are to influence the observed situation.

Recording the observation

Despite the availability of some helpful observation schedules (see FIAC and the Exeter Schedule above), researchers sometimes find it helpful to modify pre-existing schedules or develop their own categories depending on the purpose of the study and the nature of the activities that they want to observe. It may also be the case that the readymade schedules do not work for them and they want to phrase them in their own way.

Checklists and tables

Unless the observation is of an exploratory nature and is intended to inform the design of a future research project, it is advisable to keep a record of what is observed in order to pick up the nuances of the culture being studied. This can be done in a number of ways. Structured observation can be recorded quite simply by ticking pre-formulated checklists to record the frequency of a particular occurrence. For example, how many times a teacher asked questions of girls; how many times boys raised their hands to answer a question; or how many times junior lecturers made a comment during a departmental committee meeting. Such checklists can also be used to record the participation or behaviour of specific individuals.

An observer may wish to record how long an activity continued, for example, for how long the teacher read the story to infant school children, for how long the children asked questions about it and the teacher answered their questions, and how long the children took to draw pictures about the story and write words that they remember from the story. This can be done by using a table with columns for times and rows for activities, indicating the timeline for the activities. If the story started at 10.30 am and finished at 11.00, this half hour will be recorded on the table by highlighting cells representing that 30 minutes period, then the next 15 minutes for asking and answering questions and so on.

Activity / Time	10.30–10.45	10.45–11.00	11.00–11.15	11.15–11.30	11.30–11.45	11.45–12.00
Teacher reads story	▓	▓				
Children ask questions			▓			
Children write words				▓	▓	
Children draw pictures						
Children say written words						▓

On the other hand, the researcher can put a mark showing the number of times a particular activity takes place or draw a line through that time slot. This can be done quite simply by using the forward and back slashes alternately. For example if a researcher is analysing talk in the classroom, this can be recorded as follows:

Teacher explains activity	/
Pupil asks question	∧∧∧/
Teacher answers question	∧∧∧/
Teacher admonishes pupil	∧∧
Teacher asks pupil to read out the answer	∧∧/
Pupil reads out answer	∧∧∧
Teacher praises pupil	∧/
Teacher corrects pupil	∧/
Teacher makes a joke	∧
Teacher and pupils laugh	∧

Note taking

Recording unstructured observation is much more difficult than structured observation as it is easy to miss something significant. A straightforward way of recording unstructured nonparticipant observation is through note taking in the field. The researchers can sit on one side and jot down whatever they observe. They will need to be pretty adept at identifying individuals, noting verbal interaction and nonverbal cues, deciding which occurrences are significant and should be recorded and which are trivial and should be ignored. Fieldnotes offer an account which is available to the researcher immediately after the observation and enables them to start analysing the data. They are a very helpful personal record of the observation as noted by the observer and should be taken even if the observation is audio- or video-recorded.

Schensul et al. (1999: 114) highlight the challenge for the researchers in transforming observations into fieldnotes to capture a scientific record of what has been observed. Completion and accuracy of fieldnotes is important to facilitate their use as data which can then be catalogued and coded. LeCompte and Preissle (1993: 224) state that observation notes can include the following:

- Quick and fragmentary jotting of keywords and symbols
- Detailed written out observations and transcriptions
- Descriptions, when assembled, to constitute comprehensive and comprehensible accounts of what happened
- Profiles of participants
- Reconstructions of conversations
- Description of settings
- Description of events, behaviour and activities
- A description of the researcher's own behaviour and activities

Muijs (2004: 55) contends that the descriptive observation record is the easiest form to construct, yet is the most difficult to use and analyse. On this form, the researchers write down everything that they observe which is relevant to their study. The advantages of this form are that it allows the researchers to gather rich and detailed data, and record phenomena that they may not have anticipated. The disadvantages are that it requires high levels of alertness and concentration from researchers to enable them to capture the detail, and since the data collected are qualitative, it is time consuming to code them and to make comparisons across observations. Schensul et al. (1999) suggest that while writing fieldnotes, researchers remember that:

> Behaviors should be defined behaviorially, rather than in terms of what they mean to the observer. For example, fidgeting with a pencil and keeping eyes downcast in a meeting may mean several things: boredom, disagreement, lack of understanding, anger, frustration, or preoccupation with another matter. Researchers

should describe the behavior and avoid attributing meaning to it in the fieldnotes until they discover what the behavior communicates to others in the setting. (p. 115)

The use of technology

A discreet method of recording unstructured observation is by audio-recording. A high quality audio-recorder can be kept in a corner and people usually forget its presence after a little while. This is particularly useful when considerable verbal communication is taking place and when the researcher is a participant observer and cannot take notes. This gives us a verbatim record of the entire observation. However, this loses nonverbal communication, and unless voices are clear, some of the data may be lost. Further, it is difficult to identify individuals.

Video recording of observation can be highly advantageous. It can capture individuals, their voices, movements and mannerisms. It is particularly valuable if just one person is being observed, such as the teacher. Ideally, the camera should focus on the entire group being observed and should be kept in one place. However, it is difficult to use this method to record whole class or big group observations unless the observer operates the camera and continues to target the source of action. This means that the observed are conscious of the presence of the video camera and may start behaving in a superficial or simulated manner. Focusing on one subject may cause the researcher to miss an important observable instance in another part of the room. Researchers note that videoing teachers at work in their own classroom can be perceived as invasive and intrusive and a violation of what is mostly a private sphere (see for example, Jones and McNamara, 2004). However, using a video to record the observation is not a great deal more intrusive than recording the observation by note taking, though video recording will take longer to organize. It is the presence of an outsider which can be viewed as intruding on the teacher's territory. Researchers therefore need to make themselves as inconspicuous as possible when observing in a classroom.

Jones and McNamara (2004) also note that teachers prefer the video camera to be positioned in a way that it is not in their direct line of vision, and that pupils quickly learn to ignore it. They also found that teachers have considerable control over the way the recording is carried out:

It was the teachers who decided which lessons were to be recorded; moreover, they could stipulate the length of each session . . . one teacher wanted access to data that depicted her introducing a new science topic . . . to examine whether her questioning techniques allowed children opportunity to demonstrate their knowledge and understanding of the topic . . . Teachers could also veto videoing . . . one teacher asked for filming to stop because of the disruptive behaviour of some of the class. (p. 286)

Clearly, the researchers have to respect the wishes of the teacher whose class is being observed. Nevertheless, it is helpful to agree some ground rules when negotiating access to specify the kind of jurisdiction the teacher will have on the observation.

Analysis of observation data recorded in this way is time consuming. Audio- and video-recording of observation should ideally be transcribed verbatim and interpreted in conjunction with the researcher's fieldnotes as this offers a full picture of the observed scenario. However, transcribing is expensive and time consuming and the researcher may want to listen to or view the recordings and make notes of key points for analysis. The raw data will then enable us to look for meaning by utilizing the lenses that are at our disposal for this purpose (Ely, 1991).

Taking still photographs is another way of recording observation. This is particularly useful when nonverbal communication needs to be recorded over a period at short intervals. For example, this can be used to record how one particular pupil interacts with her peers in the classroom. A digital camera can be set up to take photos of the pupil every minute for the duration of a lesson. This can be supplemented by fieldnotes to document specific instances of verbal communication if necessary. Fieldnotes are also important to describe the context so that the relevance of the photographs is linked to the setting in which they are taken.

Validity and reliability

Miles and Huberman (1994: 56) highlight the fact that observation is selective as 'the observer is constantly making choices about what to register and what to leave out, without necessarily realizing that, or why one exchange or one incident is being noted, but another is not'. While some degree of selectivity is required depending on the focus of the study, and the fact that it is impossible to observe everything that is happening in a particular milieu, in order to ensure validity in observation researchers need to take care that they do not report their findings out of context. The data generated through observation have to address the research questions and deliver what the researcher set out to investigate. Observation data and analysis should also be reliable. This means that they have to be sufficiently robust to enable other researchers to replicate the study. In order to ensure reliability, researchers need to write up their fieldnotes as soon after the observation as possible, if they have not been able to do so during the observation.

Cohen et al. (2007: 411) advise that researchers make sure that the indicators of the construct under investigation are fair and operationalized, so that there is, for example, agreement on what counts as constituting qualities such as 'friendly', 'happy', 'aggressive', 'sociable' and 'unapproachable'. They recommend that for research to be reliable, the indicators of the construct under investigation have to be applied fully, consistently and securely without variation in interpretation, whether there is one observer or several observers involved in the project.

Ethical considerations

The ethical considerations discussed in Chapter 3, which pertain to all research projects regardless of the methods they use, apply to observation. Mason (2002: 99) argues that questions about the ethics of researchers' entire research practice, where their ethical position stems from, how they create and maintain relationships in the field, the resulting power dynamics and the researchers' role in them, the issue of informed consent, and the researchers' right over the data and the analysis, are all fundamental to observation. Muijs (2004: 57) highlights the dilemma faced by nonparticipant observers whether or not to become involved in the phenomenon they are observing. While it will be easy not to get involved in teaching per se when observing a classroom where a lesson is being taught by a teacher, it may not be straightforward to decide to what extent we should detach ourselves from what else is happening in the classroom. For example, it would be unethical to decline a child's request for help or to answer their question. It is therefore important to check with the teacher beforehand what they want us to do in such a situation.

Researchers need to consider whether observation should be overt or covert. Most of the time, we can tell the participants that they are being observed. However, in certain situations, informed consent of the participants, and even their knowledge that they are being observed, may render the observation data useless or even prevent the researcher from accessing the relevant group to be observed. Mitchell (1993) contends that certain kinds of knowledge are only available through covert observation, for example, when observing groups who do not wish to be observed such as bullies, racists and so forth. Covert research is also helpful to the researcher when it is likely that the participants will modify their behaviour if they are aware that they are being observed, for example, pupils demonstrating disruptive behaviour and aggression in the classroom. Covert observation presents an ethical dilemma to the researcher. Nevertheless, it is an acceptable strategy as long as it does not hurt or harm research participants and, in particular, vulnerable groups.

Research participants involved in observation studies may at times feel uncomfortable as a consequence of being constantly observed. Mason (2002: 100) maintains that while this may also be the case in research interviews, yet when people are being observed they are 'on view' for longer periods and in a wider range of activities. The researchers can therefore potentially cause more harm to the participants during data collection. On the other hand, longer time in the field may enable the researchers to make better judgements about, and more opportunities for, reducing or eliminating harm. She also anticipates researchers making a number of instantaneous ethical and moral decisions while undertaking observation.

Activity

The headteacher of the primary school where you are working has found out that some children who bring packed lunch to school have their lunch stolen or confiscated by their peers. The pupils who lose their lunch in this way are too scared to name the perpetrators. This is a school-wide problem and the headteacher has asked you to help her find the culprits. How will you design a small-scale research project to observe what is happening?

7 Documents: exploiting records of social phenomena

Using documents in research projects does not involve the researchers in the same kind of interaction that interviewing and participant observation offers, is less invasive than these two methods, and is very much a solitary activity. In a research project, documents can be used in two ways. First, existing documents can be perused to gather data and to analyse these data. Second, new documents can be produced by researchers themselves, or requests can be made by them to research participants to generate documents as part of the data collection process. Mason (2002: 111) uses the terms 'excavation' and 'construction' in relation to documents. She maintains that it is more useful to think of documents as constructions rather than excavations, embedded in or constitutive of social or cultural relations, rather than revealing facts about them.

Interestingly, documents are significant in what they record, but also with respect to what they omit about a specific period, event or phenomenon. Cohen et al. (2007) view documents as social products which are located in particular contexts and, therefore, need to be questioned and interpreted rather than merely accepted since they can be selective, intentionally excluding some information and serving purposes and audiences other than the researcher. May (2001: 176) notes that when documents are read as 'sedimentations of social practices', they can inform and structure the decisions that individuals make, and describe the aspirations and intentions of people, events, places and relationships of times when the researchers were not present or even born. McCulloch (2004) highlights the benefits of documentary research:

> Documents are often neglected and taken for granted, estranged and alienated even in their familiarity, propinquity and abundance. Nevertheless, they form a basis for a renewed understanding of our social and historical world. Perhaps, also, documentary studies may encourage mutual understanding and regard across the disciplinary barriers, and a fresh awareness of the research challenges that we have in common. (p. 131)

Lincoln and Guba (1985: 276–277) note the reasons why documents should be more consistently tapped in research:

1. They are available, either free, or on low cost, which may be researchers' time.
2. They offer a stable source of data, firstly because they may accurately reflect situations which occurred at some time in the past; and second, because they can be analysed and reanalysed without the original document undergoing changes in the interim.
3. They offer a rich source of data which are contextually relevant and grounded in the contexts they represent, and appear in the natural language of that setting.
4. They are often legally unassailable, representing formal statements that satisfy some accountability requirement.
5. Unlike human participants, they are nonreactive, though what emanates from a documentary analysis still represents the interaction between the document and the analysing researcher.

Documents produced for research purposes primarily generate qualitative data, though quantitative data are sometimes collected by this method too. May (2001) argues:

> [Documents] do not simply reflect but also construct social reality and versions of events. The search for documents' 'meanings' continues, but with researchers also exercising 'suspicion'. It is not then assumed that documents are neutral artefacts which independently report social reality . . . or that analysis must be rooted in that nebulous concept [called] common-sense reasoning . . . Documents are now viewed as media through which social power is expressed. They are approached in terms of the cultural context in which they were written. (p. 183)

The ontological and epistemological stance of the researchers determine who writes the documents and how and when they are written. Mason (2002: 106–107) notes some of the possible reasons due to which researchers use documents to gather data:

- Their *ontological* perspective suggests that written words, texts, documents, records, visual or spatial phenomena, or aspects of social organization, shape, form or so on, are meaningful constituents of the social world in themselves – more meaningful than verbal utterances – and aspects of the social world can be read through them.
- Their *epistemological* perspective suggests that words, texts, documents, written records, visual documents, visual records, visual artefacts and phenomena can provide or count as evidence of these ontological properties.
- Documents may be used in *addition* to other methods of data collection, for example, to verify, contextualize or clarify personal recollections and other forms of data derived from interviews, observation and so forth.
- The data researchers want may not be *available* in other forms.
- Documentary data may be used simply because they *exist* and are accessible.

Burgess (1984; 123–124) distinguishes between various types of documents as follows:

- Primary or Secondary sources
- Public or private documents
- Unsolicited or solicited documents.

McCulloch (2004: 128) observes the tensions and interactions between public records and private documents in research studies using documents. He concedes that the two are 'powerful constructs' representing 'distinct domains', yet argues that documentary studies can illuminate how they affect and interact with each other in practice.

Existing documents

Existing documents come in several shapes and forms. For example, these can be:

- Archives in libraries and museums
- Attendance records

- Biographies and memoirs
- Calendars
- Committee meeting agendas and minutes
- Curricula
- Diaries and journals
- Evaluations
- Examination results
- Feedback and progress reports
- Government reports
- League tables
- Letters
- Maps
- Newspaper and magazine articles
- Policy papers
- Prospectuses
- Parliamentary papers
- Statistics
- Tables and graphs.

All of the above can provide invaluable sources of secondary data, which have already been collected by someone, usually for purposes other than research, and have possibly been analysed as well. These data and analyses can be used by researchers in their own way for their own research projects. Some of these, and additional sources, are now available on the internet and can be searched and downloaded by using various search engines. Furthermore, data gathered for previous research studies in the form of interview transcripts, audio-recordings, observation checklists, fieldnotes, photographs, videos, films, charts, graphs, figures, tables and so forth can be reinterpreted by new research-ers. While most of the documents are in the form of text, visual and audio sources are also used in research studies. In addition to the above, Prior (2003: 2, 5) mentions paintings, tapestries, monuments, shopping lists, stage plays, advertisements, rail tickets, and the World Wide Web, which can also be classified as documents. She maintains that documents are usually considered as fixed and static texts, yet contemporary documents often express their contents such as ideas, arguments, and narratives in multi-modal forms which can include image and voice, as well as words. She wants researchers to take note of this and argues:

> If we are to get to grips with the nature of documents, then we have to move away from a consideration of them as stable, static and pre-defined artefacts . . .

> The status of things as 'documents' depends precisely on the ways in which such objects are integrated into fields of action, and documents can only be defined in terms of such fields. (p. 2)

Ideally, none of the above documents should be used in isolation, but rather as a source to triangulate with primary empirical data gathered by the researchers to offer another perspective on the issues under investigation. They also enable the interviewers and observers to compare their own interpretations of phenomena with those cited in documents about these or similar phenomena. McCulloch (2004) argues:

> A broader notion of triangulation and methodological pluralism is possible . . . through a combination of documentary and non-documentary sources. Probably the most common approach to developing such a combination is to relate archival records to interviews of living respondents. (p. 129)

Activity

Look at the various lists of documents above. Do you envisage drawing on any of these sources of secondary data in your research project? Explain which ones you will be using and how they will help you in your project.

Alaszewski (2006) highlights the use of documents in historical studies and maintains that diaries are a valuable yet neglected source of historical research, which can provide supporting evidence for traditional political histories. In social and anthropological studies that use historical data they are a unique source offering a way of accessing information that could not be accessed in any other way. Ponsonby (1923: 32) observes the value of previously written diaries as historical evidence:

> Notwithstanding all the immense store of facts we are compiling by means of newspapers, books, registers and official records with regard to the history of our own times, the privately written comments of an individual spontaneously scribbled and so reproducing the mood, the atmosphere, and, so to speak, the particular aroma of the moment, are priceless and can be regarded as the spice of history. (cited in McCulloch, 2004: 103)

Researchers need to contemplate a number of factors when deciding to use documents. Some social worlds, cultures and events will have been written about a great deal resulting in an abundance of documentary evidence about the participants' social world, whereas this may be less so in other cultures. Also, not all documents are written by researchers for other researchers or for research purposes; most may be written by individuals for other audiences. Researchers therefore need to consider the relevance and authenticity, and the validity and reliability, of documents and decide whether and how to use these documents most effectively for the purposes of their own research. While there may be a temptation to view text-based documents as ready made data, it is useful to ask ourselves what counts as data and how to obtain them from documents to meet the objectives of our research.

Alaszewski (2006), discussing existing documents, contends that researchers using diaries for historical research are unable to control the scope of diary keeping or the survival of the diaries, as the use of diaries as a method of data collection is opportunistic and researchers have to make the most of whatever is available. There are issues related to the survival and storage of diaries, access to them, and their relevance to the purposes of the research. Nevertheless, Fothergill (1974: 9) enthusiastically argues in favour of diaries:

> They were so concretely *there*, so firmly embedded in the centre of their own existences, each consciousness composing all the elements of its experience into a unique and incommunicable set of relations with itself as the focal point of the world. One's sense of the substance of history is turned inside out. Where one habitually thought of 'ordinary lives' forming a vast background to historical 'events', now one's vision is of the great events daily passing behind the immediate realities that comprise an individual's experience. (cited in McCulloch, 2004: 103)

Thus diaries document the immediate experiences of individuals and convey them to future generations so that they can visualize these events too. Bailey (1994: 294–296) notes that analysis of existing documents can be appealing to researchers for a number of reasons:

- It can enable them to reach otherwise inaccessible participants, as in historical research.
- There is little or no reactivity on the part of the writer, particularly if the document was not written for research purposes.
- It can show how situations evolve over time, as in longitudinal analysis.
- It can address large samples, as in registers of births, marriages and deaths; and national census.
- It can catch the dynamic situation at the time of writing, as in documents written *in situ*.

- It can capture personal details and feelings, as in letters and diaries.
- It allows them to access documents written by skilled professionals containing valuable information and insights.
- There may not be any cost involved in retrieving them, if they are held in a library or archive.

Mason (2002) maintains that during the process of deriving data, researchers need to think what they are going to take from existing documents. It can be copying whole documents for analysis, or just relevant parts of the documents, or selected literal quotations. She suggests that if researchers are interested in the literal wording, and form and sequence of text in a document, then they devise a literal method of recording these. Further, Cohen et al. (2007) argue that documents need to be studied in their context to enable us to understand their importance at the time. They give the example of a document written two centuries ago mentioning £200, which is a small amount in the twenty-first century, but represented a great deal of money when the document was written.

Yin (2009: 103) observes the explicit and significant role that documents play in data collection in case study research and highlights their use in corroborating and augmenting evidence from other sources in the following ways:

1. Documents are helpful in verifying the correct spellings and titles or names of organizations that might have been mentioned in an interview.
2. Documents can provide other specific details to corroborate information from other sources. If the documentary evidence is contradictory rather than corroboratory, you need to pursue the problem by inquiring further into the topic.
3. You can make inferences from documents. For example, by observing the distribution list for a specific document, you may find new questions about communications and networking within an organization. However, you should treat inferences only as clues worthy of further investigation rather than as definitive findings because the inferences could later turn out to be false leads.

Documents can sometimes be difficult to use and it may be hard to decide whether data collected from documents add value to the study. Bailey (1994: 296–298) points to a number of disadvantages attached to documents. They may:

- Be biased and selective
- Not have been written to be used as research data, but for a different purpose, audience and context
- Be interpretations of events rather than objective accounts

- Be an incomplete record of the situation under consideration
- Exist, but are not available to the researchers
- Be in a format which does not lend itself to standard analytical methods, such as content analysis.

According to Yin (2009: 120), the disposition of the documents used should be covered in the protocol of a study. He suggests producing an annotated bibliography of these documents to facilitate storage and retrieval by the researcher, and to make it possible for them to be shared by future investigators. Because of the likelihood of a large amount of physical space required for the storage of such documents, he proposes turning them into portable document format (PDF) files and storing them electronically. Cross-references to these documents can also be made in other data such as fieldnotes.

New documents

Documents can also be generated as primary data. The most common types are, diaries, logs, journals and fieldnotes. A contemporary tool is the weblog which has considerable potential to be used for research purposes. Some researchers distinguish between diaries, journals, memoirs and logs. However, this differentiation is not helpful as the term 'diary' encapsulates all kinds of written records by the researchers and the participants, ranging from the most simplistic to the most analytical. While some may be intended for a small or a specific audience, they may well be used for wider research purposes as secondary data and to inform future generations.

When used in classroom research, documents can provide a context for understanding the curriculum or teaching methods. Hopkins (2008: 123) notes that using documents in research have the following advantages. They:

- Illuminate issues surrounding a curriculum or teaching methods
- Provide context, background and understanding
- Provide an easy way of obtaining other people's perceptions.

However, he also points to some disadvantages in the use of documents:

- Obtaining documents can be time-consuming
- Certain documents may be difficult to obtain
- Certain persons may be unwilling to share confidential documents.

Research diaries

This section will deal with diaries that are produced as part of the research procedure. A diary is a personal narrative written over a period of time. Research diaries are written for a specific purpose by the researcher or the research participants. The researchers may write a diary to reflect on the process of research. However, the more common type is the diary solicited by the researcher and scribed by the participants noting their perceptions and experiences. Diaries can also be requested from children. For example, a class of secondary students can be asked to write a diary about their experience of and views on the teaching methods introduced by the new science teacher. Woods (1986: 111) contends that 'diaries [are] particularly useful in studying pupil cultures, and if they are interested, pupils are well prepared to cooperate . . . Pupils are good for short bursts, but find it difficult to sustain interest over a period of more than a few days.' He recommends capturing a brief cross-section of activity, event or series in the form of a brief entry, which can be followed up by interviewing.

Oppenheim (1992) views a diary as a daily record kept by the research participants at the researchers' request; and not a document containing intimate personal confidences. It is intended to obtain an accurate daily or even hourly record of the participants' activities. However, diaries do include personal confidences if they serve the purposes of the research project for which they are being written, and if the researchers have requested such data from the participants. Alaszewski (2006: 1–2) defines a diary as 'a document created by an individual who has maintained a regular, personal and contemporaneous record'. He sees the significant characteristics of diaries as follows:

- **Regular:** A diary is organized around a sequence of regular and dated entries over a period of time during which the diarist keeps or maintains the diary. Those entries may be at fixed time intervals such as each day or linked to specific events.
- **Personal:** The entries are made by an identifiable individual who controls access to the diary while he or she records it. The diarist may permit others to have access, and failure to destroy the diary indicates a tacit acceptance that others will access the diary.
- **Contemporaneous:** The entries are made at the time or close enough to the time when events or activities occurred so that the record is not distorted by problems of recall.
- **A record:** The entries record what an individual considers relevant and important and may include events, activities, interactions, impressions and feelings. The record

usually takes the form of a time-structured written document, though with the development of technology, it can also take the form of an audio or audio-visual recording.

Research spotlight

Burgess (1983) used diaries to examine events in the classroom. He adopted an unstructured approach, gave each teacher an exercise book, and asked them to keep diaries to record what occurred in their classrooms. Each exercise book contained a note providing the framework within which teachers could make their entries, and which could be used to make comparisons between entries and between diaries. He subsequently used the diary accounts of the teachers' lessons to formulate questions to ask them in interviews to gain a more thorough understanding of their lessons. He did this by underlining key words and phrases which he wanted the teachers to explain in interviews. He noted the page numbers on which these words and phrases appeared, so that easy references could be made to those pages and entries in the diaries during the interviews.

Diaries have traditionally reported behaviour, rather than attitudes or perceptions. However, increasingly, researchers are becoming interested in looking at participants' feelings, perceptions and viewpoints regarding their own or someone else's behaviour, and request such information, resulting in diary entries that are an excellent source of qualitative data. Alaszewski (2006) sees the use of diaries in not only identifying patterns of behaviour, but also providing insights into how participants interpret situations and ascribe meanings to actions and events, and therefore actions that may appear irrational to outsiders are rational to the diarist. Research diaries cover a certain time span, usually from a week to a month, but sometimes longer. Plummer (2001) argues:

> The diary is the document of life *par excellence*, chronicling as it does the immediately contemporaneous flow of public and private events that are significant to the diarist. The word 'contemporary' is very crucial here, for each diary entry – unlike life histories – is sedimented into a particular moment in time. (p. 48)

Diaries are particularly helpful if the participants are required to record behaviour and feelings immediately because they may not remember them with accuracy later on. For example, if a secondary school pupil is being bullied by her classmates on a regular basis, a researcher can ask her to keep a diary in which she will enter every night if she was bullied that day, what kind of bullying behaviour was demonstrated by the perpetrators, how she felt about the conduct of her classmates, whether she reported the incidents to anyone in authority, and if she received any support from them.

Activity

You are studying for a higher degree. Keep a diary for a week to indicate every night how much time you were able to spend on activities related to your studies every day during the week and at the weekend, noting what the different activities were and your detailed views about those activities.

Diaries are a rich and illuminating source of data gathered from participants who are shy and reticent and do not find it easy to articulate what they know or think. They may not even be aware of what they know until they start to write about it. Others may need the time and space that diary writing provides, as opposed to interviews, to compose a narrative. Also, some participants may write better than they speak. Conversely, some participants may be poor writers, and, therefore, interviews will be a better method of gathering data from them. If, however, diaries are seen as necessary in such cases, then the researchers will need to accept the diarists' idiosyncratic writing with its accompanying spelling and grammatical mistakes. We have to recognize that like different modes of speech in interviews, the participants writing diaries will have a range of writing styles. Still, whatever the style in which the diaries are written, they can offer rich depictions of the participants' perceptions. Alaszewski (2006) maintains:

> Diaries provide a rich source of data for researchers who wish to explore the development of an individual life, and the activities and relationships of particular groups in society. The utility of diaries may be restricted by their availability, but it may be possible to minimise such limitations by seeing an individual diarist or group of diarists as typical or representative of a wider group. Diaries can be used to access information within a specific society or social group and to explore the relationships between groups and even between cultures. (p. 33)

Oppenheim (1992: 253) advises researchers not to use diaries as a method of data collection unless the researchers' requirements cannot be met by using another method. He sees these requirements as:

- The timing of the activities within the day, when an hourly record is needed
- The summing up of certain activities over a period of time, noting differences in weekday and weekend behaviour
- Recording unobservable phenomena, such as dream records.

It can sometimes be difficult to persuade participants to keep a diary for a period of time and to generate the kind of data sought by the researchers. Nevertheless, there are a number of ways in which diaries can be successfully used in research. These include detailed verbal and written instructions given to the participants by the researchers, suggesting the format in which diary entries should be made, and checking by telephone once or twice during the diary-keeping period if the participants are making their entries at the required times, for example, every hour or every evening, and in sufficient detail.

Diaries can be used successfully in ethnographic research. Woods (1986) maintains:

> Diaries are an important complement to life histories, for past events may be recollected and interpreted through current mental frameworks, and quite often remembered facts may be wrong or somehow distorted. A diary can produce corroboration, or otherwise, of facts, dates, places, people, views and feelings . . . [Nevertheless], it is the ethnographer's business to be sceptical and to seek to understand the interpretative frame behind all the materials that are presented. (p. 107)

This method of data collection can also be used productively in other research approaches. While discussing the use of diaries in action research, Elliott (1991) contends that accounts in diaries should not just report the bare facts, but communicate to the reader how the participant felt in a situation. 'Anecdotes; near-verbatim accounts of conversations and verbal exchanges; introspective accounts of ones feelings, attitudes, motives, understandings in reacting to things, events, circumstances; these all help one to reconstruct what it was like at the time' (p. 77).

Both quantitative and qualitative data can be collected by diaries. Data gathered for studies using experimental design and surveys can be entered in diaries in a structured manner and a diary pro forma devised by the research-ers can be used for this purpose for every day or every hour. Diaries solicited for case study, ethnography or action research can allow more freedom to the participants to write about specific issues, which are the focus of the study, in their own way. However, it is crucial that clear instructions and guidance, which are not too prescriptive, are provided by the researchers at the onset of the study and then checks are made at regular intervals during data collection. A sample of diary entries for a day or two can be sent to the researchers to ascertain if participants' diaries are addressing the relevant issues in the correct format, so that mistakes can be prevented in subsequent entries. However, such exemplars may curtail creativity and encourage the participants to compose their entries in exactly the same way. This initial attempt at diary writing can be treated as a pilot if necessary, especially if considerable changes need to be made to the way the participants are writing the diaries.

A hardbound diary should be given to each participant, the first one or two pages of which should repeat the instructions verbally given by the researchers, including the focus of the study, the importance of putting the date and time with each entry, the issues that the diarists should concentrate on when enter-ing the data, how often the diary should be written, and when it has to be com-pleted. If diaries are being kept on the computer in a word format, then similar arrangements should be made by sending a word file to the participants with the instructions and asking them to continue typing in that file using it as a diary. Alternatively, they can use a new file for every day and send the initial files to the researchers for feedback to check if they are on the right track.

Diary data are difficult to analyse. While analysing qualitative data gathered by any method is time consuming, some of the data collected by diaries may need to be quantified and presented in a tabulated form to show averages and differences. Diaries can be used as the primary method of data collection in case study, ethnography and action research, and may be used in conjunction with interviews, questionnaires or observation. They can also be used to provide qualitative data to supplement the quantitative data gathered in experimental design and small-scale surveys which have used observation or questionnaires as the main method of data collection. Alaszewski (2006: 29–30) notes that diaries are not the dominant source of data in some research approaches because experimental research uses observation, and surveys use questionnaires or interviews. Diaries overcome the shortcomings of these methods to access the desired data that cannot be acquired otherwise because of memory problems.

Diaries can be particularly helpful to record behaviour which is seen as deviant. For example, if we want to examine the high truancy rate in a second-ary school, we may ask the truants to keep a diary for a month to record every day if they attended school or if they did not go to school. This will include their views about the days when they were in school and how they felt on that day; and the days when they did not attend, why they missed school, and what they did instead. Interviewing the truants is another method of collecting data in such a study, but the interviewees are less likely to recall the specific aspects related to truanting and attending on a day-to-day basis to provide meaningful data. According to Alaszewski (2006):

> Diaries can be used to access those facets of social life which members of social groups take for granted and are therefore not easily articulated or accessed through research methods such as interviews. Interactions within social groups imply common and shared characteristics, for example, members of the groups can competently speak the same language and have sufficient agreement about the nature of the world to facilitate meaningful communication and interaction. The shared agreements or tacit knowledge about the world . . . tend to be inter-nalised through the processes of socialisation . . . Diaries can be used to access such tacit knowledge. (p. 37)

Activity

You are conducting a project on the eating habits of university students who live away from home to find out how many of them eat healthily and how often in the day they eat junk food and why. Design a study using diaries as a method of data collection.

In educational research, it can be fairly easy to recruit a number of parti-cipants to write a diary, for example, as stated above, if it is a readymade group such as a class of students who are requested to keep a diary for a certain period to illuminate specific issues. Nevertheless, in some cases, selecting a sample of diarists can be problematic. In such instances, snowballing can be helpful in choosing a sample by asking the participants if they know of other potential participants with similar characteristics, then approaching these participants, and then further participants through them and so forth.

Alaszewski (2006) notes that diarists act as researchers' agents in situations where the latter cannot record the data themselves. He suggests selecting those participants for writing diaries who can follow the instructions; are trustworthy, honest, and competent; understand the purpose of writing the diary; are motivated; and have the skills to document data accurately. He recommends training the participants if they lack appropriate skills. However, any structured training will be beyond the scope of a small-scale study and an individual researcher, and detailed instructions and follow-up phone calls offering support and answering queries, as well as checking the progress of the diary, may be more feasible in such cases.

The blog

Participants need to have reasonable literacy skills to write diaries, though with the advent of technology, audio and video diaries are being recorded which remove the need for the participants to write the diary and they can present it in a verbal format instead. Technology has also introduced the weblog or the blog.

The blog is a novel way in which an individual writes an online diary. It is a written account, but may be composed in a relaxed manner, with the bloggers sometimes using quaint shorthand that is commonly used in email or phone text correspondence. Data can also be represented pictorially, as graphics, audios and videos. A blog is a diary which is regularly written, usually daily, in reverse chronological order similar to email correspondence, to present an update on one's activities. It is either open to public viewing, or whatever is written has restricted access to those who are on the bloggers' friends' list.

Blogs have considerable potential to be used as a research tool, mainly with young participants who are interested in electronic interaction and may be more motivated to keep a regular blog than a conventional diary. Links can be made to other blogs, photographs, videos, audios and articles to illuminate particular statements made by the blogger. The unique feature of the blog is the interactive nature of the diary, whereby readers of the blog can comment on the entries. In some ways it is similar to an internet/email interview (see Chapter 5), though the blog has a greater potential to gather data from multiple participants. Popular blogging websites, such as Blogger (http://www.blogger.com) can be used for this purpose. Further, Facebook (http://www.facebook.com) comprises a blog feature as well as a number of other social interaction tools.

Activity

Contemplate a research topic in which you can use a blog to gather data from a group of participants. Discuss in detail how you will design your study.

Fieldnotes

As opposed to the new documents discussed above, which are scribed by research participants, fieldnotes are a reflective diary which are kept by the researchers during a research project to note what cannot be captured by traditional methods of data collection. They are a key component of researchers' fieldwork and a method of recording the researchers' contemporaneous reflections during or soon after an observation or interview, so that researchers can easily recall and document significant facts about their fieldwork. Some researchers differentiate between fieldnotes and a reflective diary, but they are very similar. The simplest version is an *aide memoire* to remind ourselves of various obvious and obscure facts in the field, whereas the more sophisticated form encapsulates the researchers' analytical reflections. Schatzman and Strauss (1973) view the researchers' diary or fieldnotes as comprising the following:

- *Methodological notes:* to show the planning or completion of an operational activity; a reminder or instruction to oneself; or a critique of one's tactics
- *Theoretical notes:* self-conscious, controlled attempts to derive meaning from any observational notes
- *Analytical memos:* to elaborate on an inference or tie up several inferences in an abstract statement
- *Observational notes:* to record events experienced through watching and listening, without any interpretation so as to make them reliable.

Activity

Look at the fieldnotes or reflective diary that you produced during your last fieldwork session. Into which categories noted by Schatzman and Strauss above do your data fall?

Bogdan and Biklen (1992: 122) view the reflective aspects of fieldnotes as follows:

- Reflections on the descriptions and analyses done
- Reflections on methods of data collection and analysis
- Reflections on ethical issues, tensions, problems and dilemmas
- Reactions of researchers on what is recorded
- Points of clarification made or need to be made
- Reflection on possible avenues of further inquiry

Such musings are clearly helpful in research studies in which data are gathered empirically. Fetterman (1998) views fieldnotes as an essential aspect of ethnographic research:

> Fieldnotes are the bricks and mortar of an ethnographic edifice. These notes consist primarily of data from interviews and daily observations [and] inundates the ethnographer with information, ideas and events. Ethnographic work is exhausting, and the fieldworker will be tempted to stop taking notes or to postpone typing the day's hieroglyphics each night. Memory fades quickly, however, and unrecorded information will soon be overshadowed by subsequent events. Too long a delay sacrifices the rich immediacy of concurrent notes. (p. 114)

This shows the urgency of writing fieldnotes promptly to capture the essence of action in the field before the researchers forget the salient points that need to be noted. Fieldnotes can also be used for various purposes in action research in the classroom, as Hopkins (2008: 105) maintains, they can:

- Focus on a particular issue or teaching behaviour over a period of time
- Reflect general impressions of the classroom and its climate
- Provide an ongoing description of an individual child that is amenable to interpretation and use in case study
- Record our development as teachers.

Further, Emerson et al. (2001) argue:

> Fieldnotes are a form of *representation*, that is, a way of reducing just-observed events, persons and places to written accounts. And in reducing the welter and confusion of the social world to written words, fieldnotes (re)constitute that world in preserved forms that can be reviewed, studied and thought about time and time again. (p. 353)

Validity and reliability

Documents must be carefully used, should not be accepted as unmitigated truth and literal recordings of events that have taken place, and researchers should not be overly reliant on them (Yin, 2009: 103, 105). Before choosing specific documents for analysis, we need to ascertain their authenticity and credibility. Mason (2002) notes the importance of text-based data in social research, but cautions researchers to take a critical stance when dealing with such data:

> The idea that observations and interviews become *data* when they are transformed into text is a very influential one in the social sciences. This probably has the effect of over-emphasising the inherent credibility of documentary and particularly textual data, and under-playing that of visual and other non-text based forms of data. The implication is that text has a superior or concrete and indisputable quality, but you should not uncritically accept such a claim about any document . . . You should ensure that you subject all documents, including those you have produced, to exactly the same degree of critical scrutiny. (p. 106)

While validity may be strong in documents written in first person or for a specific reason, that reason may not coincide with the purpose of the research and thereby undermine the validity of the documents for research purposes (Bailey, 1994: 317). McCulloch (2004: 44) suggests that in order to overcome potential problems of reliability and bias, researchers use a wide range of different kinds of documents representing alternative perspectives – that is, a form of triangulation. This helps to expose any inaccuracies of sources and allows the researchers to corroborate the inferences that they draw from their data. Different documents have different strengths and weaknesses and using them together in a research project to compare and contrast the evidence presented by them will give us a fuller and truer portrayal of the social world.

Nevertheless, participants' interest in writing a diary may cause them to modify the very behaviour we wish them to record. For example, if we want to look at whether parents of infant school pupils read to their children, we can ask the parents to keep a diary for a fortnight. However, the parents may decide to read to their children every night, when previously they only read to them once in a while, and read for longer, and choose better books to read, so that their diary entries can be impressive.

Like most qualitative data, there can be an issue about generalizability in data generated through diaries. We may not want to claim that the behaviour noted in diaries is typical of the participants, and rather state that it is likely to vary from day to day. It may be difficult to assert, for example, that the diaries of 20 FE students commenting on their experience of further education in a new college, are characteristic of all FE students in that college. What we might be able to claim, though, is that the experiences of these FE students may be similar to some other FE students' experiences in the same college and in other FE colleges. Alaszewski (2006) argues that:

> If the focus is on a specific historical case study or on the nature of narratives in specific diaries, then the issue of representativeness may not be important. However, if the researcher is seeking to generalize from a specific diary or group of diaries to the experiences of a wider group then the researcher needs to explore the typicality or representativeness of the diarists. (p. 49)

Ethical considerations

Ethical considerations discussed in Chapter 3 apply to the use of documents in educational research too. Documentary analysis requires the researcher to access the required documents and while some documents may be fairly easy to get, others may be of a confidential nature and may mean that we have to sign a declaration promising to guard the confidentiality of the data, which is indeed good ethical practice. It may be difficult to persuade potential participants to write diaries, but they should not be pressurized into participating in the study. Perusing personal records of other people may be viewed as highly intrusive and researchers should ensure that the data are anonymized and used for research purposes only.

McCulloch (2004: 48) maintains that 'a potentially key issue in document analysis that has been neglected as a result of the general lack of recognition of documentary research as a social process is the ethical dimension of such research.' He highlights issues of copyright, freedom of information, data protection and intellectual ownership of data, and recommends researchers deal with these matters early on in documentary research. Obtaining informed consent for the use of documents can be problematic. Sometimes documents refer to people other than those who own these documents. Researchers need to decide whether permission to utilize the document from the owner is sufficient to proceed with its use. Advice can be sought from the ethics committee of the researchers' institutions.

Part 3
Making Sense of Data

Quantitative Data Analysis: seeking breadth and generalizability

8

Both quantitative and qualitative data need to be analysed to make sense of the information that they are conveying to us. Quantitative data are seen as offering precision whereas qualitative data are viewed as presenting depth. Both kinds of data are ultimately expected to fulfil our objective of searching for the truth and addressing our research questions. Quantitative data are generated by researchers working within the positivist paradigm, mainly using research approaches such as surveys and experimental design, but also case study and action research. These data will either already be in a numerical form or can easily be converted into numerals. Data collected in studies utilizing a quantitative methodology are analysed to look for similarities and differences, patterns, distribution, significance and correlation. It is important to consider how the data will be analysed before we commence data collection, as the method of analysis will inform the structure of the research instruments.

The process of handling quantitative data is essentially cyclical with the following stages:

1. Specifying the problem – asking the question(s)
2. Planning – what data to collect, how to collect, whom to collect it from
3. Fieldwork – gathering data quickly, efficiently and effectively
4. Processing – summarizing data in the form of models, lists, tables, figures
5. Interpreting – analysing data and examining them to see if our questions are answered – by going back to the problem and questions (1) and planning (2) to gather more data (3) if our data do not address our questions, and so forth.

Researchers are sometimes tempted to quantify qualitative data and vice versa when they are analysing their data. There is somehow a tacit obligation to show that what we have got is more than what we actually have. For example, we may feel that the numerical data that we have generated do not have sufficient depth, so we need to explain in a qualitative manner what the data are conveying to us. Conversely, we may not be confident that the in-depth data provided by the small numbers of participants in a qualitative study are convincing enough for our readers unless we show in numerical forms how many participants felt this or believed that. Researchers who have such misgivings and are not sufficiently confident about their methodology should undertake research using mixed methods, or an eclectic methodology, which will allow them to use both quantitative and qualitative methodologies appropriately. Nevertheless, this is a decision that we should take at the design stage and before we embark on the pilot study.

Punch (2003) contends:

> A central feature of empirical research, which applies very much to the quantita-tive-survey-relating-variables, is that data exist and are collected at a very specific or concrete level, but that the purpose or objective of the research is to reach conclusions and make statements at a much higher level of generality or abstraction. This means that there are specific pieces of data at the lowest level, abstract concepts at the highest level, and a gap between these levels. Disciplined research requires that we establish logical connections between these levels. (pp. 27–28)

The most common ways in which quantitative data are generated in educational contexts are through closed questions in questionnaires, structured interviews, structured observations, structured documents, school-based tests and quasi-experimental research. Quantitative data deal with variables, which can be independent or dependent, and the relationship between these variables.

Variables

A Variable is a construct or particular characteristic which the researchers are interested in, and which they observe, measure or manipulate. Variables can vary from individual to individual, from one group to another, or from one organization to another. Examples include gender, age, ethnicity, social class, occupation, attainment and so forth.

Independent variable

An independent variable is the input variable, and is the one which causes a specific outcome. It is a stimulus that affects a response, an antecedent or a feature which can be modified (e.g. under experimental conditions) to bring about an outcome.

Dependent variable

A dependent variable is the outcome variable, and is the one which is caused by the input, precursor variable. It is the effect or consequence of experimental treatment to the independent variable.

Muijs (2004) argues:

> While it may be tempting to start looking at relationships between variables straightaway, it is a good idea to look at our individual variables first . . . how our respondents have replied to particular questions, or how many times a teacher has asked a particular question . . . before we can go and look at relationships with other variables. We might often just want to know how many boys and girls are in our sample . . . Because we are looking at individual variables, this type of analysis is called *univariate analysis*. As well as providing important information, univariate analysis can help us to look out for mistakes that may have been made during data input, for example. (p. 91)

Kinds of quantitative data

These are the levels of measurement. Muijs (2004: 97) contends that 'levels of measurement are basically categories of variables. This categorization is important because it fundamentally affects the meaning of the variables and what we can do with them statistically.' Punch (2005) maintains:

> Statistics is one of the many tools the researcher needs. Like other tools, it can be used very effectively without the user having a full knowledge of how it works. What is needed, however, is an understanding of the logic behind the various statistical tools, and an appreciation of how and when to use them in actual research situations. (pp. 108–109)

Quantitative data that are generated in research are in four main forms:

Nominal

Numerical values are assigned to categories in the data as codes, hence their alternative name, Categorical Data. The categories have no ranking, ordering or meaning, and are mutually exclusive. For example, a pupil labelled as 5 is not necessarily a better or worse pupil than the one labelled as 3. In coding a questionnaire for computer analysis, the response 'male' might be coded as '1' and 'female' as '2'. These data represent discrete variables, i.e. totally separate categories of 1, 2, 3 and so on, and cannot be 1.50 or 2.75.

Ordinal

Numerical values are assigned to the data in accordance with a qualitative scale. The data are classified and are in some kind of order, such as rating scales, to elicit attitudes and opinions. For example, in coding a questionnaire, the responses, 'very satisfactory', 'satisfactory', 'neither satisfactory, nor unsatisfactory', 'unsatisfactory', and 'very unsatisfactory' may be coded '5', '4', '3', '2', and '1' respectively. Indeed, these values can be included in the scale used in a questionnaire, for example, the Likert Scale. However, these data do not have a measure using equal intervals or a metric. And therefore they cannot assume that the distance between each point of the scale is equal. The ordering of the responses is retained in the coding.

Interval

The ordering of, and the distance between, values is given in the form of regular and equal intervals, thus introducing a metric, but also retaining the aspects of the nominal and ordinal scales, i.e. classification and order. Measurements are made on a quantitative scale, in which the differences between points are consistently of the same size. However, the base point is arbitrary and there is no true zero, as some measurements do not start from a zero, such as the freezing point of water on a Fahrenheit scale is not zero degrees, but 32 degrees, and the boiling point of water is 100 degrees Fahrenheit. However, since the zero is arbitrary, we cannot assume that water which is at 50 degrees Fahrenheit is half as hot as that which is at 100 degrees Fahrenheit. The Interval scale is not often used.

Ratio

This has the major components of the previous three scales, i.e. classification, order and equal interval metric, but also has a true zero. Measurements are made on a quantitative scale in which the differences between points are consistently of the same size. The advantage is that data of this type allow us to ascertain proportions easily, and all mathematical procedures of addition, subtraction, multiplication and division can be applied, making them the most powerful kind of data. Distances, incomes, lengths, money, exam marks, time spent on activities, are all ratio measures because they can have a true zero. For example, student A spent £30 on books in a month; which is twice as much as student B, who spent £15; and which is three times the amount of £10 spent by student C.

Analysis of quantitative data may involve employing one of the following:

Descriptive statistics
These include nominal and ordinal data – frequencies, proportions, percentages, ratios; Interval data – measures of central tendency, i.e. mean, median, mode;

and Measures of dispersion – range, interquartile range, standard deviation. They allow the researchers to explore the data by summarizing, describing and presenting them, but without making any inferences or predictions.

Inferential statistics

These are more powerful than descriptive statistics and allow the researchers to use various tests to check their findings and report them with confidence. They make inferences and predictions from the data and calculate the significance of the data and the findings. They include hypotheses testing; correlations; regression and multiple regression; analysis of variance; factor analysis; chi-square – to compare sets of values; Kolmogorov-Smirnov – to compare two samples; t-test – single-sample test of mean or two-sample test of means.

It may be appropriate for researchers conducting small-scale quantitative studies to analyse their data quite simply by using descriptive statistics and by examining the relationship between some of the variables. Others, particularly those undertaking research for doctoral work, may need to go further and carry out sophisticated statistical analyses of the data. This, however, will mean working with larger samples. Statistical analysis is often concerned with statistical significance, that is, to say with confidence that the result is not the outcome of chance. Quantitative research subscribes to the hypothetico-deductive model and is concerned with devising and testing hypotheses (see Chapter 2) through research approaches such as experiments or surveys, and by using methods of collecting data such as questionnaires, observation and so forth. Wragg (1999: 122) argues that if researchers want to use statistical techniques to analyse the data generated through observation, then it is important that they start with questions instead of techniques. For example, if the observer wants to know whether the contacts between the teacher and various Year 11 students are significantly different in some way, or if one teaching method leads to more effective learning than another teaching method, then there are several appropriate statistical methods of analysing the data that can be used provided the data are in a numerical form.

Types of tests

It is important that researchers are aware of the distinct features of their data as the form of data will determine the type of statistical test to be applied to analyse them. The two main categories of tests are nonparametric and parametric.

Nonparametric tests

Nominal and Ordinal data are regarded as nonparametric, which means data that do not make assumptions about the population because the characteristics of the population are not known to the researchers. Such data are usually obtained from questionnaires. These tests can be adapted to be used in particular circumstances and contexts. For example, they can help teachers and education managers to verify their findings on student and staff performance respectively.

Parametric tests

Interval and ratio data are regarded as parametric data, which means data that have knowledge of the characteristics of a population and researchers are therefore able to make inferences from such data. These data are viewed as more robust and are often obtained from experiments. It is important that researchers are more cognizant of issues pertaining to validity, reliability and the characteristics of the population.

There are a number of statistical tests that researchers can carry out to analyse their data. Some of the important tests are briefly discussed below:

The chi-square test
This is a test that is carried out to examine association or difference, though it is more often used as a test of difference. It measures the difference between a statistically derived expected result and an actual result to ascertain whether there is a significant difference between the two.

The t-test
This test is conducted to determine if there are statistically significant differences between the means of two groups. It is carried out to look at comparisons between two randomly chosen groups, with a normal distribution of scores, using parametric data. There are two variations of the t-test and the sample may be independent or dependent subject to the hypothesis:

- Independent samples are usually two randomly selected groups
- Dependent samples are matched on some variable, or are the same people tested twice.

For example, if we examine the results of 100 twin boy and girl Year 9 SATs mathematics test marks, this will be a dependent t-test because it is a paired sample with a relationship. Alternatively, if we test 100 boys' and 100 girls' Year 9 SATs mathematics test marks, it will be an independent t-test as there is no relationship between the sample.

Analysis of variance (ANOVA)

Sometimes the t-test does not serve our purpose as it is confined to two groups, two variables or two points in time. The analysis of variance allows us to compare and examine the differences between more than two groups which have been chosen by random sampling, with normal distribution, and parametric data. The two common types of analysis of variance are the one-way analysis of variance – to examine the difference between the means of three or more groups on one independent variable; and the two-way analysis of variance – to investigate the consequence of two independent variables on one variable.

Research spotlight

Smith and Tomlinson (1989) conducted the very first study to analyse data with the method of variance component analysis. They knew every one of their 3,000 pupil participants' results when going into schools, during their school career at 14, and their school leaving results; plus parental class, ethnicity, background and so forth (as they interviewed the parents). All this showed the school effect and which schools were doing better for which pupils. This research was conducted before the British government introduced the Pupil Level Annual School Census (PLASC) in 2002.

The Mann-Whitney U and the Wilcoxon tests

These two tests are the nonparametric equivalent of the t-test and are used with one categorical variable and at least one ordinal variable. The Mann-Whitney test is used for two independent groups and the Wilcoxon test is used for two related groups. Both tests are based on ranks. The Mann-Whitney test checks how often the score from one group is ranked higher than the score from the other group, and the Wilcoxon test compares how the same sample has responded to two different items or on two different occasions. In the two tests, not finding a statistically significant difference between the samples is as important as finding a statistically significant difference between them.

The Kruskal-Wallis and the Friedman tests

These two tests are the nonparametric equivalent of the analysis of variance and are used with one categorical variable and one ordinal variable. The Kruskal-Wallis test is used for three or more independent groups and the Friedman test is used for three or more related groups. These tests are also based on rankings and function in the same way as the Mann-Whitney test.

Factor analysis

This is a method in which variables which have some common characteristics are grouped together. It allows the researchers to reduce a group of variables to fewer underlying factors, thus accounting for several variables. The researchers are able to identify structures and commonalities in the relationship between variables, and discover whether different variables are addressing the same concept. For example, one variable may measure a child's weight in kilograms and another may measure it in pounds. The underlying latent factor uniting both variables is weight. There are two forms of factor analysis:

- **Exploratory factor analysis:** that explores previously unknown groupings of variables to detect underlying patterns and clusters.
- **Confirmatory factor analysis:** that is more rigorous and tests a set of factors against a hypothesized model of groupings and relationships.

Analysing questionnaire data

Oppenheim (1992) observes that researchers need to recognize that regardless of how subtle the questions in their questionnaire were, and notwithstanding how cooperative the respondents had been, the main purpose of the questions, the questionnaire, and indeed the entire survey, is measurement. The end result of this will comprise tabulations and statistical analyses, which, along with illustrative quotations from the raw data, will form a report to demonstrate how our findings support our hypotheses.

Punch (2003: 45) reminds the researchers that before starting the analysis, the survey data needs to be prepared, which involves data cleaning and data entry. Data cleaning means tidying up the data, such as proofreading the responses; making decisions about unclear responses, where multiple alternatives have been ticked, and unanswered questions result in missing data. Then the questionnaire responses have to be entered into the computer software for analysis.

For large-scale surveys, in which data are sought from a sizeable number of respondents by means of questionnaires, data should be analysed statistically using one of the tests noted above. However, for a small-scale survey, case study or action research, deriving quantitative data from a few questionnaires, a small number of structured observations, or structured interviews, data can be analysed using the measures of central tendency, measures of spread and dispersion, or standard deviation.

Measures of central tendency

Mean, mode and median

The *mean* is obtained by adding all the items or values and then dividing them by the total number of values. For example, if we want to look at the mean age at which our 12 master's students at the School of Education began their master's studies, we will add their ages given in the questionnaire: 21, 22, 22, 23, 25, 25, 25, 27, 29, 31, 31, 32 which will come to 313, which divided by 12 gives us the mean age of the students as 26 years.

The *median* gives us the middle value in a range. To find the median, the items must be listed in order. If the range comprises an odd number of values, then the middle value is the median. If there is an even number, then the average of the two middle values is taken, which in the example above is 25 + 25, which gives us the median age of 25.

The *mode*, which is not commonly used in small-scale studies represents the most frequently occurring value, which in our range above is 25.

Measures of spread and dispersion

Range, interquartile range and standard deviation

Range is the difference between the highest and the lowest value in the range (32–21), which is 11 years in our example above.

Interquartile range places less importance on the two extremes of the range and presents a more precise figure. The highest and lowest 25 per cent are ignored and the middle 50 per cent of the values is cited. In the example above, the lowest 25 per cent is 21, 22, 22, and the highest 25 per cent is 31, 31, 32. This shows the interquartile range of 23–29, which is six years.

Standard deviation shows the spread and the degree to which the values differ from the mean. It uses values for the whole group and not just one section. A small standard deviation shows that frequency distribution is closely concentrated around the mean, whereas a large standard deviation indicates that the distribution is widely spread out from the mean. This can be calculated with a calculator. The steps below show how it can be done by using the 12 values in our example above, i.e.

21, 22, 22, 23, 25, 25, 25, 27, 29, 31, 31, 32.

- *Step* 1: calculate the mean = 26
- *Step* 2: calculate how much each value differs from the mean =
  -5, -4, -4, -3, -1, -1, -1, +1, +3, +5, +5, +6
  If these differences are added, taking the add and subtract signs into account, the sum must equal zero, as it does in our example, i.e. -19 +19 = 0
- *Step* 3: square each deviation from the mean =
  25, 16, 16, 9, 1, 1, 1, 1, 9, 25, 25, 36
- *Step* 4: Add the above squared values = 165
- *Step* 5: Divide the sum by the number of responses, i.e. 165 / 12 = 13.5
- *Step* 6: 13.5 is the variance and the square root of this gives us the standard deviation, which is 3.67

Presenting the analysis

Having looked at the data that they have derived from questionnaires, researchers need to make informed decisions about how to conduct and present the analysis of their data. Punch (2003: 45) maintains that there are three main data analysis steps that can be applied in the analysis of quantitative survey data, and which follow a logical order:

- Summarizing and reducing data – creating the variables
- Descriptive level analysis – the distribution of the variables across the sample
- Relationships analysis – relationships between the variables, first bi-variately, then (as appropriate) jointly.

During the analysis of quantitative data, respondents' written words are turned into figures and symbols that are counted and added, and entered into tables, to allow us to draw conclusions. Initial coding of survey data can be done on the completed questionnaires in the right hand margin. See Table 8.1 below:

Table 8.1 Frequency of meeting with dissertation supervisor – Please tick

Once a fortnight	Once a month	Other – please state	Coding (For official use only)
	√		2

Here the coding numeral for once a fortnight is 1, once a month is 2, and other is 3. Oppenheim (1992) recommends researchers anticipate the data processing requirements. If, for example, they intend to put data-processing indications in the right hand column or margin of the questionnaires, with the heading, 'For official use only', then this layout should be introduced during the pilot study to check if it is distracting for the respondents. He also draws attention to the possibility of using bar codes for each response category, or making the responses machine readable in other ways, so that the data can be directly entered into a computer.

As noted above, researchers should contemplate the methods of analysis before the data are collected. Cresswell (2003: 159–161), discussing the analysis of data in a survey, suggests presenting information in the research proposal about quantitative data analysis in a series of steps as follows:

1. Report information about the number of members of the sample who did and did not return the survey. A table with numbers and percentages is a useful tool to present this information.
2. Discuss the method by which response bias, i.e. the effect of nonresponses on survey estimates will be determined. Bias means that if nonrespondents had responded, their responses would have substantially changed the overall results of the survey.
3. Discuss a plan to provide a descriptive analysis of data for all independent and dependent variables in the study, indicating the means, standard deviations, and range of scores for these variables.
4. If the proposal contains an instrument with scales or a plan to develop scales, identify the statistical procedure (i.e. factor analysis) to do it.
5. Identify the statistics and the statistical computer programme for testing the major questions or hypotheses in the proposed study. Provide a rationale for the choice of statistical test and mention the assumptions associated with the statistics.

At the simplest level, the quantitative data collected by questionnaires can be entered onto summary sheets and then presented in a tabulated form. Data can also be represented as bar charts, pie charts, histograms or graphs, indicating spatial rather than numerical values and relationships, which some readers may find more convincing.

Tables

Tables are a good way of managing a great deal of data by summarizing and presenting them in a straightforward way. A well-presented table will include a main heading which will relate to the question asked in the questionnaire and state the total number of responses on the top. All the columns and/or rows will also have labels indicating what the data that are displayed relate to. For example, if we have 100 completed questionnaires returned to us, and one of the questions asked is:

How old are you?
Under 26 years ☐
26–30 ☐
31–35 ☐
36–40 ☐
41–45 ☐
46–50 ☐
51–55 ☐
Over 55 ☐

The summary sheet will look something like this (Table 8.2), with each column indicating the different age ranges of doctoral students at the university:

Table 8.2 Summary sheet

Under 26	26–30	31–35	36–40	41–45	46–50	51–55	Over 55
## ##	## ##	## ##	## ##	##	## ////	////	//
## ##	## ##	## //					
## ##	///						

And the data can then be presented in a table with a heading (Table 8.3):

Table 8.3 Age of doctoral students at the university – n = 100

Under 26	26–30	31–35	36–40	41–45	46–50	51–55	Over 55	Total
30	23	17	10	5	9	4	2	100

Tables can show the frequencies of the responses or the percentages as well as the frequencies. For example, the table below (Table 8.4) shows whether the students were able to get admission in the higher education institution (HEI) which was their first choice, as stated by them in a questionnaire:

Table 8.4 Gained admission in first choice HEI

GROUP		1st choice HEI?		
		Yes	No	Total
Majority	Count	76	9	85
	% within GROUP	89.4%	10.6%	
Minority	Count	78	21	99
	% within GROUP	78.8%	21.2%	
Control	Count	15	2	17
	% within GROUP	88.2%	11.8%	
Total	Count	**169**	**32**	**201**
	% within GROUP	**84.1%**	**15.9%**	**100%**

Bar charts

Quantitative data can also be presented in a bar chart. For example, Figure 8.1 below shows the responses of the participants when they were asked if they felt they had faced discrimination because of their ethnicity:

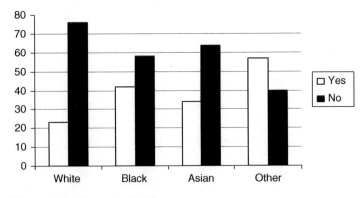

Figure 8.1 Discrimination and ethnicity

Pie charts

A pie chart is particularly useful to illustrate data such as the proportion of students who fall into the different age groups. In this case, frequencies are changed to percentages, though frequencies can also be displayed. A pie chart can be drawn by using a computer programme. For example, Figure 8.2 below shows the age distribution of the questionnaire respondents, in a research project, which was 14–24 years:

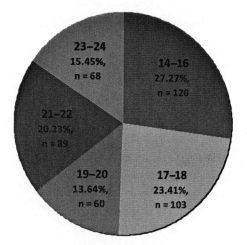

Figure 8.2 Participants' age distribution

It can show the distribution across groups and also within groups. For example, Figure 8.3 below shows the ethnic origin of the respondents, and also a break down of one ethnic group:

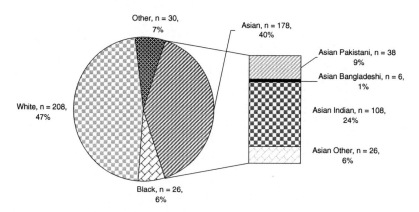

Figure 8.3 Participants' ethnic origin

Analysing structured interview data

Data generated by structured interviews can be analysed in the same way as those derived from questionnaires. However, because of the usually small numbers of participants interviewed, statistical analyses are not an option. Such data can be presented in tables, pie charts and so forth.

Analysing observation data

Quantitative data in observations can be collected by using some of the scales that are used in questions to rank or rate occurrences. If the researchers are using pre-formulated checklists or counting the frequency of events, then they will generate simple quantifiable data which can be analysed in the same way as questionnaire data derived from closed questions.

Wragg (1999) gives an example of the quantitative data collected while conducting action research in the classroom:

> Suppose that teachers in a school are concerned about the amount of disruption from pupils who misbehave, so they want to see if they can reduce it. [An] observer . . . might decide to watch classes of pupils counting up how many appear to be disruptive, noting who the disruptives are and what they do. It might be anticipated in advance that disruption often follows when children get out of their seat without permission and then distract others, so this could be one of the categories noted. The observation phase might then be followed by some kind of action programme during which teachers try to reinforce and recognise good behaviour whenever it occurs, or take out pupils who misbehave for special counselling. The observer might then go into the classroom after the programme using the same observation schedules as previously, to see if the incidence of misbehaviour had increased, decreased or remained the same. (p. 21)

Wragg (1999: 124–126) notes the reasons why researchers use statistical analyses to confirm their findings. These include establishing the relationship between measures, making a comparison between groups, measuring change, making predictions, reducing complexity, and aggregating findings, as summarized below:

1. Relationship between measures

Wragg (1999) observes that when the researchers are seeking a relationship between two variables, for example, the incidence of misbehaviour and number of pupils who are misbehaving, a correlation coefficient will be used. He notes that there are many forms of correlation, depending on the nature of the data, Pearson's r is the most common for two sets of continuous measures, like test scores. Two sets of rank orders, or the comparison between a score and a yes/ no measure, would involve different forms, such as Spearman's rho and point biserial correlations. An example of calculating correlation is reported by A-Latif (1992) who measured the relationship between two sets of scores obtained by medical students in an objective structured clinical examination (OSCE) and the traditional clinical examination by means of a correlation coefficient using the Spearman rank-difference method. Muijs (2004: 91) maintains that in educational research we often look at the relationship between two variables. For example, if boys are better at reading than girls, or if there is a relationship between school attendance and children's self-concept. This will involve bi-variate analyses. We will want to know if the relationship is statistically significant, and how large the effect size or the strength of the relationship is.

2. Comparing groups

Wragg (1999) contends that this depends on the type of measure involved. If a frequency count has been taken, then a chi square might be appropriate. If the occurrence of reprimands in the lessons of teachers in four different age groups were to be compared, then a 'goodness of fit' chi square would look at the distribution actually obtained and compare it with what might have been expected. When the scores of two groups on something like a rating scale are compared, then if the distribution is roughly normal, a t-test would be appropriate. For three or more groups or for measures which are repeated several times, analysis of variance may be used. If the distribution of scores is not normal, then nonparametric forms of analysis will be needed, like the Mann-Whitney U for two groups, and the Kruskal-Wallis analysis of variance for three or more groups.

3. Measuring change

Wragg (1999) maintains that the measurement of change is extremely problematic when groups do not have an equal starting point. He gives the example of raw unadjusted league tables of schools' test results which pose the problem of inferring effectiveness from final rather than initial scores. If initial scores are known, then it is possible to calculate change, otherwise it is difficult.

He suggests that various statistics can be used to try to partial out the effects of initial differences, such as analysis of covariance and regression analysis. The usual procedure is to take a measure which is thought to affect initial differences, like social class, and use that as part of the procedure in an attempt to even up the groups, though he acknowledges that using this approach is controversial.

4. Predicting

Wragg (1999:) argues that regression, particularly multiple regression analysis, is often used to make a prediction. One variant of it is stepwise multiple regression, which involves taking the predictor which shows the highest correlation with the outcome measure and then combining it step by step with others to improve the correlation. An example would be if the observer wanted to know how best to predict scores on a pupil 'attitude to science' test. There might be a correlation of +0.5 between the attitude scores and a rating measure of teachers' enthusiasm in the classroom.

5. Reducing complexity

Wragg (1999) notes that sometimes the data that have been gathered look complex and need reducing in complexity so that researchers can make sense of them. He suggests using factor analysis and cluster analysis with large datasets. Factor analysis is a way of putting together sets of measures that correlate with each other in order to reduce them to fewer factors. Scores gathered by classroom observation might show that short teacher questions, brief pupil answers and praise all correlated quite highly and came together in the same factor. This might be then given a name like 'programmed learning' to reflect the stimulus–response–reinforcement nature of the interactions. Cluster analysis is another way of putting together scores in a more economical way, but in this individual teachers' profiles can be grouped together because they share similar characteristics.

6. Aggregating findings

Wragg (1999) maintains that findings from different research studies based on classroom observation can be put together in many ways. Meta analysis is a process used to aggregate the findings of different studies to check the consistency or inconsistency in their findings. There are two stages of meta analysis.

The first is the process of putting together data from projects that have used different statistical procedures and need converting for aggregation. The second involves developing an overall effect size which can be calculated for all the studies under review. This can calculate separate effect sizes to see if certain types of studies have different effect sizes, such as larger or smaller studies, older and newer studies. Wragg (1999), however, points out that different researchers analysing similar studies may arrive at different conclusions depending on the criteria they use for aggregation.

Tizard and Hughes (1991) point to the complexities involved in data analysis when they comment on the way they analysed the quantitative data in a mixed methods study of 30 four-year-old girls at home and at nursery school. They focused in particular on the conversations between the girls and their mothers at home, and the girls and their teachers at school:

> In the first phase we worked in an essentially quantitative style, coding the transcripts according to reliably determined criteria and carrying out statistical tests on the results . . . The most time-consuming aspect of the quantitative phase was the process of working up a coding system which could be reliably used by four coders. The codes themselves were mainly chosen in order to test our hypotheses . . . All the team would start by coding parts of the transcripts according to a fledgling coding system: we would then compare our preliminary codings. (p. 28)

Tizard and Hughes (1991: 28) then state two problems that they faced during the process:

1. There might be passages which could not be dealt with by the coding system as it stood, and the number of codes would have to be expanded accordingly.
2. There might be large discrepancies between our different interpretations of the coding system: this was particularly likely to happen in the early stages of working up a system.

As a result they had to start again. This needed several attempts before they could get it right, which is not dissimilar to what many of us need to do during data analysis. They note:

> We would then alter our definitions, and try again on a new set of extracts. This process of reworking the coding, trying it out, comparing notes, and reworking yet again would frequently pass through several cycles until we had reached a satisfactory level of agreement – usually a figure of around 80–90 per cent

> inter-coder agreement. Having reached the final version of the coding system, we would then code all the transcripts according to this system. (Tizard and Hughes, 1991: 28–29)

They then looked at their hypotheses to determine if the analyses supported the hypotheses and found that their quantitative analyses provided substantial support for the first part of their original hypothesis – that there are important differences in the quality of parent–child and teacher–child dialogues (Tizard and Hughes, 1991: 29).

Analysing documentary data

Quantitative data generated or derived from documents are either already in numerical forms or can easily be converted into numbers. Diaries are one of the ways in which such data can be generated. Moser and Kalton (1971: 414) observe that data produced in diaries represent specific forms of social reality and researchers are interested in making sense of the patterns in these data; patterns which are readily distinguishable if the data are recorded in the form of numbers. They suggest that researchers using diaries in surveys and experimental research use structured forms of diaries in order to facilitate conversion of data into numbers for coding.

Alaszewski (2006) maintains that the purpose of the analysis is identifying relationships between variables and demonstrating that these relationships are unlikely to be a product of chance. He explains how structured textual data can be converted into numerical values:

> The data within each case are organised into categories or variables, and the data relevant to each variable for each case are coded as a number. This creates a data-set which can be analysed using statistical techniques. (p. 85)

Analysing data from experiments and quasi-experiments

Gorard (2003: 180–181) observes that good experimental designs which test quite narrowly defined hypotheses, to minimize puzzling variables, are powerful. This power is not related only to the design, but also from the power of the questions that the experiments can address. Data generated through experimental research are usually analysed by using statistical methods. Cresswell (2003: 172–173) recommends that researchers explain to the reader the types of statistical analysis that will be used during the experiment:

- Report the descriptive statistics calculated for observations and measures at the pre-test and post-test stage of experimental designs. These statistics are means, standard deviations and ranges.
- Indicate the inferential statistical tests used to examine the hypotheses in the study. For experimental designs with categorical information (groups) on the independent variable and continuous information on the dependent variable, researchers use *t-tests* or *univariate analysis of variance (ANOVA), analysis of covariance (ANCOVA),* or *multivariate analysis of variance (MANOVA-multiple dependent measures).* In factorial designs, both interaction and main effects of ANOVA are used. When data on a pre-test or post-test show marked deviation from a normal distribution, use nonparametric statistical tests.
- For single-subject research designs, use line graphs for baseline and treatment observations for abscissa (horizontal axis) units of time and the ordinate (vertical axis) target behaviour. Each data point is plotted separately on the graph, and the data points are connected by lines. Occasionally, tests of statistical significance, such as t-tests, are used to compare the pooled mean of the baseline and the treatment phases.

There are a number of software packages that can be used to analyse quantitative data. The most frequently used software for statistical analyses is the Statistical Package for Social Sciences (SPSS). Muijs (2004) maintains:

> SPSS is probably the most common statistical data analysis software package used in educational research and is available at most institutions of higher education. It is also quite user-friendly and does everything we need it to do. This does not mean that it is necessarily 'better' than any of the other packages. Other packages may be better in some areas, but SPSS is by far the most commonly used statistical data analysis software. SPSS is a Windows-based software. A Mac version is also available. (p. 85)

It is beyond the scope of this chapter to discuss the various methods of statistical analyses in detail. Readers may want to refer to texts such as Wragg (1999), Cresswell (2003), Gorard (2003), Muijs (2004), and Cohen et al. (2007) for detailed guidance on how to analyse quantitative data using statistical methods.

Research spotlight

Al-Saadi (2009) conducted a study to examine the cultural tolerance of young Omani female students. She designed a quasi-experimental study using an intervention, involving two experimental and two control schools. A questionnaire was administered before and after the intervention to a sample of 241 girls, of whom 116 were in the experimental group and 125 in the control group. A semi-structured interview was conducted before and after the intervention with 16 participants, of whom 8 were from the experimental group and 8 from the control group. SPSS was used to analyse the quantitative data. Analysis of the quantitative data in post-intervention round revealed statistically significant differences between the experimental group and the control group in tolerance towards others. Analysis of the qualitative data from the pre-intervention interviews conducted with the participants in both the experimental and the control group revealed low tolerance towards those who had different beliefs and practices. Yet in the post-intervention interviews the experimental groups showed greater tolerance.

Qualitative Data Analysis: achieving depth and richness

9

Once we have completed the exciting phase of data collection by interviewing or observing our research participants, or deriving documentary data from documents or human participants, we have to embark on the task of analysing these data to make sense of them. 'Raw data can be very interesting to look at, yet they do not help the reader to understand the social world under scrutiny, and the way the participants view it, unless such data have been systematically analysed to illuminate an existent situation' (Basit, 2003: 144). Marshall and Rossman (2006: 157) observe that raw data have no meaning, and the act of interpretation brings meaning to raw, inexpressive data which is a necessary process. Miles and Huberman (1994) observe:

> The reporting of qualitative data may be one of the most fertile fields going; there are no fixed formats, and the ways data are being analyzed and interpreted are

> getting more and more various . . . The challenge is to combine theoretical elegance and credibility appropriately with the many ways social events can be described; to find intersections between the propositional thinking of most conventional studies and more figurative thinking. (p. 299)

Quantitative data are derived from a large number of participants and may be broad and sketchy; qualitative data are gathered from smaller numbers, but are likely to be detailed and in-depth. However, fewer numbers do not make the analysis easier. Making sense of qualitative data is not straightforward but is a complex exercise, as I note elsewhere:

> The analysis of qualitative data is usually seen as arduous. The reason why it is found to be difficult is that it is not fundamentally a mechanical or technical exercise. It is a dynamic, intuitive and creative process of inductive reasoning, thinking and theorizing. (Basit, 2003: 143)

Researchers need to contemplate the analysis of data before they start collecting them since this will inform the process of analysis later. Marshall and Rossman (2006: 154) maintain that the researchers should convince the readers that they have thought about the process of analysis and are aware of what it involves. This should be done at the research proposal stage and illustrate that the researchers' knowledge of analysis includes the organization of data, the development and interpretation of themes, and writing the report. However, Feldman (1995: 64) cautions against adopting an analytical framework prior to gathering data. She argues that while this may simplify and shorten the process of data collection, researchers ought to resist this temptation because:

> Succumbing to it may considerably reduce the effectiveness of the research as it may reduce the ability of the researcher to understand the relevant phenomena from the perspectives of the members of the culture. (p. 64)

The researchers' stance and positioning is important in the process of analysis. Cohen et al. (2007: 469) observe that the analysis and findings may say more about the researchers than the data, and the researchers, therefore, need to be cautious and conscious of their role as researchers. It is the researchers who design the research, choose the methodology, and select the categories for the analysis of qualitative data. Yin (2009: 127) argues that researchers frequently begin case studies without any notion of how the data are to be analysed. There is very little guidance available, and much depends on the researchers' own styles of rigorous thinking, presentation of evidence, and contemplation of alternative interpretations.

The object of analysing qualitative data is to determine the categories, relationships and assumptions that inform the respondents' view of the world in general, and of the topic in particular. These categories are hoped to be isolated and defined during the process of research (McCracken, 1988). 'The researcher should use preliminary research questions and the related literature developed earlier in the proposal as guidelines for data analysis' (Marshall and Rossman, 2006: 156). 'Writing up notes or transcribing tapes and simply listening to the conversations assist the important analytical stage of becoming familiar with the data' (May, 2001: 139). Analysis of qualitative data starts early on in the fieldwork, even as early as when one interview or observation or diary request has been completed. The significant task in analysis is to seek explanations from descriptions. Researchers need to use their research skills to decide what data are relevant to their research questions and analyse them accordingly.

Patton (2002: 432) uses metaphors to explain the process of analysis and the role of the researcher in qualitative research. He observes:

- Analysis begins during a larval stage, that if fully developed, metamorphoses from caterpillar-like beginnings into the splendour of the mature butterfly.
- The inquirer acts as catalyst on raw data, generating an interaction that synthesizes new substance born alive from the catalytic conversion.
- Findings emerge like an artistic mural created from collage-like pieces that make sense in new ways when seen and understood as part of a greater whole.
- Transformation, synthesis and sense making run through analysis like golden threads in a royal garment.

Patton (2002: 432), nevertheless, argues that 'no abstract processes of analysis, no matter how eloquently named and finely described, can substitute for the skill, knowledge, experience, creativity, diligence, and work of the qualitative analyst.'

Reading data

Qualitative data are mainly textual, or are usually converted into textual form, and before researchers engage in the task of analysing these data, they need to read them. Mason (2002: 149) recommends that researchers take the following approaches to reading their data:

1. *Literal reading:* This will involve looking at the content, structure, style and layout of the data. In interview transcripts, researchers may look at the words and language, the sequence of interaction, and the form and structure of the dialogue. In documents and visual data, researchers may wish to document a literal version of the data that are available.
2. *Interpretive reading:* This will entail constructing or documenting a version of what the researchers believe the data represent and what they can infer from the data. Researchers will be concerned with how the interviewees make sense of the social world and how they then interpret the interviewees' perceptions of the social world. In documents, the researchers will interpret the documentary evidence to understand what the data are conveying to them.
3. *Reflexive reading:* This will locate the researchers as part of the data that they have generated, exploring their role and viewpoint in the collection and interpretation of the data, and thus depicting their relationship with the data.

Analysing documents also requires us to read them first. Documents do not just produce social reality or allow people to accomplish social order, but enable them to employ their cultural understandings to engage with meanings embedded in the documents that they read and analyse. Being part of the social world that they inhabit is an advantage for researchers and not something they should apologize for. Documents should be read in an engaged, not detached, manner. This kind of emphasis on hermeneutics allows the researchers to examine the similarities and differences between their own interpretation of the meanings and those found in the document during the process of analysis (May, 2001: 182–183).

Ball (1991: 182) suggests researchers get intimately familiar with the data when working from documents, observation notes and interview transcripts. This will involve the reading and rereading of text in order to find out what is what, and where things are. He notes that it is surprising that when researchers read interview transcripts, they identify issues that were overlooked in the interviews themselves.

Stages of analysis

Grbich (2007: 25) highlights the importance of preliminary data analysis in qualitative research, which is an ongoing process carried out every time data are gathered. This is simply tracking and checking the data to see what they are telling us, and which areas need to be followed up; and interrogating the data to see where they are leading the researcher. This is more an engagement with the text, rather than a critical examination of it, to comprehend the values and meanings within it. This reveals emerging issues and gives direction for seeking further data. She further notes:

> The usefulness of preliminary data analysis [is] in filling the gaps and completing the holistic view of the research area . . . By the end of data collection you should be on top of the data as opposed to being buried under them. If this process has not been undertaken, you are likely to end up with a room full of data with which you have largely lost contact, and further analysis then exposes the holes and unpursued signposts which may require further sampling and additional data collection to complete. (Grbich, 2007: 31)

Mason (2002: 179) argues that theory permeates qualitative research from start to finish, as decisions made by qualitative researchers have both theoretical grounds and theoretical consequences. She notes (2002: 180) three possible ways in which theory plays a role in research:

1. Theory comes first, before empirical research and is measured against data. The researchers do not develop the theory from data, but may refine it by looking at previous research which may have proved or disproved earlier theories. The researchers will state their hypotheses in advance and will inspect their data in relation to these hypotheses.
2. Theory comes last and is derived from or through data gathering and analysis. The researchers will start the analysis during data collection and examine their data to build explanations to fit the data.
3. Theory, data generation and data analysis are developed concurrently and dialectically. The researchers will move back and forth between data analysis, explanation and theory construction.

Qualitative research has the potential to gather abundant amounts of data, which we can use to our advantage. Researchers can exploit the rich, illuminating, data generated in qualitative research in the form of verbatim quotations to be presented in their writings. We need to be selective in quoting directly from interviews, diaries and observation fieldnotes, link them to appropriate themes and ensure that they are followed by analysis. Becker (1958: 653; cited in Hopkins, 2008) describes four stages in the analysis of fieldwork data. These include three distinct stages of analysis carried out in the field and a fourth one when the fieldwork has been completed. These are as follows:

1. The selection and definition of problems, concepts and indices.
2. The check on the frequency and distribution of phenomena.
3. The incorporation of individual findings into a model of the organization under study.
4. The problems of presentation of evidence and proof.

Becker stresses that these stages are differentiated in various ways:

- By their logical sequence as each succeeding stage depends on some kind of analysis in the preceding stage
- By the fact that different kinds of conclusions are arrived at in each stage
- By the different uses that these conclusions are put to in the continuing research
- By the different criteria that are used to assess evidence and reach conclusions in each stage.

Miles and Huberman (1994) recommend a number of ways in which researchers can derive meaning from qualitative data once they have been transcribed. These include counting the frequency of occurrences; noting patterns and themes; looking for plausibility; clustering, categorizing and classifying data; using metaphors to reduce the data; splitting the themes to elaborate on and differentiate between them; considering particularities and generalities; identifying relationships between themes; and explaining phenomena by moving from metaphors to constructs to theories. Wolcott (1994) views data analysis in the form of three activities, but acknowledges that they are not discrete:

> By no means do I suggest that the three categories – description, analysis, and interpretation – are mutually exclusive. Nor are lines clearly drawn where description ends and analysis begins, or where analysis becomes interpretation . . . [However,] identifying and distinguishing among the three may serve a useful purpose, especially if the categories can be regarded as varying emphases that qualitative researchers employ to organise and present data. (p. 11)

Mason (2002: 150–171) offers a comprehensive discussion of three broad approaches to sorting and organizing qualitative data, though she does not see them as mutually exclusive and acknowledges that researchers may want to use elements of all three. These are as follows:

1. *Cross-sectional and categorical indexing:* This means developing a uniform system for indexing, categorizing or coding the entire data set using common principles. This is similar to headings and subheadings in a book chapter or journal article, telling the readers what each section comprises.

2. *Non-cross-sectional data organization:* In non-cross-sectional, contextual or case study forms of data organization, the researchers do not use the same lens throughout their entire data set, i.e. they do not use the same set of indexing categories for all the data the way they do in cross-sectional data indexing. In this kind of data organization, the researchers look at discrete parts or cases in the data and comment on specific rather than common themes in the data.

3. *Diagrams and charts:* These can be used as tools in their own right or as an aid to cross-sectional and non-cross-sectional ways of data organization. Sometimes researchers find it easier to make sense of data if they are represented diagrammatically.

Grounded theory

Theory grounded in the data is a powerful way of generating theory which is inductively derived in the process of data collection and analysis in qualitative research. This assumes the inherent and embedded nature of theory which is to be discovered by the researcher. Glaser and Strauss (1967) contend that the researcher's job is not to provide a description of an area, but to develop a theory that accounts for much of the relevant behaviour. They highlight the fact that since each stage is transformed into the next after some time, this method of theory generation is a constantly developing process. However, earlier stages of analysis operate simultaneously with later stages, providing continuous development to the next stage until the analysis is complete. Strauss (1987) argues:

> The methodological thrust of the grounded theory approach to qualitative data is toward the development of theory, without any particular commitment to specific kinds of data, lines of research, or theoretical interests. So, it is not really a specific method or technique. Rather, it is a style of doing qualitative analysis that includes a number of distinct features, such as theoretical sampling, and certain methodological guidelines, such as the making of constant comparisons and the use of a coding paradigm, to ensure conceptual development and density. (p. 5)

Strauss and Corbin (1994) maintain that 'theory consists of plausible relationships produced among concepts and sets of concepts' (p. 278). It does not force data to fit with a predetermined theory (Glaser and Strauss, 1967: 3), but instead must fit the situation which is being investigated (Lincoln and Guba, 1985: 205). The significant features of grounded theory are that it emerges from the data, instead of the data collection being dictated by the theory. In fact, data collection, analysis, and theory stand in reciprocal relationship to each other (Strauss and Corbin, 1998). This kind of theory does not need to be tested through data collection, but is the outcome of collection and analysis of data which have been carried out in a systematic way to identify themes, patterns, concepts and theories which are contained within the data. It takes into account the interconnectedness and interactions in the social world and considers the complexity, consistency and contradiction in social contexts and relationships. Strauss and Corbin (1998) observe that grounded theorists are not as interested in individual actors as with discovering patterns of actions and interactions, and with changes in internal or external conditions to the process.

Theoretical sampling

Theoretical sampling is an important component of grounded theory. This involves gathering data in a continuous and iterative manner until sufficient data have been gathered to illuminate the phenomena under investigation and theoretical saturation has been reached. The researchers have to determine the point at which they have collected enough data to enable them to make theoretical interpretations and discover the theory emerging from the data. Glaser and Strauss (1967: 61) maintain that saturation is reached when no new categories or insights are generated even when new data are introduced.

The aim of theoretical sampling is to sample events, incidents and so forth that are indicative of categories, their properties and dimensions so that researchers can develop them and conceptually relate them. Concepts are the basis of analysis in grounded theory, and procedures in grounded theory are directed towards the identification, development and exploration of the relationships between concepts. Theoretical sampling indicates sampling on the basis of the concepts which are proved to be theoretically relevant to the emerging and developing theory. Strauss and Corbin (1998: 202) maintain that proven theoretical relevance means that certain concepts are considered significant for two reasons:

1. They are repeatedly present or notably absent when comparing incident after incident.
2. Through the coding procedures they earn the status of categories.

Strauss and Corbin (1990) recommend that researchers develop theoretical sensitivity, as it is because of this that they generate a theory that is grounded, conceptually dense, and well-integrated. They contend that theoretical sensitivity:

- Refers to a personal quality of the researcher
- Signifies the attribute of having insight and understanding
- Represents the skill to separate the pertinent from that which is irrelevant
- Indicates an awareness of the subtleties of data and the ability to give meaning to data
- Is dependent on previous reading and experience with an area
- Can also be developed further during the research process.

Coding

Coding is another significant element of the grounded theory approach, the purpose of which is to break down and deconstruct the data to make sense of them and then to reconstruct and synthesize the data to consider the links, similarities and differences. Miles and Huberman (1994) note that:

> Codes are tags or labels for assigning units of meaning to the descriptive or infer-ential information compiled during a study. Codes usually are attached to chunks of varying size – words, phrases, sentences, or whole paragraphs, connected or unconnected to a specific setting. They can take the form of a straightforward category label or a more complex one (e.g. a metaphor). (p. 56)

Strauss and Corbin (1998) argue that researchers do not necessarily need to code whole paragraphs, but can also analyse a word, phrase or sentence:

> This technique is especially valuable because it enables the analyst to raise questions about possible meanings, whether assumed or intended. It can also help bring into awareness an analyst's assumptions about what is being said

or observed while demonstrating to him or her that there are other possible meanings and interpretations. This exercise is invaluable as an opening gambit even for
experienced researchers as a way of checking themselves against their preconcep-
tions. (p. 92)

Thus codes enable us to engage with our data to identify and highlight text and
give it names and by doing so, help us to proceed with the process of analysis.
Strauss (1987: 55–56) contends that coding:

- Both leads to and follows generative questions
- Fractures the data, thereby freeing the researchers from description and forcing
  interpretation to higher levels of abstraction
- Is the pivotal operation for moving towards the discovery of core categories
- Progresses towards ultimate integration of the entire analysis
- Yields the desired conceptual density, i.e. the development of codes and the
  relationships between them.

Two important concepts to consider here are:

- **Induction:** which 'refers to the actions that lead to discovery of a hypothesis – that
  is, having a hunch or an idea, then converting it into a hypothesis and assessing
  whether it might provisionally work as at least a partial condition for a type of
  event, act, relationship, strategy, etc.' (Strauss, 1987: 11–12). 'The general principle
  underlying inductive approaches to coding is a desire to prevent existing theoretical
  concepts from over-defining the analysis and obscuring the possibility of identifying
  and developing new concepts and theories' (Lewins and Silver, 2007: 85).
- **Deduction:** which 'consists of the drawing of implications from hypotheses or
  larger systems of them for purposes of verification' (Strauss, 1987: 11–12). 'Deduc-
  tive approaches to coding are more explicit about the themes or categories to be
  considered at the outset of the coding process . . . for example, where the intention
  is to test an existing theory or hypothesis on newly collected data or to investigate
  its transferability to a different social context' (Lewins and Silver, 2007: 85).

Below is an example of themes that were generated by coding data in a
study in which I examined the educational, social and career aspirations of
adolescent British Muslim girls. Figure 9.1 shows the diagrammatic represen-
tation of the final stage, subsequent to the categorizing of the dataset, which
resulted in 23 sub-themes and culminated in 6 decisive themes (for details,
see Basit, 2003).

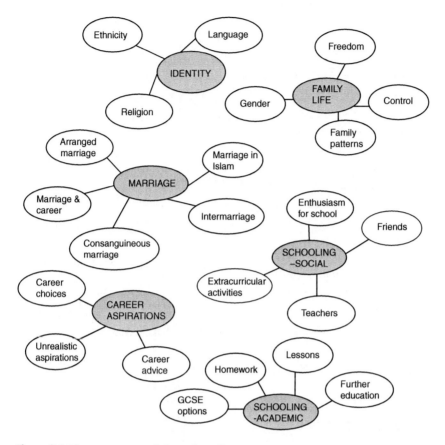

Figure 9.1 Themes generated through coding

Lewins and Silver (2007) view coding of qualitative data as:

> The process by which segments of data are identified as relating to, or being an example of, a more general idea, instance, theme or category. Segments of data from across the whole dataset are placed together in order to be retrieved together at a later stage. Whether coding manually or using software, you will build up a system to organize data and your ideas about it . . . Coding therefore manages and orders qualitative data. It enables easier searching of data for similarities, differences, patterns and relationships. As such coding is often an integral part of the analytic process, but it is not analysis in itself. (pp. 81–82)

Coding is of three main kinds:

Open coding
In this kind of coding, data and units of analysis are coded to identify meanings, perceptions, experiences and so forth. This involves breaking down, examining, comparing, conceptualizing and categorizing data, and by creating categories and subcategories.

Axial coding
This links categories and codes around the axes of the main categories, interconnecting them, and comparing them to the existing theory. This utilizes a coding paradigm involving conditions, context, interactional strategies and consequences.

Selective coding
This identifies the principal code, explores its relationship with other codes, validates those relationships, and compares the coding format with existing theory. The researchers discover a theme on which they write a story integrating the categories in axial coding.

(Source: Cresswell, 1998; Strauss and Corbin, 1998;
Ezzy, 2002; Cohen et al., 2007)

Making comparisons

Grounded theory has been referred to as 'the constant comparative method of analysis' (Glaser and Strauss, 1967: 101). The making of comparisons is crucial in order to identify and categorize concepts. Strauss and Corbin (1990) maintain that the purpose of comparison is to help the researcher break through assumptions and uncover specific dimensions. To make these comparisons, researchers draw on personal and professional knowledge and the relevant literature on the subject. (For an example of the use of the constant comparative method, see Ball, 1991).

Constant comparison is made when open, axial and selective coding methods are applied in grounded theory. The researchers are constantly comparing new data and categories with existing data and categories to ascertain the suitability or fitness between them, until there is no further variation and data saturation is reached. However, if the data, categories and theory do not fit, then the researchers need to modify their categories until they correspond with data and all data are categorized. The four stages in the constant comparative method stated by Glaser and Strauss (1967: 105) to analyse data are the following:

1. Comparing incidents and data applicable to each category
2. Integrating categories and their properties
3. Delimiting and bounding the theory
4. Setting out and writing the theory.

Hopkins (2008: 131) compares the methods of analysis of Glaser and Strauss with those of Becker, stated earlier in the chapter, and argues that while Glaser and Strauss' constant comparative method is a more dynamic model than Becker's linear stages, they are basically similar in the way in which they consider the analysis of data. He sees them as similar because each views the analytical process as four discrete phases representing the standard practice for the analysis of data as follows:

1. Data collection and the initial generation of categories
2. Validation of categories
3. Interpretation of categories
4. Action.

Glaser and Strauss (1967: 237) propose four key criteria to evaluate theory grounded in the data. These are as follows:

1. **Fit:** The closeness of the fit between the theory and data.
2. **Understanding:** The readiness with which the theory is understandable to the researcher.
3. **Generality:** The ability of the theory to be general to different and diverse situations within the substantive area, rather than only to a specific situation.
4. **Control:** The need for theory to allow partial control of situations as they change over time in order to make its application worthwhile.

Research spotlight

An example of grounded theory is presented by Stronach and Piper (2008), whose approach to data analysis in their study combined a deconstructively inflected grounded approach with a sensitivity to metaphors, concepts and theories regarding self, learning and schooling. They viewed their approach as deconstructive, rather than analytical as it treated boundaries as a beginning, rather than an end of something. The analysis involved transcribing all data, which was then read and analysed by both researchers, who identified the emerging themes. These emerging themes in turn provoked emerging theory grounded in the data.

However, the decision to use the grounded theory approach should not be taken lightly. It is time consuming and requires considerable insight and imagination. Because of the fragmentation of data through coding, the researchers may lose sight of the fuller picture and wider contextual factors. It is difficult to plan ahead. Theoretical sampling prevents the researchers from predicting the kind of sample to be used. Also, the need to recognize theoretical saturation means that the final sample size cannot be determined in advance. As researchers using the grounded theory approach rely heavily on data generated through their empirical research, they sometimes overlook the complex relationship between earlier theories and theories grounded in their own data.

Content analysis

Content analysis involves an examination of spoken or written communication. It is a method of analysing qualitative data, and can be carried out on any kind of written, published or transcribed data. It reports textual data in a summarized form by examining the frequency of occurrences in the text. It entails coding or categorizing sentences, statements or phrases, and making links and comparisons between these categories. It can be the analysis of diary data, interviews, speeches, newspaper or magazine articles on a particular theme, the number of such articles, the location of these articles in the newspaper or magazine, the size of the article, the size of the headlines, the accompanying pictures and so forth. Prior (2003: 4) argues that 'documents are not just manufactured, they are consumed. Further, as with all tools, they are manipulated in organized settings for many different ends, and they also function in different ways – irrespective of human manipulations.' She observes that researchers should not merely concentrate on what documents contain, but need to ask questions about how documents affect and function in particular situations.

Grbich (2007) views the purpose of content analysis as follows:

> Content analysis is a systematic coding and categorising approach which you can use to unobtrusively explore large amounts of textual information in order to ascertain the trends and patterns of words used, their frequency, their relationships and the structures and discourses of communication. You can use this approach to analyse media and policy documents, visual images and actions, medical and other personal records, speeches and transcripts. The researcher's creation of coding frames highlights certain aspects of the text, providing the reader with one particular view, but other views are possible and different researchers may achieve varying results because of different protocols developed and imposed. (p. 112)

Grbich, thus, points to the multiplicity of meanings in a text which researchers may perceive differently. Researchers analyse texts into various components to understand the inherent meaning in them and then synthesize these components in their own way to tell the complete story as they understand it. Alaszewski (2006) maintains that:

> Content analysis involves taking a number of written texts such as diaries, breaking them into their constituent parts, and reassembling these parts into a new scientific text. The starting point for the analysis is the identification of constituent units of the text. (p. 86)

However, instead of applying the term 'content analysis' to all forms of textual analysis, Alaszewski (2006: 86) uses it in a more restricted sense. He views it as utilizing the information implicit within the text to identify a reality external to the text.

Krippendorp (2004: 22–24) notes that there are a number of features of texts relating to content analysis. This includes the fact that texts do not have objective reader-independent qualities, but comprise multiple meanings, resulting from multiple readings and interpretations which can be personal. These meanings need to be understood in context as they are situated in particular contexts, discourses and purposes. May (2001: 191) argues that documents cannot be viewed as standalone entities, but have to be situated within a theoretical frame of reference to enable researchers to comprehend their content. He maintains that the use of content analysis comprises three stages:

1. Stating the research problem
2. Retrieving the text and employing sampling methods
3. Interpretation and analysis.

This method identifies the characteristics of a document by looking at the frequency of occurrence of certain words or phrases in it. The consequent analytical framework allows researchers to interpret the data through the theoretical categories generated by this method. Alaszewski (2006) contends that:

> Researchers who use content analysis to identify the themes and categories contained within the text have some common ground with researchers using statistical techniques to analyse the numbers generated by structured questions contained within some diaries. Both groups of researchers see the material recorded

> in the diary as the record of some aspect of social reality that is external to the text they are analysing, and the text describes and can be used to build up a picture of this external reality whatever its precise form, e.g. events, actions, perceptions, emotions. Thus the researcher is concerned about the relationship between the reality as recorded in the text and the reality external to the text. (p. 87)

According to this, as well as analysing textual data following the qualitative traditions, content analysis takes a quantitative approach to data analysis by counting concepts, occurrences and words in a text. This can then be illustrated diagrammatically or in a tabular form. This is sometimes viewed as a way of imposing quantitative analysis on qualitative data by using numerical categories to explain textual data. Ezzy (2002: 83) observes that content analysis begins with a sample of texts, defines the units of analysis such as words or sentences, defines the categories to be used for analysis, reviews the text to code and categorize it, and counts and records the occurrence of words and codes. Units of analysis can be of different types. Krippendorp (2004: 99–101) differentiates between the units of analysis as follows:

1. **Sampling units:** which are units of selection that are included in, or excluded from the analysis.
2. **Recording or coding units:** which are units of description that are smaller than, and are present within, sampling units, and are therefore less complex.
3. **Context units:** which delimit the data to be analysed in the recording units and delineate the scope of the data that researchers need to refer to in order to characterize the recording units.

The use of software

Computer packages such as NVivo, Atlas and Ethnograph can be helpful in qualitative data analysis. They can be used, for example, to search, retrieve, label, annotate, sort, count, group, code, compare and link data and categories. Coding is perhaps the most useful function of these software packages. Lewins and Silver (2007) discuss the various aspects of Computer Assisted Qualitative Data AnalysiS (CAQDAS) and state how coding works in qualitative software:

> When a code is applied to a data segment in a CAQDAS package, a link is created between the segment and the code. Software packages comprise two elements of a database system. The first holds the data files, and the second houses the codes . . . When a link is created between the code sitting on one side of the database and the data segment on the other, the quick retrieval of coded text has

been enabled. Any number of codes can be applied to a single segment of text of any size and to overlapping/embedded segments. Codes can be defined and analytic memos attached. (p. 82)

Research spotlight

Gipps et al. (2000) conducted a study in which they worked with 'expert' teachers of 7-year-olds in Year 2, and 11-year-olds in Year 6, of primary school over four school terms. The purpose was to explore teaching, assessment, feedback and learning. This involved 90 interviews with headteachers or teachers, 108 lesson observations, 23 Four Card activities and 22 Quote Sorts. Interviews, observations, Four Card, and Quote Sort activity data were merged and analysed using the software package, NUDIST.

Below is an example of a study, in which I was involved, which used software to analyse data. It investigated the transition of final year BEd students from teacher trainee to mathematics teacher in a primary school. The data were coded using the software package NVivo (for details, see Basit, 2003). The list shows the codes (or Nodes, as they are called in NVivo) which were generated during the process of coding in NVivo.

NVivo revision 1.1.127
Project: Fourth Phase
Date: 30/11/01 – 11: 44: 15
Nodes in Set: All Nodes
Modified: 30/04/01–14: 04: 07

Licensee: Tehmina Basit
User: Administrator
NODE LISTING
Created: 30/04/01–14: 04: 07
Number of Nodes: 52

1 notion of play
2 real vs ideal
3 school vs college structures
4 theory vs practice
5 (1)/self
6 (1 1)/self/resource
7 (1 1 1)/self/resource/subject knowledge
8 (1 2)/self/student
9 (1 2 1)/self/student/college structures

⇨

10 (1 2 1 1)/self/student/college structures/career entry profile
11 (1 2 1 2)/self/student/college structures/reflection
12 (1 2 2)/self/student/in relation to others
13 (1 2 2 1)/self/student/in relation to others/peers
14 (1 2 2 2)/self/student/in relation to others/tutors
15 (1 3)/self/individual
16 (1 4)/self/teacher
17 (1 4 1)/self/teacher/professional
18 (1 4 2)/self/teacher/developing sense of being a teacher
19 (1 4 2 1)/self/teacher/developing sense of being a teacher/initial coping strategies
20 (1 4 2 2)/self/teacher/developing sense of being a teacher/classroom management
21 (1 4 2 3)/self/teacher/developing sense of being a teacher/ownership
22 (1 4 2 4)/self/teacher/developing sense of being a teacher/responsibility
23 (1 4 2 5)/self/teacher/developing sense of being a teacher/multiplicity of tasks
24 (1 4 2 6)/self/teacher/developing sense of being a teacher/skills
25 (1 4 3)/self/teacher/relation to others
26 (1 4 3 1)/self/teacher/relation to others/pupils
27 (1 4 3 2)/self/teacher/relation to others/colleagues
28 (1 4 3 3)/self/teacher/relation to others/parents
29 (1 4 4)/self/teacher/relation to school structures
30 (1 4 5)/self/teacher/maths teacher
31 (1 4 6)/self/teacher/motivation to teach
32 (1 4 6 1)/self/teacher/motivation to teach/specialism
33 (1 4 6 2)/self/teacher/motivation to teach/parents
34 (1 4 6 3)/self/teacher/motivation to teach/own teachers
35 (1 4 6 4)/self/teacher/motivation to teach/love of children
36 (2)/teaching and learning
37 (2 1)/teaching and learning/maths
38 (2 1 1)/teaching and learning/maths/conceptions of maths
39 (2 1 2)/teaching and learning/maths/experience of maths
40 (2 1 2 1)/teaching and learning/maths/experience of maths/as pupil
41 (2 1 2 2)/teaching and learning/maths/experience of maths/as university student
42 (2 1 2 3)/teaching and learning/maths/experience of maths/as trainee teacher
43 (2 1 2 4)/teaching and learning/maths/experience of maths/as NQT
44 (2 2)/teaching and learning/working theories
45 (2 3)/teaching and learning/memories of schooling
46 (3)/policy
47 (3 1)/policy/assessment
48 (3 1 1)/policy/assessment/audits
49 (3 1 2)/policy/assessment/tests
50 (3 2)/policy/National Numeracy Strategy
51 (3 3)/policy/inspection
52 (3 4)/policy/induction

Source: Basit (2003: 150–151)

I comment on the process of coding, by using the software, NVivo, as follows:

> There was considerable flexibility in coding within NVivo. I could uncode excerpts as easily as I coded them. I could even remove a code from the node listing quite simply, which in turn uncoded the quotations which had been coded using that node. A node could also be renamed or moved from one tree [main code] to another or become the child node [sub-code] of a sibling node, or vice versa. An extract could be coded as many times as required if more than one node was applicable. I could also start coding an extract with a different node in the middle of something which had already been coded. Since we worked as a team and wanted to contemplate the codes together, while only one of us was going to undertake the coding in NVivo, we had to predetermine many of our categories. Nevertheless, a researcher working independently could readily create nodes and code documents directly in NVivo, eliminating the need for prior thorough perusal of transcripts. (Basit, 2003: 151)

Interpreting the data

Data do not only need to be analysed but they have to be interpreted as well. Feldman (1995: 64) contends that the difficulty in interpreting qualitative data is not in learning how to build interpretations, but in learning how to stay away from pre-established interpretations. She observes that there are two main kinds of pre-established interpretations that are hard to avoid. These are as follows:

- The interpretations made by people in the setting being studied
- The interpretations made by other researchers and theorists about phenomena similar to those being examined.

She notes that while qualitative researchers will have considerable knowledge about both kinds of interpretations, which is undoubtedly essential, it is necessary that they move away from this knowledge to enable themselves to gain new understandings of the phenomena that are reflected in the data that they have gathered.

In qualitative research data analysis and interpretation usually happen simultaneously, and the interpretation of data is dependent on the context in which those data were collected. Cohen et al. (2007) argue that:

> Words carry many meanings; they are nuanced and highly context-sensitive. In qualitative data analysis, it is often the case that interpretation and analysis are

fused and, indeed, concurrent. It is naïve to suppose that the qualitative data analyst can separate analysis from interpretation, because words themselves are interpretation and are to be interpreted. Further, texts themselves carry many levels of meaning, and the qualitative researcher has to strive to catch these different levels or layers. (p. 495)

Nevertheless, Wolcott (2001: 32–33) distinguishes between analysis and interpretation as follows:

Analysis: It has a more limited, precise and clearly defined role, which follows typical procedures for measuring, observing, interviewing and communicating the reality of the social world to others. Qualitative and quantitative data are analysed in standardized ways according to the conventions of data analysis in these two methodologies. So, putting quantitative data into a software package such as SPSS, and putting qualitative data into NVivo for coding, and the outcome of these activities is seen as analysis.

Interpretation: This is more relaxed, less rigorous, and does not follow specific procedures. This is the consequence of our endeavours as researchers to discern the patterns in a study and make sense of human interaction and experiences, and express it in our own words. This needs deliberation and examination and is informed by our own personal and professional experiences, attributes, emotions and intuition.

We need to interpret the data in a way that they enable us to tell a coherent story about the phenomena that we are investigating. In discussing the analysis of case study data, Yin (2009: 130) contends that all empirical research studies need to tell a story which embraces the data and has a beginning, middle and end, and researchers require an analytical strategy to guide them to craft this story as the data do not always construct this story for them. He believes that this strategy will help them to treat the evidence fairly, produce compelling analytic conclusions, rule out alternative interpretations, and use tools to manipulate the data more effectively and efficiently. Ball (1991: 182–183) maintains that writing about data is a vital discipline as it encourages the interrogation of data and facilitates creative thinking. He further notes that:

The data-bits are important in two ways as the writing begins. First, they serve for illustration of categories and issues . . . Second, the deployment of the data drives the analysis as exactly what it is about each extract that is meaningful is explained . . . New nuances, complexity or contradictions emerge, especially as each new piece of data is added to what is already displayed and said. (Ball, 1991: 187)

Patton (2002: 513) maintains that 'qualitative inquiry draws on both critical and creative thinking – both the science and art of analysis. But the technical, procedural and scientific side of analysis is easier to present and teach. Creativity, while easy to prescribe, is harder to teach, and perhaps harder to learn.' Yet, ultimately we need to learn to write in a critical and creative manner because that is what writing at postgraduate level demands.

10 Writing Up: the potency of written argument

When we have carried out the penultimate phase of our research, i.e. the final data analysis, we need to write up our findings and what we can conclude from the research. Writing up our research is perhaps the most important phase during our research project, though this phase is likely to extend throughout the lifecycle of the research. This is one of the main avenues, similar to the verbal presentation of our work, through which we can tell our audience what our research is about. Regardless of how wonderful our research questions or hypotheses were, how competently we chose and approached our participants, how capably we gathered the data, how proficiently we analysed them, and how ethical the entire research process was, unless we write about these activities and issues in a persuasive manner, our readers will not be able to comprehend and evaluate our research, and learn from it. Nevertheless, we need to choose judiciously what we write and how we write it. Richardson (1990) observes that:

> In our work as researchers, we weigh and sift experiences, make choices regard-ing what is significant, what is trivial, what to include and what to exclude. We do not simply chronicle what happened next, but place the next in a meaningful context. By doing so, we craft narratives and we write lives. (p. 10)

Reading and thinking

As noted earlier (see Chapter 2), one of the purposes of reading is to learn to write. This is important, as Strauss (1987) argues:

> Not everyone knows how to examine [research publications] for the analytic struc-ture embedded in them . . . [i.e.] whether the publication is organized around proof or causality, or concern for consequences, or a setting out of strategies or of topologies. (p. 249)

Strauss (1987: 249) suggests that researchers develop the skill 'to read and think in terms of the logic of analysis'. He believes this will help them to 'think more clearly about their own writing, to organize it with more facility, and to give critical attention to the presentation of its underlying analysis' (p. 249). Further, researchers need to practise reflexivity when writing up their research. Delamont (1992) observes that writing up is part of the same reflexive process that has carried the researchers from the planning stage through the fieldwork and the analysis. Stronach et al. (2007) draw on the reflexive practices of doctoral students whose theses reflect the ways in which these students choose to appropriate reflexive methodological texts. They argue that the socially constructed nature of all knowledge, which includes scientific knowledge, entails the introduction of a reflexive dimension to accounts written about the discovery of such knowledge.

Ideally, and in similarity with qualitative data analysis, the discovery and writing up of new knowledge should not be a separate and self-contained phase. Miles and Huberman (1994: 299) argue that 'reporting is not separate from thinking, from analysis. Rather, it *is* analysis'. Walford's (1998) comments on his own writing resonate with the writing experiences of many of us:

> Writing does not just improve my thinking, but it allows me to think. It is only when a draft is finished that I begin to be clear about what I am trying to

> say – even if only at that particular moment. Writing forces me to confront at least some of my illogicalities, such that a temporary truce is constructed. What I write is always open to reassessment and development. (p. 197)

The need to write early

Researchers need to start writing as soon as they have collected and analysed some data and can link the data and analysis to their research questions, or hypotheses, and to previous research in the field. Becker (2007: 17–18) recommends researchers start writing before they have all their data to clear their thinking. This will tell them what they want to discuss and what data they will have to get, thus shaping their research design. 'Academic writing is not a final stage of doing research that occurs once all the data construction, thought and analysis has finished' (Walford, 1998: 197). Punch (2005) contends that as opposed to the traditional model of research writing, when researchers write up after they have completed the research, writing should be viewed as a learning experience:

> A different view sees writing as a way of learning, a way of knowing, a form of analysis and inquiry. This is the idea of 'writing in order to work it out'. In this view, I don't delay the writing until I have it all figured out. On the contrary, I use the process of writing itself to help me figure it out, since I learn by writing . . . Thus writing becomes an integral part of the research, and not just an add-on once the 'real research' is completed. This is writing to learn. (p. 275)

We can easily underestimate the time required for writing up an empirical study. It will need several attempts to get it right and will thus necessitate rewriting. Feedback from supervisors and critical colleagues is crucial at this stage. For dissertations and theses written in the conventional way, a first draft of the chapters on Literature Review and Methodology should be completed before the commencement of data collection. (For a different format, see Basit, 1995). These will undoubtedly be revisited a few times during the course of the study, but the bulk of the work for these two chapters will have been done.

Brown and Jones (2001) maintain:

> In engaging in educational research, we are invariably engaged in a task of capturing the experience of the research process in some tangible and collectible form. Depending on the style of research in question, this might include: extracts of

people's speech, statistical analyses, lesson plans, examples of children's work, presentations or critiques of theoretical positions, interpretations of data etc. In developing or reporting on a research enquiry, there is a need to find ways of looking back on this tangible product in deciding how best to select and combine components of it in creating further tangible product. (p. 36)

Brown and Jones (2001: 36) proceed to propose that the research process should be seen as the production of a sequence of pieces of writing, because the accountability of research activity, and the statements made regarding this activity, are closely linked with the production of writing.

Planning to write

While writing comes naturally to some, not all of us are born writers who have writing flowing through their pen, or their keyboard as it now happens. It is therefore useful to plan what and how to write. Strauss and Corbin (1990) maintain that over the course of the research project, researchers gain increased theoretical sensitivity to the many facets of the phenomena, a great deal substantively about the phenomena, and about essential analytical procedures. This will lead them to the first phase of writing which requires:

- A clear analytic story
- Writing on a conceptual level, with description kept secondary
- The clear specification of relationships among categories, with levels of conceptualization also kept clear
- The specification of variations and their relevant conditions, consequences, and so forth, including the broader ones.

Wolcott (2001: 16–21) suggests three components of the writing plan. These include the following:

1. Writing the statement of the purpose at the beginning to tell ourselves and our readers what the purpose of our study is. Admittedly, this purpose will be rewritten and refined a few times during our writing.
2. Writing a detailed outline or list of topics, written sequentially, telling the reader what to expect from our writing, in which order. This list also shows the difference between the key and the secondary points or issues that will be discussed under the main headings and subheadings. This will then be turned into a table of contents.

3. Carefully contemplating what story we are going to tell and how we are going to tell it. While storytelling is more pertinent to writing qualitative research, quantitative research narrates a story in its own way.

Once we have planned what and how to write, we may want to delay writing up through various forms of procrastination, for example, making a couple of phone calls, checking our emails, sending a few texts, making a cup of coffee, tidying our desk, consulting another book or two, and so forth. Nevertheless, we need to get going as we can never write until we make a start, however bad it is. Becker (2007: 48–49) maintains that writing difficulties commonly originate from the problem of getting started and deciding how to organize the writing. This is because writers think there is only one right way to begin, and unless they find that way, they cannot write.

On no account should we assume that what we write now will necessarily appear in the final version of our writing. The process of writing is just as important as the product. No writing is perfect in its initial form, but the important thing is to write whatever comes to our mind and which is somewhat related to what our research is about. It is expected that most of what we write initially will be edited and revised later on, as writing is a developmental process. We need to have written something in order to improve it, so that we eventually produce writing which is of master's or doctoral standard, or worthy of publication in a refereed journal, depending on the purpose for which it is produced. The dissertation, thesis or research report should be structured and written in a way that it represents a coherent product. Wallace and Wray (2006) suggests that:

> Every part of a defensible account of empirical research should link logically together, from the title, with its keywords indicating the focus of the study, through the central question being addressed, the critical literature reviews, the research design, the data collection instruments, the presentation and discussion of the findings, the conclusion and any recommendations, to the reference list and any appendices. (pp. 174–175)

When planning to write, researchers should sketch an overall logic outline of their analytical story. Additional procedures which will help the researchers to translate their analysis into writing include thinking about the analytic logic that informs the story; and constructing outlines, including a logical ordering of chapters and sections (Strauss and Corbin, 1990). A master's dissertation or doctoral thesis written in a conventional way has certain chapters in a particular sequence. This guideline is usually followed in theses in which both quantitative and qualitative research are written up. A rough guide to dividing the percentage of total wordage is as follows:

Abstract
Acknowledgements

1. Introduction`	10%
2. Review of Literature	25%
3. Methodology	20%
4. Findings and Analysis	35%
5. Conclusion	10%

References
Appendices

The abstract, acknowledgements, reference list and appendices are usually not included in the word count. The substantive chapters will comprise the following:

Chapter One – Introduction

This chapter should set the scene by introducing the research issue and the research context and why this particular subject is worthy of investigation. This should be written in light of what previous research has been undertaken in the area and if any gaps exist which our study will aim to fill. It should also state the structure of the dissertation or thesis and how it is organized.

Chapter Two – Review of literature

This should review the existing literature on the subject in a critical and analytical fashion. Researchers should develop a conceptual framework in relation to the literature they review, and discuss the relevant literature in logically designed sections under headings and subheadings. A wide range of literature should be discussed, the majority of which should be recent, but seminal studies should also be included. If the study draws on a theoretical framework, then it should be discussed in this chapter and its relevance to our research made evident. Crucially, the review of literature must not be descriptive.

Chapter Three – Methodology

This should start by stating the key and secondary research questions, or the hypotheses, developed as a result of the literature review. The aims and objectives of the study should also be stated in this chapter. This should be followed by a brief discussion of the research paradigms, methodologies, approaches and methods, with a detailed critique of the chosen paradigm, methodology, approach and method(s) used for our research, with a clear justification for our choice. Issues of sampling, validity, reliability and ethics should be discussed, followed by methods of analysing the data. Everything regarding the research design should be discussed with reference to the research methods literature.

Chapter Four – Findings and analysis

In this chapter, we should present the findings of our study and the analysis of our data in relation to our research questions or hypotheses. While this can be dealt with in a single chapter in a master's dissertation, it may be better to split this into two or three chapters for a doctoral study. For example, the analysis and findings can be discussed in one chapter and a discussion of these in another chapter. Alternately, the findings, analysis and discussion can be discussed in three different chapters, each based on a key research question that we have addressed through our study. We should refer back to the literature on the subject to show where our findings correspond with the literature, and where they are at variance with previous research in the field.

Chapter Five – Conclusion

This chapter should summarize and draw together the significant themes and arguments presented in the study. It should show the relevance of our title and research questions to the wider research in the field, and how it is similar and/or different to what other researchers have done. In case of a doctoral study, we need to demonstrate which aspect of our research makes an original contribution to knowledge. Recommendations for educational policy and practice can be made, and limitations to the study should be noted.

Abstract

This should be the last thing that we write, after the entire dissertation or thesis has been written. Ideally written on one side of the page, this should present the reader with an overview of the dissertation or thesis, encompassing every aspect of the study. This should be at the beginning, after the title page.

Acknowledgements

This section should follow the abstract, and be used to express our gratitude to the people who made our study possible. These could be our research participants (who should be thanked without being named), supervisors, advisors and anybody else who helped us during the course of our research.

Reference list

Written in alphabetical order according to the authors' surnames, this should be after the Conclusion chapter and should include only those sources which have been cited in the main body of the dissertation or thesis. (See the section on 'Citations and the reference list' later in the chapter).

Appendices

Letters used to gain access for the fieldwork; covering letters sent with questionnaires; and research instruments such as interview schedules, questionnaires, observation checklists can be included as an appendix. Anything else that we think is useful for the reader, but not important enough to be included in the main body of the study can be put here.

Starting to write

Researchers think in different manners and write in different styles. Despite our best intentions, not all of us plan what to write. While some of us prefer to have a detailed writing plan before our writing commences, some others choose to get on with it and write whatever comes to mind. Researchers have a range of optimal writing styles and it is best to experiment a little to establish what suits our purposes and personality. Still, even when we are ready to write up our research, it is not a straightforward task, done smoothly. Nias (1991) describes her experience of writing up a research project, which is not too different from what many of us go through:

> Writing was difficult for many reasons . . . I am a slow and painstaking writer, most of whose work goes through four drafts. I do not find writing easy, but I like to do it as well as I can. In consequence, producing a manuscript which I feel is fit for publication is hard and tiresome work, inducing broken nights, bad temper, and the kind of preoccupation, which is often difficult to distinguish from utter egocentricity. I can truthfully say that whereas data collection is generally enjoyable and analysis is intellectually rewarding, writing is painful drudgery. I persist in it for only two reasons: I feel I have something to say that

> I want others to read (this itself is normally dependent on other people telling me that they think it is worth saying); and I take a craft pride in the finished product. (pp. 160–161)

Since it is fairly easy to use computers to write and save our writing, we are expected to present our drafts and the final version of our writing as typescript. This is a huge improvement on drafts of manuscripts written in longhand a quarter of a century ago, and which were then typed on a typewriter and saved as a carbon copy. Familiarizing ourselves with the format and style in which we should be writing is important. University guidelines about the way a dissertation or thesis should be structured must be perused before we start writing. If it is a paper for a journal, or a report for an external funder, then advice will be provided by the journal or the funding authority. It is customary to use A4 size paper, with ample margins on all four sides, and to use 1.5 or double line spacing. Pages should be numbered. References in the text and in the reference list should be cited in the required style. Writing in the correct format from the beginning will save researchers time later on. Whatever the purpose of writing, researchers need to write in a way that is acceptable for that particular genre of writing. For example, Delamont (1992) notes:

> The thesis, whether for a masters degree or a doctorate, is usually the first sustained text its author has tried to produce . . . The first thing to do is to discover what the rules about theses are, and the second is to read some theses which have been successfully completed under those rules. (p. 164)

We should always save our work at least once a day. It can be at the end of the day when we know we are not going to write any more. Saving it on at least one USB disk/memory stick every day is essential. Most of us have more than one email address. We can email the updated version to ourselves at the end of each day. This will mean that our files will remain in the Sent folder of one of our email accounts and the Inbox of our other email account. Older versions of the writing can be deleted regularly from the email accounts as we produce newer ones.

We do not necessarily have to write in the sequence in which our chapters will appear in our dissertation or thesis or report. As noted above, it is important to complete a first draft of the chapters on Literature Review and Methodology at the initial stages, which will of course undergo a few revisions later. The Methodology will have further sections added to it after the completion of the research, stating the research procedure including the data collection and analysis. In addition to these sections, the researchers' fieldnotes and summaries of transcripts will prove to be helpful, especially at various stages of writing about data analysis. The purpose of writing these chapters early on is to refine our research questions and to gain a sense of the most appropriate research design for our study before we go into the field. The Introduction, which will be the first chapter does not need to be written at this point. In fact, it is quite common for researchers to leave this until the end when all the chapters, including the Conclusion, have been written in a dissertation or thesis.

Once we have started to write, we need to keep up the momentum. It is useful to set aside some time to do at least a little writing every day even when we are involved in fieldwork, transcribing our interviews or entering our data into a software package. Even making detailed notes which will be incorporated into the chapters later will be useful. It is a good idea to read what we have written on the previous day, before continuing with our writing. Contemplating our earlier work gives us ideas about where our writing should be going. Writing allows us to reflect on our work and as our power of reflection improves, so does our writing.

Lavelle and Bushrow (2007) highlight the complexity of writing at postgraduate level which requires students to move beyond the strategies used in undergraduate writing. They observe that expectations regarding breadth and depth call for new insights and higher levels of skills. They note the need to look at models of writing, genre familiarity, discussing writers and writers' beliefs, and how academic writing functions at postgraduate level as both a tool of learning and a medium of communication. They suggest we recognize the fact that students' negotiation of academic understandings and the way they express and structure their ideas is largely framed, or even driven, by the quality of writing.

How to write

Writing up our research essentially means composing potent arguments to convince our readers about the merits of our research. How we write up our research will be determined by who our audience are. For master's or doctoral students, this will initially be their examiners. The examiners will need to be persuaded by the students through their writing that their study meets the required criteria for the specific postgraduate degree, can justify its methodology, shows the ability to analyse and synthesize, and is written in a critical manner. Lichtman (2006) contends:

> The strength of what you write is revealed in your ability to convince the reader that your interpretations are reasonable and supported by the data. The acceptance of your writing comes down to how you weave your data into concepts . . . The writing act is inextricably woven with the task of organising and making sense of your data. (p. 178)

A doctoral thesis must be much more rigorous than a master's dissertation. In addition to being based on more in-depth research carried out over a longer period, a doctoral thesis will need to demonstrate originality and contribution to knowledge in the field to which it relates. The student will also have to show the readers that the claims that the master's or doctoral study is making are based on evidence. The dissertation or thesis will then be perused by future master's or doctoral students respectively who will doubtless learn from it. Subsequently, for students, and for researchers carrying out postdoctoral work, the audience will be the wider research and academic community, especially those who have an interest in the same area of research. It will also appeal to other groups, for example, policy makers, practitioners and those who have funded the research. The researchers therefore need to communicate with their specific audience in a persuasive way, and ensure that their writing is credible and comprehensible to those audience. Wallace and Wray (2006) maintain:

> Awareness of audience is a generic skill. It demands different emphases according to the purpose and destination of the material. However, in all cases, unless you can adequately back up your claims, your readers will find them unconvincing. If they do, it will undermine the achievement of your purpose in writing the text. (p. 41)

Miles and Huberman (1994: 300) suggest that researchers ask themselves which type of readers they are targeting and what kind of effects they want their research report to have on their audience. They note the different effects that a qualitative research report can aim to generate:

Aesthetic:
- Entertain, amuse, arouse feeling
- Enable vicarious experiencing

Scientific:
- Heighten insight, illuminate, deepen understanding
- Add to existing information on a topic
- Expand or revise existing concepts, theory, explanations
- Convince the reader of the report's worth, truth and value
- Advance the methodological craft of research

Moral:
- Clarify and sharpen moral issues
- Emancipate, raise consciousness, free the reader from unrealized oppression

Activist:
- Enable improved decisions, provide guidance for action
- Show connections between findings and local problems
- Empower the reader, increase the sense of control
- Mobilize specific action
- Support the reader in future use of the findings.

Our completed manuscript needs to present a lucid story. An important aspect of writing involves scrutinizing it regularly to ensure that the various chapters and sections present a coherent whole. Several times during the writing the research questions should be inspected to ensure that the writing deals with the focus of the research. Having our working title in front of us at all times is helpful as whatever we write ultimately needs to address what our study is about. The title and the research questions will lead us to make relevant claims about our research, based on our findings. Punch (2003: 68) maintains that 'when writing a research report, it is important to keep in mind that its main purpose is the clear and accessible communication of the project's *objectives*, its *methods* and its *findings*'.

A necessary feature of writing at postgraduate level is to present a compelling argument throughout. This can be written in the first person or the third person, but we need to be consistent. The argument evolves as the writing progresses and is underpinned by references to previous research and theory. It is further strengthened by our own empirical research and what we deduce from it in the light of our evidence. Academic writing demands that we write in a critical manner and avoid description. According to Taylor (1989: 67) the common motives governing academic writing include the following:

- Agreeing with, acceding to, defending or confirming a particular viewpoint
- Proposing a new standpoint

- Conceding that an existing perspective has some merits, but it needs to be qualified in significant ways
- Reformulating an existing viewpoint in a way that the new version presents a better explanation
- Dismissing an argument on account of its inadequacy, irrelevance, incoherence or other similar criteria
- Rejecting, rebutting or refuting a standpoint on various reasoned grounds
- Reconciling two perspectives which may seem to be at variance by appeal to a higher or deeper principle
- Retracting or recanting one's own previous position in light of new evidence or arguments.

Strauss (1987: 260) observes the apprehension of researchers, in particular those who use grounded theory, regarding their writing when approaching, or even during, the writing period, as they doubt whether they can write effectively. He gives the following reasons for the researchers' anxiety:

- They are perfectionists and cannot settle for less than an ideal performance. This can result in no performance at all or a very delayed performance.
- They lack confidence in themselves and believe they are incapable of accomplishing this kind of task.
- They have styles and habits of writing developed through essay writing during their school years, when writing is done quickly and simplistically to meet deadlines, and without revising the drafts.

Strauss (1987: 260) argues that even though researchers have to complete their writing within a certain period, a 'facile style of writing is quite antithetical to the rather complicated, dense, tightly organized style appropriate to the grounded theory methodology, especially when writing theses and monographs'. Strauss and Corbin (1990: 232), too, note this problem, which may be encountered by researchers writing grounded theory theses, as the source of such theses is the fairly complex analysis generated through the entire research process.

Strauss and Corbin (1990: 232–233) highlight the difficulty faced by researchers in compressing the copious grounded theory analysis and recognizing the depth in which one needs to go when writing about the research. They believe that firstly researchers should identify their main analytic message, and then provide sufficient conceptual detail to convey this message to the readers. They suggest researchers using grounded theory methodology learn two skills simultaneously: how to present in written form the various analyses generated by this complex research process, and to integrate them all again in written form. They maintain that the actual form of the central chapters in a thesis ought to be consistent with the analytic message and its components (for an example of a thesis using the grounded theory approach, see Basit, 1995).

Claiming originality

As stated above, a doctoral study needs to illustrate that it is original. Originality pertains to creativity, innovation and freshness of ideas and practices in research. As the examiners have not seen how well the research procedure was carried out, researchers need to convince their examiners and readers about the significance and usefulness of their research through their writing. It is almost impossible to conduct totally original research as a doctoral student, mainly because in the vast majority of cases doctoral research is our first step towards original and rigorous research. In fact, very few experienced educational researchers can claim that their research is completely original. Nevertheless, originality can be demonstrated through at least one element within the research process.

Phillips and Pugh (2005: 62) offer a number of suggestions based on a synthesis of various sources and state the different ways in which a research study can illustrate its originality:

- It sets down important new information in writing for the first time
- It provides an original idea, method, result or interpretation
- It continues an original research undertaken previously
- It shows originality in testing an idea belonging to someone else
- It carries out empirical work that has not been done before
- It provides a synthesis that has not been made before
- It offers a new interpretation of already known material
- It tries out something in a country which has only been done in another country
- It applies a technique to a new area of research
- It brings new evidence to bear on an old issue
- It uses different methodologies in cross-disciplinary research
- It investigates an area that researchers in a discipline have not looked at before
- It adds to knowledge in a way that has not been done before.

Thus originality in doctoral research can be shown in any one of the ways stated above. Cryer (2006) offers an analogy to help us understand the concept of originality in research by depicting the research student as an explorer and the research programme as an expedition. In congruence with the suggestions of Phillips and Pugh (2005) noted above, she maintains that researchers can demonstrate originality in different ways, for example, in tools, techniques and procedures; in exploring the unknown, unexplored or unanticipated; in the collection of data; in the outcomes and unforeseen by-products; and in applying a research design in a different context or country. Denscombe (2002: 90–91) maintains that originality can be illustrated by choosing new subject matter and a topic that has not previously been studied; a novel application of a method; new information that does not already exist, which goes beyond a straightforward description of the information, and looks at why things are the way they look instead of just stating what they are. He argues that such analysis leads to generation of knowledge rather than mere information and contributes to the originality of the research.

Citations and the reference list

Researchers will refer to a wide and diverse range of literature in their final manuscript. The sources of literature cited in the writing need to be duly acknowledged in the text, or the researchers may be accused of plagiarism. Passing off someone else's work is unethical and if researchers have failed to note the reference details of certain publications, then verbatim extracts from, or critiques of, those publications should not be included. All references should be cited briefly in the main text with the author's surname and date of publication in parenthesis. If it is a direct quotation, then the number of the page(s) from which it was taken must follow. If there are two authors, then both the names should be inserted here. If there are more than two authors, then the name of the principal author should be given followed by 'et al.' The names of all the authors should then be noted in the reference list at the end.

As noted earlier, the reference list should be compiled in alphabetical order according to the authors' surnames. It is crucial that the reference list is composed as we write and cite new references, so that a full reference list is ready at the completion of the writing. This should include the full reference to each source in the required style, such as the Harvard style of referencing, or the APA style. Under no circumstances should the reference list be left until the writing up is complete. This will be extremely time consuming as researchers will need to dig out the sources which they used perhaps several months ago, and may find that some of them are not readily available.

Most commonly used sources of literature that researchers refer to are books, journal articles, chapters and internet sources. Each reference to the source in the Reference List should include the following:

For books

The surname and initials of the author(s); the title of the book; the edition of the book if it is not the first edition; the place of publication; and the name of the publisher. The title of the book should be written in italics.

For journal articles

The surname and initials of the author(s); the title of the article; the name of the journal; the volume number and issue number; and the range of pages on which the article appears in the journal. The name of the journal needs to be written in italics.

For book chapters

The surname and initials of the chapter author(s); the title of the chapter; the initials and surname of the editor(s); the title of the book; the edition of the book if it is not the first edition; the place of publication; and the name of the publisher. The title of the book should be written in italics.

For internet sources

The surname and initials of the author(s); the title of the article; any other information available, for example, if the article was published in a report, then the title of the report; the full address of the website on which the article appeared; and the date on which we retrieved the article from the website.

If we cite a number of publications of the same author, then these need to be listed in chronological order, first itemizing all the single-authored publications of the author, and then noting the dual- or multiple-authored publications in which the author's name appears first, again in chronological order. Other sources that researchers might refer to include unpublished material, policy papers, government reports, conference presentations, official documents and so forth. Universities' and journal publishers' guidelines provide advice on how to refer to these various sources. Researchers can use software programmes such as Endnote and Refworks to keep track of the references.

Editing

When we first start to write, we believe that what we are writing is flawless. This is significant as we need to have faith in ourselves as writers in order to write. Nevertheless, almost everything we write at the outset will be edited.

This will involve reading it a few times, deleting what we see as irrelevant or imprecise, and substituting it with statements and arguments which are more convincing, and are more pertinent to our study. We may also want to cut text from one section and paste it in another section if it makes our arguments more logical. When word processing our work, we should always save each draft separately, rather than editing an only copy, as we sometimes need to go back to earlier drafts to check and compare our writing. Earlier drafts can then be deleted regularly as we accumulate more revised drafts of our writing.

Despite constant editing, at the end of the writing up phase, researchers usually find that they have written twice their word limit. In most cases, it is the result of repeating ourselves when we are arguing for or against something; duplicating similar viewpoints from various authors; including lengthy, verbatim quotations from the literature; or, in qualitative studies, citing several large quotations from the data, which are from different participants, but are mainly similar. All this is remediable, but needs major pruning. We can tighten our arguments and remove the repetition; and discuss similar viewpoints by writing them once and attributing them to a number of authors at the same time, rather than presenting several direct citations. We can paraphrase some of the arguments in the literature, incorporating them into the paragraphs, and giving the full reference to the source; and give a flavour of the dominant themes by offering only selected quotations from the interviews or fieldnotes, followed by analysis. This is not easy as we get attached to our data and want to use as much of them as possible in our writing, particularly if we have carried out a qualitative study. We want to give our readers the true flavour of the participants' sentiments, but we need to exercise care and recognize the importance of brevity and selectivity. As Nias (1991) notes:

> Writing for publication . . . presented me with the problem of selecting illustrative examples, especially given the constraints of length and the need to balance against each other the reader's likely interest in abstractions on the one hand and living detail on the other. For the most part, I set myself the arbitrary limit of three or four illustrative comments for any given point and pared these down to essentials. I was painfully aware of all the data I did not, and probably shall never directly use. (p. 161)

There comes a point in our writing when we have to stop editing. No writing is perfect and researchers cannot carry on improving it endlessly. For students producing a dissertation or a thesis, the supervisors will provide regular feedback on the writings. For others, critical friends, such as colleagues working in the same area, can look at our work and advise on how it can be improved. Strauss and Corbin (1990: 236) note the logic of letting go, avoiding the trap of dreaming of the perfect manuscript, and striking a balance between profitable reworking of drafts and disentangling ourselves from our research.

We also need to acknowledge that we cannot do everything in a study. We may have thought initially that we would be able to examine a wide range of issues, but later found that we needed to narrow our focus. This is fine, and quite common in research, and is an important part of our development as a researcher. We may also find that because we have to comply with a maximum word count in our thesis or dissertation, we need to reduce the number of categories or variables that we analyse and report. We should state at the end of our writing what we could not investigate, analyse or write about, and why, and identify those issues as areas for future research.

Dissemination

Knowledge generation is a crucial objective of educational and other social science research. Hammersley (2003) contends:

> It would not be logically contradictory, or even obviously irrational, to argue that the best way for a researcher to contribute to the improvement of education would be to build sociological and psychological knowledge in this field . . . Within [research], the production of knowledge is the sole immediate goal. (pp. 12, 14)

This knowledge then needs to be disseminated to those who can benefit from it. Educational researchers must be passionate about the research they are conducting, believe in the momentous nature of its findings, and have the motivation to disseminate its outcomes to a wider audience. The final report, dissertation, or thesis should be gripping, potent and persuasive, and tell our readers all they want to know about our study. Yin (2009: 189), discussing case study research, maintains that 'the report should be engaging [with] a clear writing style, but one that constantly entices the reader to continue reading. A good manuscript is one that seduces the eye . . . [so that you] continue to read.' He maintains that:

> Engagement, enticement and seduction – these are unusual characteristics of case studies. To produce such a case study requires an investigator to be enthusiastic

> about the investigation and to want to communicate the results widely. In fact, the good investigator might even think that the case study contains earth-shattering conclusions. This sort of inspiration should pervade the entire investigation and will indeed lead to an exemplary case study. (p. 190)

This kind of enthusiasm and engagement will encourage the researchers to disseminate their findings to a wider audience verbally by presenting papers at conferences, and in writing by publishing their research. Pring (2004) argues:

> Research, as that is normally understood, requires a 'research forum' – a group of people with whom the conclusions can be tested out and examined critically. Without such openness to criticism, one might have missed the evidence or the counter argument, which casts doubts on the conclusions drawn. Hence the importance of dissemination through publications and seminars. (p. 133)

The British Educational Research Association recommends that researchers disseminate the findings to research participants. In its Revised Ethical Guidelines (BERA, 2004), it states:

> The Association considers it good practice for researchers to debrief participants at the conclusion of the research and to provide them with copies of any reports or other publications arising from their participation. Where the scale of the research makes such a consideration impractical, alternative means such as a website should be used to ensure participants are informed of the outcome. (p. 10)

The way we disseminate our findings, what we present in seminars and conferences, and what we write in our publications, will not only convey to our audience what our research is about, but also what kind of researchers we are. We have to accept that researchers are inevitably part of the social world that they study. They need to be cognizant of this reality, as it will encourage them to become reflexive researchers. Reflexivity entails reflection, introspection and critical self-analysis during the research. It engages the researchers in acknowledging and examining their subjectivities, based on their background, prior knowledge and experiences. This will lead them to recognize the unavoidable impact of these biases on the choices that they make during the process of research; on their own behaviour and that of the research participants during the study; and on the way the data are collected, analysed and interpreted; and the research is written up and disseminated.

References

Adelman, C.; Kemmis, S. and Jenkins, D. (1980) Rethinking case study: Notes from the Second Cambridge Conference, in H. Simons (ed.) *Towards a Science of the Singular*. Norwich: Centre for Applied Research in Education, University of East Anglia.

Adler, P. A. and Adler, P. (1994) Observational techniques, in N. K. Denzin and Y. S. Lincoln (eds) *Handbook of Qualitative Research*. London: Sage.

Alaszewski, A. (2006) *Using Diaries for Social Research*. London: Sage.

A-Latif, A. (1992) An examination of the examinations: the reliability of the objective structured clinical examination and clinical examination, *Medical Teacher*, 14, 179–183.

Al-Saadi, F. H. (2009) The Effect of 'Our Brothers and Sisters in Humanity' Program on Omani Secondary School Girls' Cultural Tolerance. PhD Thesis, University of Leicester.

Anfara, V. A. and Mertz, N. T. (eds) (2006) *Theoretical Frameworks in Qualitative Research*. Thousand Oaks, CA: Sage.

Argyris, C. and Schon, D. A. (1974) *Theory in Practice: Increasing Professional Effectiveness*. San Francisco, CA: Jossey-Bass.

Bailey, C. A. (1996) *A Guide to Field Research*. Thousand Oaks, CA: Pine Forge.

Bailey, K. D. (1994) *Methods of Social Research* (fourth edition). New York: Free Press.

Ball, S. J. (1981) *Beachside Comprehensive: A Case Study of Secondary Schooling*. Cambridge: Cambridge University Press.

Ball, S. J. (1991) Power, conflict, micropolitics and all that, in G. Walford (ed.) *Doing Educational Research*. London: Routledge.

Barker, C. and Johnson, G. (1998) Interview talk as professional practice, *Language and Education*, 12, 229–242 (cited in Cohen et al., 2007).

Basit, T. N. (1995) Educational, Social and Career Aspirations of Teenage Muslim Girls in Britain: An Ethnographic Case Study. PhD Thesis, University of Cambridge.

Basit, T. N. (1997) *Eastern Values, Western Milieu: Identities and Aspirations of Adolescent British Muslim Girls*. Aldershot: Ashgate.

Basit, T. N. (2003) Manual or electronic: the role of coding in qualitative data analysis, *Educational Research*, 45, 143–154.

Basit, T. N.; Roberts, L.; McNamara, O.; Carrington, B.; Maguire, M. and Woodrow, D. (2006) Did they jump or were they pushed? Reasons why Minority Ethnic Trainees withdraw from Initial Teacher Training Courses, *British Educational Research Journal*, 32, 387–410.

Bassey, M. (1999) *Case Study Research in Educational Settings.* Buckingham: Open University Press.

Becker, H. (1958) Problems of inference and proof in participant observation, *American Sociological Review*, 28, 652–660 (cited in Hopkins, 2008).

Becker, H. S. (2007) *Writing for Social Scientists* (second edition). Chicago, IL: University of Chicago Press.

BERA (2004) *Revised Ethical Guidelines for Educational Research.* British Educational Research Association www.bera.ac.uk/files/2008/09/ethical.pdf accessed on 27 December 2008.

Bogdan, R. G. and Biklen, S. K. (1992) *Qualitative Research for Education* (second edition). Boston, MA: Allyn and Bacon.

Brown, L. M. and Gilligan, C. (1992) *Meeting at the Crossroads.* Cambridge, MA: Harvard University Press.

Brown, T. and Jones, L. (2001) *Action Research and Postmodernism: Congruence and Critique.* Buckingham: Open University Press.

Burgess, R. G. (1983) *Experiencing Comprehensive Education: A Study of Bishop McGregor School.* London: Methuen.

Burgess, R. G. (1984) *In the Field: An Introduction to Field Research.* London: George, Allen and Unwin.

Burrell, G. and Morgan, G. (1979) *Sociological Paradigms and Organizational Analysis.* London: Heinemann.

Campbell, D. and Stanley, J. (1963) *Experimental and Quasi-Experimental Designs for Research.* Boston: Houghton Mifflin (cited in Gorard, 2003).

Carr, W. and Kemmis, S. (1986) *Becoming Critical: Education, Knowledge and Action Research.* Lewes: Falmer.

Carspecken, P. F. (1996) *Critical Ethnography in Educational Research.* London: Routledge.

Cohen, L.; Manion, L. and Morrison, K. (2007) *Research Methods in Education* (sixth edition). London: Routledge.

Colley, A. and Comber, C. (2003) Age and gender differences in computer use and attitudes among secondary school students: what has changed? *Educational Research,* 45, 115–165.

Cook, T. and Campbell, D. (1979) *Quasi-Experimentation: Design and Analysis Issues for Field Settings.* Chicago: Rand McNally (cited in Gorard, 2003).

Cresswell, J. W. (1998) *Qualitative Inquiry and Research Design.* Thousand Oaks, CA: Sage.

Cresswell, J. W. (2003) *Research Design: Qualitative, Quantitative, and Mixed Methods Approaches* (second edition). Thousand Oaks, CA: Sage.

Croll, P. (2008) Occupational choice, socio-economic status and educational attainment: a study of the occupational choices and destinations of young people in the British Household Panel Survey, *Research Papers in Education,* 23, 243–268.

Cryer, P. (2006) *The Research Student's Guide to Success* (third edition). Maidenhead: Open University Press.

David, M.; Edwards, R.; and Alldred, P. (2001) Children and school-based research: 'informed consent' or 'educated consent'? *British Educational Research Journal,* 27, 347–365.

Delamont, S. (1992) *Fieldwork in Educational Settings.* London: Falmer.

Denscombe, M. (2002) *Ground Rules for Good Research*. Buckingham: Open University Press.

Denzin, N. and Lincoln, Y. (1998) *The Landscape of Qualitative Research*. Thousand Oaks, CA: Sage.

Ebbutt, D. and Elliott, J. (eds) (1985) *Issues in Teaching for Understanding*. Longman/Schools Curriculum Development Committee (SCDC).

Edwards, D. and Mercer, N. (1987) *Common Knowledge: The Development of Understanding in the Classroom*. London: Routledge.

Eid, F. H. (2008) Preparing Youth for Citizenship and Democracy: Young Bahrainis' Civic and Political Knowledge and Understanding. PhD Thesis, University of Leicester.

Elliott, J. (1991) *Action Research for Educational Change*. Buckingham: Open University Press.

Elliott, J. (2005) *Using Narrative in Social Research*. London: Sage.

Elliott, J. and Adelman, C. (1976) *Innovation at the Classroom level: A Case Study of the Ford Teaching Project*. Course CE203. Milton Keynes: Open University.

Ely, M. (1991) *Doing Qualitative Research*. Basingstoke: Falmer.

Emerson, R. M.; Fretz, R. I. and Shaw, L. L. (2001) Participant observation and fieldnotes, in P. Atkinson; A. Coffey; S. Delamont; J. Lofland and L. Lofland (eds) *Handbook of Ethnography*. London: Sage.

ESRC (2005) *Research Ethics Framework*. Swindon: Economic and Social Research Council www. esrcsocietytoday.ac.uk/ESRCInfoCentre/Images/ESRC_Re_Ethics_Frame_tcm6-11291.pdf accessed on 27 December 2008.

Ezzy, D. (2002) *Qualitative Analysis: Practice and Innovation*. London: Routledge.

Fairbairn, G. and Winch, C. (1991) *Reading, Writing and Reasoning: A Guide for Students*. Buckingham: Open University Press.

Feldman, M. S. (1995) *Strategies for Interpreting Qualitative Data*. Thousand Oaks, CA: Sage.

Fetterman, D. M. (1998) *Ethnography: Step by Step* (second edition). Thousand Oaks, CA: Sage.

Fielding, N. G. and Fielding, J. L. (1986) *Linking Data*. London: Sage.

Finch, J. (1984) It's great to have someone to talk to: the ethics and politics of interviewing women, in C. Bell and H. Roberts (eds) *Social Researching: Politics, Problems and Practice*. London: Routledge and Kegan Paul.

Flanders, N. A. (1970) *Analysing Teaching Behaviour*. Reading, MA: Addison-Wesley.

Flick, U. (1998) *An Introduction to Qualitative Research*. London: Sage.

Fothergill, R. A. (1974) *Private Chronicles: A Study of English Diaries*. London: Oxford University Press (cited in McCulloch, 2004).

Fraenkel, J. R. and Wallen, N. E. (1990) *How to Design and Evaluate Research in Education*. New York: McGraw-Hill.

Galton, M.; Simon, B. and Croll, P. (1980) *Inside the Primary Classroom*. London: Routledge and Kegan Paul.

Galton, M.; Hargreaves, L.; Comber, C.; Wall, D. and Pell, A. (1999) *Inside the Primary Classroom: Twenty Years on*. London: Routledge.

Giddens, A. (1979) *Central Problems in Social Theory*. London: Macmillan.

Gipps, C.; McCallum, B. and Hargreaves, E. (2000) *What Makes a Good Primary School Teacher? Expert Classroom Strategies*. London: RoutledgeFalmer.

Glaser, B. G. and Strauss, A. L. (1967) *The Discovery of Grounded Theory: Strategies for Qualitative Research*. Chicago: Aldine.

Gorard, S. (2003) *Quantitative Methods in Social Sciences*. London: Continuum.

Grbich, C. (2007) *Qualitative Data Analysis: An Introduction*. London: Sage.

Habermas, J. (1984) *The Theory of Communicative Action* (Vol. 1) *Reason and the rationalization of Society*. Translated by T. McCarthy. Boston, MA: Beacon.

Hammersley, M. (1992) *What's Wrong with Ethnography*. London: Routledge.

Hammersley, M. (2003) Can and should educational research be educative? *Oxford Review of Education*, 29, 3–25.

Hammersley, M. and Atkinson, P. (1983) *Ethnography: Principles in Practice*. London: Tavistock.

Hargreaves, D. (1967) *Social Relations in a Secondary School*. London: Routledge and Kegan Paul.

Hart, C. (1998) *Doing a Literature Review: Releasing the Social Science Imagination*. London: Sage.

Hart, C. (2005) *Doing Your Masters Dissertation*. London: Sage.

Hitchcock, G. and Hughes, D (1995) *Research and the Teacher* (second edition). London: Routledge.

Holliday, A. (2007) *Doing and Writing Qualitative Research* (second edition). London: Sage.

Hopkins, D. (2008) *A Teacher's Guide to Classroom Research* (fourth edition). Maidenhead: Open University Press.

House, E. R. (1993) *Professional Evaluation: Social Impact and Political Consequences*. Newbury Park, CA: Sage.

Howard, K. and Sharpe, J. A. (1983) *The Management of a Student Research Project*. Aldershot: Gower.

James, N. (2007) The use of email interviewing as a qualitative method of inquiry in educational research, *British Educational Research Journal*, 33, 963–976.

Jones, L. and McNamara, O. (2004) The possibilities and constraints of multimedia as a basis for critical reflection, *Cambridge Journal of Education*, 34, 279–296.

Kaplan, A. (1973) *The Conduct of Inquiry*. Aylesbury: Intertext.

Kemmis, S. and McTaggart, R. (eds) (1988) *The Action Research Planner*. Geelong, Vic: Deakin University Press.

Kerlinger, F. N. (1986) *Foundations of Behavioural Research* (third edition). New York: Holt, Rinehart and Winston.

Kipling, R. (1902, reprinted 1974) *Just So Stories*. London: Macmillan.

Kirk, J. and Miller, M. L. (1986) *Reliability and Validity in Qualitative Research*. Beverly Hills, CA: Sage.

Krippendorp, K. (2004) *Content Analysis: An Introduction to its Methodology*. Thousand Oaks, CA: Sage.

Kvale, S. (1996) *Interviews*. London: Sage.

Lacey, C. (1970) *Hightown Grammar*. Manchester: Manchester University Press.

Lambert, P.; Scourfield, J.; Smalley, N. and Jones, R. (2008) The social context of school bullying: evidence from a survey of children in South Wales, *Research Papers in Education*, 23, 269–292.

Lavelle, E. and Bushrow, K. (2007) Writing approaches of graduate students. *Educational Psychology*, 27, 807–822.

LeCompte, M. and Preissle, J. (1993) *Ethnography and Qualitative Design in Educational Research* (second edition). London: Academic.

Lewins, A. and Silver, C. (2007) *Using Software in Qualitative Research: A Step-by-Step Guide*. London: Sage.

Lichtman, M. (2006) *Qualitative Research in Education*. Thousand Oaks, CA: Sage.

Lin, N. (1976) *Foundations of Social Research*. New York: McGraw-Hill.

Lincoln, Y. S. and Guba, E. (1985) *Naturalistic Inquiry*. Newbury Park, CA: Sage.

Lofland, J. (1971) *Analysing Social Settings*. Belmont, CA: Wadsworth.

Mac an Ghaill, M. (1988) *Young, Gifted and Black: Student-Teacher Relations in the Schooling of Black Youth*. Milton Keynes: Open University Press.

Marsden, E. (2007) Can educational experiments both test a theory and inform practice? *British Educational Research Journal*, 33, 565–588.

Marshall, C. and Rossman, G. B. (2006) *Designing Qualitative Research* (fourth edition). Thousand Oaks, CA: Sage.

Maslow, A. H. (1954) *Motivation and Personality*. New York: Harper and Row.

Mason, J. (2002) *Qualitative Researching* (second edition). London: Sage.

May, T. (2001) *Social Research: Issues, Methods and Process* (third edition). Maidenhead: Open University press.

McCracken, G. (1988) *The Long Interview*. Sage University Paper Series on Qualitative Research Methods, 13. Newbury park, CA: Sage.

McCulloch, G. (2004) *Documentary Research: In Education, History and the Social Sciences*. London: RoutledgeFalmer.

McMillan, J. H. and Schumacher, S. (2001) *Research in Education: A Conceptual Introduction* (fifth edition). New York: Longman.

McNamara, O. (2002) Evidence-based practice through practice-based evidence, in O. McNamara (ed.) *Becoming an Evidence-based Practitioner*. London: RoutledgeFalmer.

Mercer, N (1991) Researching common knowledge: Studying the content and context of educational discourse, in G. Walford (ed.) *Doing Educational Research*. London: Routledge.

Merriam, S. B. (1988) *Case Study Research in Education*. San Francisco, CA: Jossey Bass.

Merriam, S. B. (1998) *Qualitative Research and Case Study Applications*. San Francisco, CA: Jossey-Bass.

Middlewood, D.; Coleman, M. and Lumby, J. (1999) *Practitioner Research in Education*. London: Paul Chapman.

Miles, M. B. and Huberman, A. M. (1994) *Qualitative Data Analysis* (second edition). Thousand Oaks, CA: Sage.

Mitchell, R. G. (1993) *Secrecy in Fieldwork*. London: Sage.

Morgan, D. (1988) *Focus Groups as Qualitative Research*. Beverley Hills, CA: Sage.

Moser, C. and Kalton, G. (1971) *Survey Methods in Social Investigations* (second edition). London: Heinemann.

Mouly, G. J. (1978) *Educational Research: The Art and Science of Investigation*. Boston, MA: Allyn and Bacon.

Muijs, D. (2004) *Doing Quantitative Research in Education with SPSS*. London: Sage.

Nias, J. (1991) Primary teachers talking: a reflexive account of longitudinal research, in G. Walford (ed.) *Doing Educational Research*. London: Routledge.

Oakley, A (1981) Interviewing women: a contradiction in terms, in H. Roberts (ed.) *Doing Feminist Research*. London: Routledge and Kegan Paul.

O'Brien, M. (1993) Social research and sociology, in N. Gilbert (ed.) *Researching Social Life*. London: Sage.

Oppenheim, A. N. (1992) *Questionnaire Design, Interviewing and Attitude Measurement* (New edition). London: Continuum.

Patton, M. Q. (2002) *Qualitative Research and Evaluation Methods* (third edition). Thousand Oaks, CA: Sage.

Phillips, E. M. and Pugh, D. S. (2005) *How to Get a PhD* (fourth edition). Maidenhead: Open University Press.

Plummer, K. (2001) *Documents of Life 2: An Invitation to Critical Humanism*. London: Sage.

Ponsonby, A. (1923) *English Diaries: A Review of English Diaries from the Sixteenth to the Twentieth Century with an Introduction on Diary Writing*. London: Metheun (cited in McCulloch, 2004).

Pring, R. (2004) *Philosophy of Educational Research* (second edition). London: Continuum.

Prior, L. (2003) *Using Documents in Social Research*. London: Sage.

Punch, K. F. (2003) *Survey Research: The Basics*. London: Sage.

Punch, K. F. (2005) *Introduction to Social Research: Quantitative and Qualitative Approaches* (second edition). London: Sage.

Richardson, L. (1990) *Writing Strategies: Reaching Diverse Audiences*. Thousand Oaks, CA: Sage.

Richardson, L. (1994) Writing: a method of enquiry, in N. K. Denzin and Y. S. Lincoln (eds) *Handbook of Qualitative Research*. Thousand Oaks, CA: Sage.

Robson, C. (2002) *Real World Research* (second edition). Oxford: Blackwell.

Rutter, M.; Maugham, B.; Mortimore, P.; Ouston, J. and Smith, A. (1979) *Fifteen Thousand Hours*. London: Open Books.

Said, E. (1978) *Orientalism*. London: Routledge and Kegan Paul.

Sapsford, R. and Jupp, V. (1996) *Data Collection and Analysis*. London: Sage.

Schatzman, L. and Strauss, A. (1973) *Field Research: Strategies for a Natural Sociology*. Englewood Cliffs, NJ: Prentice Hall.

Schensul, S. L.; Schensul, J. J. and LeCompte, M. D. (1999) *Essential Ethnographic Methods*. Walnut Creek, CA: AltaMira.

Schostak, J. F. (2002) *Understanding, Designing and Conducting Qualitative Research in Education*. Buckingham: Open University Press.

Shah, S. (2004) The researcher/interviewer in intercultural context: a social intruder! *British Educational Research Journal*, 30, 549–575.

Silver, P. (1983) *Educational Administration: Theoretical Perspectives on Practice and Research*. New York: Harper and Row.

Simons, H. (1995) The politics and ethics of educational research in England: contemporary issues, *British Educational Research Journal*, 21, 435–450.

Smith, D. J. and Tomlinson, S. (1989) *The School Effect.* London: Policy Studies Institute.

Smith, J. M. (2007) Life Histories and Career Decisions of Women Teachers. PhD Thesis, University of Leeds.

Spradley, J. P. (1980) *Participant Observation.* New York: Holt, Rinehart and Winston.

Stake, R. E. (1994) Case Studies, in N. K. Denzin and Y. S. Lincoln (eds) *Handbook of Qualitative Research.* London: Sage.

Stake, R. E. (1995) *The Art of Case Study Research.* Thousand Oaks, CA: Sage.

Stenhouse, L. (1975) *An Introduction to Curriculum Research and Development.* London: Heinemann.

Stenhouse, L. (1979) *What is Action Research?* Norwich: Classroom Action Research Network.

Strauss, A. L. (1987) *Qualitative Analysis for Social Scientists.* Cambridge: Cambridge University press.

Strauss, A. and Corbin, J. (1990) *Basics of Qualitative Research* (first edition) Thousand Oaks, CA: Sage.

Strauss, A. and Corbin, J. (1994) Grounded theory methodology: an overview, in N. Denzin and Y. Lincoln (eds) *Handbook of Qualitative Research.* Thousand Oaks, CA: Sage.

Strauss, A. and Corbin, J. (1998) *Basics of Qualitative Research* (second edition) Thousand Oaks, CA: Sage.

Stronach, I. and MacLure, M. (1997) *Educational Research Undone: The Postmodern Embrace.* Buckingham: Open University Press.

Stronach, I. and Piper, H. (2008) Can liberal education make a comeback? The case of 'relational touch' at Summerhill School, *American Educational Research Journal,* 45, 6–37.

Stronach, I.; Garratt, D.; Pearce, C. and Piper, H. (2007) Reflexivity, the picturing of selves: the forging of method, *Qualitative Inquiry,* 13, 179–203.

Taylor, G. (1989) *The Student's Writing Guide for the Arts and Social Sciences.* Cambridge: Cambridge University Press.

Tizard, B. and Hughes, M. (1984) *Young Children Learning: Talking and Thinking at Home and at School.* London: Fontana.

Tizard, B. and Hughes, M. (1991) Reflections on young children learning, in G. Walford (ed.) *Doing Educational Research.* London: Routledge.

Tuckman, B. W. (1994) *Conducting Educational Research* (fourth edition). Orlando, FL: Harcourt Brace.

Walford, G. (1991) Researching the City technology College, Kinghurst, in G. Walford (ed.) *Doing Educational Research.* London: Routledge.

Walford, G. (1998) Compulsive writing behaviour: getting it published, in G. Walford (ed.) *Doing Research about Education.* London: Falmer.

Walford, G. (2001) *Doing Qualitative Educational Research: A Personal Guide to the Research Process.* London: Continuum.

Walker, R. (1985) *Doing Research: A Handbook for Teachers.* London: Methuen.

Wallace, M. and Wray, A. (2006) *Critical Reading and Writing for Postgraduates.* London: Sage.

Willis, P. (1977) *Learning to Labour: How Working Class Kids Get Working Class Jobs.* Farnborough: Saxon House.

Wolcott, H. F. (1994) *Transforming Qualitative Data: Description, Analysis and Interpretation.* Thousand Oaks, CA: Sage.

Wolcott, H. F. (2001) *Writing Up Qualitative Research* (second edition). Thousand Oaks, CA: Sage.

Woods, P. (1979) *The Divided School*. London: Routledge and Kegan Paul.

Woods, P. (1986) *Inside Schools: Ethnography in Educational Research*. London: Routledge and Kegan Paul.

Woods, P. (1998) Critical moments in the Creative Teaching research, in G. Walford (ed.) *Doing Research about Education*. London: Falmer.

Wragg, E. C. (1999) *An Introduction to Classroom Observation* (second edition). London: RoutledgeFlamer.

Yin, R. (1993) *Applications of Case Study Research*. Newbury Park, CA: Sage.

Yin, R. K. (2009) *Case Study Research: Design and Methods* (fourth edition). Thousand Oaks, CA: Sage.

Author Index

Subject Index